Three Course
MENUS
A Wealth of Appetising Ideas for Every Occasion

FRASER STEWART

HOW TO USE THE RECIPES

Weights and measures

Both metric and imperial measurements are given, but are not exact equivalents; work from one set only. Use graded measuring spoons levelled across.

Ingredients

- Flour is plain white flour unless otherwise stated
- Sugar is granulated unless otherwise stated
- Eggs are medium (EEC size 4) unless otherwise stated
- Vegetables and fruits are medium-sized and prepared, and onions, garlic and root vegetables are peeled unless otherwise stated
- Butter for sweet dishes should be unsalted
- Block margarine may be substituted for butter, although the results may be different in flavour, appearance and keeping qualities.

Cooking

Dishes should be placed in the centre of the oven unless otherwise stated.

This edition published by
Fraser Stewart Book Wholesale Ltd
Abbey Chambers
4 Highbridge Street
Waltham Abbey
Essex EN9 1DQ

Produced by Marshall Cavendish Books
(a division of Marshall Cavendish Partworks Ltd)
119 Wardour Street
London W1V 3TD

Contents

Introduction

ENTERTAINING AT HOME MAY TAKE many forms – an informal Sunday brunch for the family, a casual dinner with friends, a picnic or a formal evening meal. Whichever it is, *Three Course Menus* will help you to plan and prepare meals with flair.

It aims to take the guesswork out of cooking for a crowd by offering a wide range of menus to suit all occasions, formal or informal, from breakfast to supper. Each menu provides a carefully-selected combination of dishes – starters, soups, main courses, desserts – and suggestions for drinks. These tasty dishes are specially chosen to complement others on the menu, ensuring each menu is a complete culinary experience. The menus in *Three Course Meals* offer new approaches to favourite meals – the traditional family roast lamb, for example, is transformed when it is cooked in the French style – the meat infused with the subtle aroma of delicious fresh herbs.

Time is always precious, so the recipes in *Three Course Menus* have been selected for ease and speed of preparation. Each menu comes with a schedule, showing when to begin preparing each dish in order to time the meal to perfection. To complement the recipes themselves, *Three Course Menus* also provides suggestions for wine and other accompaniments, along with ideas for setting the scene in order to create exactly the right ambience for the occasion.

The menus are, of course, only suggestions. Rather than use them exactly as shown, you may prefer to combine different dishes from the book to create a menu for your own tastes.

SUNDAY BRUNCH FOR FOUR *Bloody Mary · Fruit compôte · Scrambled eggs with smoked salmon · Piquant kidneys · Bacon and onion bread*

BRUNCH IS THAT delightful meal which combines breakfast and lunch – more satisfying than the usual hurried coffee and toast that most of us barely have time for in the morning, and less formal (and earlier) than a proper lunch with separate courses.

If you are planning to have your brunch after a late Saturday night you might need to take a 'hair of the dog', so in our recommended, starred menu we show you how to mix a Bloody Mary, a traditional hangover cure. A dish of Scrambled eggs with smoked salmon is wonderfully easy to cook and very stylish. For something special with a bit of bite, Piquant kidneys fit the bill and are also very easy to put together. Have a loaf of Bacon and onion bread ready to cut into thick slices and spread with butter. This savoury and substantial loaf is definitely worth making, as you can't often buy such an original and tasty bread.

The combination of sweet and savoury dishes at brunch is particularly delicious – a Fruit compôte of apricots, prunes, honey and port can be served at the beginning of the meal and will complement the scrambled eggs and salmon beautifully.

Setting the Scene

You may well be serving brunch to a few good friends who are staying for the weekend. You might go out or just stay up late on Saturday night and will not want to get up early the next day. You can save yourself time and trouble on Sunday morning by making the Bacon and onion bread the day before. Don't worry about setting the table, just put all the crockery and cutlery out, with napkins, onto the table; people can help themselves.

Wine Ideas

This meal will not be a particularly alcoholic affair, due to the time of day you are eating. Indeed, the vodka in the Bloody Mary might be too much for some, so mix up a non-alcoholic batch as well. If you have drunk too much the night before you will need plenty of liquid and vitamin C, so jugs of orange juice would be ideal, freshly squeezed if you can. Tea and coffee, too, are obvious drinks to have at any brunch.

Countdown

Two days before
Soak the prunes for the compôte.

The day before
Bake the Bacon and onion bread and leave to cool. Store in an airtight container.
Simmer the prunes and apricots in their soaking liquid and honey to taste. Transfer to a serving dish, add the alcohol, leave to cool, cover and chill.

Forty five minutes before
Make up the Bloody Mary, omitting the celery garnish, cover with stretch wrap and chill.
Cut the smoked salmon into thin strips.

Thirty minutes before
Slice and rinse the kidneys, prepare the piquant sauce and start cooking the kidneys.
Break the eggs for the scrambled eggs, stir well and season.

Before serving the Bloody Mary
Stir well and garnish with celery stalks.

Before serving the Fruit compôte
Decorate with orange slices, grapes and flaked almonds.

Before serving the scrambled eggs
Heat the salmon strips and lightly cook the scrambled eggs. Stir in the chives and lemon juice.

Before serving the Piquant kidneys
Stir in the cream and garnish with parsley.

Bloody Mary

● ***Preparation: 5 minutes*** ● ***Serves 4***

ICE CUBES or CRUSHED ICE
225ml/8fl oz VODKA
600ml/1pt TOMATO JUICE
4tsp LEMON JUICE
large pinch of CAYENNE PEPPER
large pinch of CELERY SALT
few dashes of HOT PEPPER SAUCE
1tbls WORCESTERSHIRE SAUCE
4 CELERY STALKS, to serve

1 Put a generous amount of ice cubes or crushed ice in a large jug. Add the vodka, tomato juice, lemon juice, cayenne pepper, celery salt, hot pepper sauce and Worcestershire sauce and stir well.

2 Pour the cocktail into large tumblers and garnish with celery stalks. Add straws and serve at once.

Variations

Make individual Bloody Marys in the tumblers, adding a quarter of the ingredients to each glass.

★ Fruit compôte

● ***Preparation:*** *15 minutes, plus 8 hours soaking*

● ***Cooking:*** *15 minutes, plus chilling* ● *Serves 4*

225g/8oz PRUNES, stoned
600ml/1pt HOT, STRONG TEA
225g/8oz NO-SOAK DRIED APRICOTS
about 2tbls HONEY
2tbls PORT or DRY SHERRY

For the decoration:
½ ORANGE, thinly sliced
SEEDLESS WHITE GRAPES
2tbls FLAKED ALMONDS, toasted

1 Place the prunes in a bowl and pour the tea over them. Cover and leave to soak for 8 hours or overnight.

2 Turn the prunes and their soaking liquid into a saucepan, together with the apricots. Add honey to taste. Set the pan over medium heat and simmer for 10-15 minutes or until the prunes and apricots are tender and the syrup has thickened slightly.

3 Using a slotted spoon, transfer the prunes and apricots to a glass serving dish. Sprinkle over the port or sherry, then spoon over a little of the cooking liquids. Cover and leave until cold, then chill in the refrigerator for at least 1 hour or until required.

4 Just before serving, cut the orange slices in quarters and use, together with the grapes and flaked, toasted almonds, to decorate the compôte.

Serving ideas

Chilled whipped cream, custard or yoghurt make the ideal accompaniment to this dish.

Freezer

Normally when freezing fruit you have to add ascorbic acid or lemon juice to the syrup and fruit to prevent the fruit colouring. As this compôte has its own syrup and tawny colouring, no extra steps are necessary. Just prepare the compôte, omitting the alcohol and the decorations, allow to cool, then freeze in a rigid container for up to 4 months. Defrost overnight in the fridge.

★ Scrambled eggs with smoked salmon

● ***Preparation:*** *5 minutes*

● ***Cooking:*** *5 minutes* ● *Serves 4*

9 LARGE EGGS
SALT and PEPPER
4tbls SINGLE CREAM
40-50g/1½-2oz BUTTER
175g/6oz SMOKED SALMON, cut into thin strips
few drops of LEMON JUICE
3tbls FINELY SNIPPED CHIVES

1 Break the eggs into a bowl. Add salt and pepper to taste and stir well with a fork (don't beat) until the yolks and whites are thoroughly mixed. Stir in the cream.

2 Heat the butter in a medium-sized frying pan. Add the strips of smoked salmon and toss gently with a wooden spoon over low heat for a few seconds only, until they change colour. Quickly pour in the eggs. Stir constantly with a wooden spoon, keeping all the egg mixture on the move. Continue to stir until the eggs are thick and creamy and almost set.

3 Stir in the drops of lemon juice and the snipped chives. Serve immediately, as the eggs will become rubbery very quickly.

Variations

The addition of single cream to the eggs makes rich, smooth scrambled eggs. You could, of course, use double cream for an even richer, smoother mixture or, for a more health-conscious dish, leave out the cream altogether and add a little water instead, which makes extremely fluffy scrambled eggs.

Poached haddock and eggs

- ***Preparation: 15 minutes***
- ***Cooking: 25 minutes*** • ***Serves 4***

450g/1lb SMOKED HADDOCK, skinned and cut into four equal pieces
SALT and PEPPER
MILK and WATER, for poaching
4tbls WHITE WINE VINEGAR
4 LARGE EGGS
1 CANNED PIMIENTO

1 Season the haddock with a pinch of salt and pepper to taste. Select a saucepan large enough to take the haddock pieces comfortably in a single layer. Place the fish in the pan and cover with equal amounts of water and milk.

2 Cover the pan and poach gently for 10-12 minutes or until the haddock flakes easily with a fork. Drain well and keep warm.

3 Meanwhile, poach the eggs. Pour 7.5cm/3in water into a large saucepan. Add the white wine vinegar and bring to the boil. Reduce to a simmer. Break an egg into a cup, then slip it into the water. Repeat with the other eggs, making a mental note of the order in which you put them in the pan.

4 Raise the heat until the water bubbles up. Draw the white round the yolk of each egg with a slotted spoon. Reduce the heat and simmer very gently for 3-4 minutes.

5 Remove the eggs with the slotted spoon. Rinse in hot water, then pat dry with absorbent paper and trim the edges neatly with scissors.

6 To serve, arrange the haddock on a serving platter and put a poached egg on top of each piece. Cut the pimiento into thin strips and arrange in a lattice on top of each egg. Serve immediately.

★ *Piquant kidneys*

- ***Preparation: 10 minutes***
- ***Cooking: 25 minutes*** • ***Serves 4***

450g/1lb LAMB'S KIDNEYS
25g/1oz BUTTER, melted
2tsp WORCESTERSHIRE SAUCE
dash of HOT PEPPER SAUCE
2tsp MUSHROOM KETCHUP
1tbls DIJON MUSTARD
1tbls LEMON JUICE
¼tsp GROUND ALLSPICE
SALT and PEPPER
pinch of CAYENNE PEPPER
3tbls DOUBLE CREAM
1tbls CHOPPED PARSLEY, to garnish

1 Slice the kidneys in half through the centre and snip out the white core with pointed scissors. Rinse thoroughly in cold water and pat dry with absorbent paper.

2 Make the piquant sauce: put the melted butter in a bowl and add the Worcestershire and hot pepper sauces, mushroom ketchup, mustard, lemon juice, allspice, salt, pepper and cayenne pepper. Stir well.

3 Pour the sauce mixture into a large, heavy frying pan and place over moderate heat. When it starts to bubble, lower the heat, then add the kidneys and cook for 15-20 minutes, turning once or twice.

5 Stir in the cream and adjust the seasoning. Pile the kidneys onto a warmed serving dish, sprinkle with parsley and serve at once.

Freezer

You can freeze the dish at the end of step 3 for up to 3 months: omit the salt and add 150ml/¼pt chicken stock to the sauce, so that the kidneys are well covered. Defrost overnight in the refrigerator, then remove the kidneys from the sauce. Reduce the sauce by fast boiling. Add the kidneys to reheat thoroughly, then stir in the cream and heat through.

Bacon and egg pancakes

● *Preparation: 20 minutes, plus 30 minutes standing*

● *Cooking: 40 minutes* ● *Serves 4*

3tbls OIL
1 ONION, finely chopped
1 GARLIC CLOVE, crushed
225g/8oz LEAN COOKED BACON, finely diced
350g/12oz TOMATOES, skinned, seeded and chopped
4tbls DRY WHITE WINE
1tbls TOMATO PURÉE
1tbls CHOPPED FRESH BASIL or 1tsp dried
2tbls CHOPPED PARSLEY
2tbls GRATED PARMESAN CHEESE
FLAT-LEAVED PARSLEY, to garnish (optional)

For the pancakes:
100g/4oz FLOUR
pinch of SALT
1 EGG
150ml/¼pt MILK

For the filling:
25g/1oz BUTTER
4 SMALL EGGS, lightly beaten

1 To make the pancake batter, put the flour and salt into a bowl and make a well in the centre. Break the egg into the well and gradually stir into the flour, working the flour in from the sides.

2 Mix together the milk and 150ml/¼pt water. Add the liquid gradually to the flour and beat until thoroughly mixed. Leave to stand in a cool place for 30 minutes.

3 Meanwhile, make the sauce. Heat 2tbls oil in a saucepan over low heat, add the onion and garlic and cook for 5 minutes or until softened. Add the bacon, tomatoes, wine, tomato purée and herbs. Cover and cook gently for 5-10 minutes, stirring occasionally, until thick. Season well.

4 Next, cook the pancakes: heat 1tbls oil in a heavy frying pan. Stir the batter well, then pour in 3tbls of batter and tip the pan to spread it out evenly. Cook over moderate heat until the underside is golden brown, then raise the pan at the handle end and turn the pancake with a palette knife. Cook the other side until golden. Slide the pancake onto a flat plate. Keep warm while you cook the remaining pancakes in the same way.

5 Heat the grill to high. To prepare the egg filling, melt the butter in a saucepan over low heat. Pour in the eggs and stir them into the butter until lightly scrambled. Remove from the heat and season.

6 Spoon about 1tbls of the egg mixture into the centre of each pancake. Fold one edge over and roll up carefully. Arrange the pancakes on a flameproof serving plate. Spoon the bacon sauce over the pancakes and sprinkle Parmesan cheese over the top. Grill for about 5 minutes or until the cheese has browned slightly. Garnish and serve immediately.

Ham and fruit platter

● *Preparation: 15 minutes* ● *Serves 4*

4 THIN SLICES of PARMA HAM
4 THIN SLICES of COOKED HAM
1 LARGE, RIPE AVOCADO
LEMON JUICE
4 RIPE FIGS
½ HONEYDEW MELON
2 RIPE PEARS
PEPPER
GROUND CORIANDER

1 Lay one slice of Parma ham and one slice of cooked ham each on four flat plates, taking care not to break the paper-thin Parma ham.

2 Halve, stone and peel the avocado. Cut each half into four slices and arrange two slices opposite each other on each plate. Brush them with lemon juice to prevent them discolouring.

3 Cut each fig into six thin slices and place three slices on each avocado slice, overlapping each piece of fig slightly.

4 Remove the skin from the melon. Cut lengthways into slices and place two slices on each plate.

5 Peel, halve and core the pears. Cut into thin, neat slices and arrange four or five on each plate. Brush them with lemon juice. Sprinkle with pepper and coriander just before serving.

Variations

If you have a spice mill, buy coriander seeds rather than ground coriander and serve the Ham and fruit platter with the coriander seeds in the mill, along with black peppercorns in a pepper mill. These can then be ground over each platter according to taste.

Bacon and onion bread

• ***Preparation: 45 minutes, plus proving***

• ***Cooking: 50 minutes, plus cooling*** • ***Serves 4-6***

75g/3oz BACON, finely chopped
15g/½oz LARD
1 ONION, thinly sliced
225g/8oz WHOLEMEAL FLOUR, plus extra for dredging
1tsp MUSTARD POWDER
2tsp EASY-BLEND DRIED YEAST
1tsp SALT
1tsp DRIED RUBBED SAGE
2tbls DRY CIDER
OIL, for greasing
1tsp HONEY
1 EGG, lightly beaten

1 Put the bacon into a large frying pan over low heat. When the fat begins to run, add half the lard and the sliced onion. Cook for 5 minutes or until the onion is soft.

2 Add the rest of the lard. When it melts, remove the pan from the heat and let the contents cool.

3 In a large bowl, combine the flour, mustard powder, yeast and salt. Stir in the bacon and onion mixture and the sage. Make a well in the centre and pour in the cider and honey, and about 150ml/¼pt warm water. Mix well to form a dough.

4 Turn the dough out onto a floured surface and knead until smooth, form it into a ball, then put it into a lightly oiled bowl, cover it loosely with oiled stretch wrap and put it in a warm place for 40 minutes-1 hour or until it is doubled in size.

5 Heat the oven to 200C/400F/gas 6. Knead the dough again for about 5 minutes and shape it into a loaf. Place on a greased baking sheet and brush it with the beaten egg.

6 Cover it loosely with oiled stretch wrap and leave in a warm place for about 20 minutes or until it begins to rise. Bake for 30-40 minutes or until it is browned and sounds hollow when you remove it from the baking sheet and rap the base with your knuckles. If it browns too quickly, cover with foil to prevent further browning. Cool the loaf on a wire rack.

Freezer

Most breads freeze well, and this one is no exception. Wrap the cooled but freshly baked loaf well in polythene, then freeze for up to 3 months. Defrost, in its wrappings, at room temperature for about 4-5 hours.

Blueberry muffins

• ***Preparation: 15 minutes***

• ***Cooking: 20 minutes*** • ***Makes 12***

25ml/1fl oz CORN OIL, plus extra for greasing
150g/5oz FLOUR
65g/2½oz CASTER SUGAR
2tsp BAKING POWDER
PINCH of SALT
1 EGG
150ml/¼pt MILK
50g/2oz BLUEBERRIES or BLACKCURRANTS
BUTTER, for serving (optional)

1 Heat the oven to 200C/400F/gas 6. Grease a bun or muffin tin with corn oil.

2 Sift the flour, baking powder and salt into a bowl and stir in the caster sugar. In another bowl, lightly beat the egg, then stir in the milk and oil.

3 Add all the liquid to the flour mixture and beat until evenly mixed and smooth. Fold in the blueberries or blackcurrants.

4 Spoon the mixture into the tin. Bake for 15-20 minutes or until well risen and a fine skewer inserted in the centre comes out clean. Serve the muffins hot, with butter, if wished.

Cook's tips

These muffins are an American speciality, and very different from English muffins. They are rather like little sponge cakes but are usually eaten for breakfast or brunch.

Blueberries are the larger, sweeter and more succulent North American cousins of the bilberry. They have similar blue-black skins with a misty-grey bloom. Fresh blueberries can be bought in late summer, and are also available frozen.

SUNDAY LUNCH FOR SIX

Cucumber and watercress salad ·

French-style lamb with haricots · Broccoli with cheese sauce ·

Fruity treacle tart

PEOPLE EXPECT A Sunday lunch to be a rather traditional meal, with a roast followed by a substantial sweet. But a good cook likes to prepare something special when guests are invited. This menu is planned to balance the traditional and the unusual in equal proportions. The starter is refreshingly light and pretty. Roast lamb is a conventional choice, but the recipe for French-style lamb with haricots gives it an unusual flavour and presentation. (Continue the French influence by cooking the lamb so it is pink in the middle, not fully cooked in the English manner.) Broccoli with a cheesy sauce is the perfect accompaniment — a plain vegetable served in an unusual way. Finish with Fruity treacle tart, as traditional as the custom of a hearty Sunday lunch itself, but with the kick of orange and lemon added.

Setting the Scene

Sunday lunch, unlike a dinner party, is a much more relaxed, informal affair, often with relatives and small children present. So set the scene accordingly, with everyday table linen and cutlery, brightened up with a centrepiece of simple flowers or a bowl of polished apples. Have some toys and games around to keep the children amused while the grown-ups enjoy their pre-lunch drinks and exchange news. Give the children a soft drink, served in the same type of glasses.

Wine Ideas

To complement the French-style roast lamb, choose a French red wine: St Estèphe from the Médoc region, or a Loire wine such as Saumur-Champigny or Chinon. Alternatively, choose an unpretentious *vin de table* or *vin de pays:* a Merlot or Cabernet Sauvignon from the Ardèche region, or the ever-popular Piat d'Or. The Cabernet is extremely fruity and full-bodied, the Merlot smooth and medium-bodied, while the Piat d'Or suits those who prefer to drink a much lighter wine.

Countdown

The night before
Rinse the haricot beans, then place them in a large bowl and cover with cold water. Leave to soak overnight.

In the morning
Cook the haricot beans in fresh cold water and leave them to cool in the cooking liquid.
Prepare and cook the treacle tart.
Make the vinaigrette dressing and add the mustard.

2 hours 20 minutes before
Heat the oven.

2 hours before
Start cooking the lamb and fry the chopped onion.

1 hour before
Add the beans, tomatoes, onion, parsley, seasoning and oil to the lamb and return to the oven.
Make the cheese sauce for the broccoli and keep warm over hot water.

30 minutes before
Prepare the salad but do not add the dressing.
Cook the broccoli, drain and keep warm.

Before serving the first course
Turn off the oven and leave the lamb to rest. Keep the bean mixture hot.
Add the dressing to the salad.

Before serving the main course
Add the bean mixture to the lamb.
Spoon the cheese sauce over the broccoli.

★ Cucumber and watercress salad

• *Preparation: 20 minutes* **• *Serves 6***

1 LARGE CUCUMBER
1 BUNCH of WATERCRESS
4 SPRING ONION TOPS, cut into 1cm/½ in segments
125ml/4fl oz VINAIGRETTE (see Red, white and green salad, page 29)

1 Slice the cucumber into very thin rounds. Arrange in a shallow serving dish, layering up the slices in neat overlapping rows.

2 Remove and discard the watercress stems, then arrange clusters of leaves over the cucumber, pushing the stem ends between the slices so that the watercress stands up. Sprinkle with spring onions.

3 In a bowl, mix together the ingredients for the vinaigrette, beating with a fork. Pour over the salad and serve immediately.

Cook's tips

The easiest way to obtain even slices of cucumber is with a good sharp knife and a non-slip chopping board. But a mandolin slicer will save time and turn out slices of identical thickness.

Mushroom salad with soured cream

● *Preparation: 30 minutes* ● *Serves 6*

450g/1lb BUTTON MUSHROOMS
300ml/½pt SOURED CREAM
4tbls MILK
1tbls LEMON JUICE
2tbls SNIPPED CHIVES
SALT and PEPPER

For the garnish:
LETTUCE LEAVES
WATERCRESS SPRIGS
TOMATO WEDGES or ROSES
BLACK OLIVES

1 Trim off the mushroom stalks so that they are level with the caps. Put the soured cream, milk, lemon juice and chives in a bowl and stir until well mixed. Season with salt and pepper to taste.

2 Slice the mushrooms thinly and add them to the dressing, tossing with a fork so that the slices are evenly coated. Check the seasoning.

3 Pile the mushroom mixture into a shallow serving dish and garnish with lettuce and watercress. Arrange tomato wedges, or 'roses' — made out of carefully cut tomato peel wound around in spirals — and black olives on the salad. Serve at once.

Cook's tips

If you cannot buy soured cream, use double cream mixing in a little lemon juice to sour it.

Do not combine the mushrooms and dressing until just before serving — the juice from the mushrooms will cause the dressing to run.

★ French-style lamb with haricots

● *Preparation: 25 minutes, plus overnight soaking*

● *Cooking: 2¾ hours, plus 15 minutes resting* ● *Serves 6*

350g/12oz DRIED HARICOT BEANS, soaked overnight
SALT and PEPPER
BUTTER, for greasing
2.3kg/5lb LEG of LAMB
2 GARLIC CLOVES, cut into thin slivers
2tbls MELTED BUTTER
1 SPANISH ONION, coarsely chopped
6tbls OLIVE OIL
400g/14oz CANNED CHOPPED TOMATOES
4tbls FINELY CHOPPED PARSLEY
MINT SPRIGS and PARSLEY, to garnish
CARROTS and TURNIPS, to serve

1 Put the soaked beans into a large pan of unsalted water, bring to the boil, boil vigorously for 10 minutes, then cover and simmer for 1 ½ hours or until tender. Add salt towards the end of the cooking time.

2 Meanwhile, start cooking the lamb: heat the oven to 170C/325F/gas 3. Butter a shallow, flameproof casserole or roasting tin just large enough to hold the leg comfortably. Prick the lamb all over with the point of a sharp knife and insert a sliver of garlic in each incision. Season generously with salt and pepper. Put the lamb in the greased dish and sprinkle with the melted butter. Roast for 1 hour.

3 Meanwhile, fry the onion in 2tbls oil over low heat until transparent, about 10 minutes.

4 Spoon the drained beans, tomatoes, onion, salt and pepper to taste and the remaining oil around the lamb and cook for a further 30 minutes. Give the bean mixture a stir, then continue roasting for another 30 minutes or until the lamb is tender and the juices run pink when the meat is pierced. (If you prefer medium-cooked lamb, add 20-30 minutes to the cooking time.)

5 When the lamb is cooked, place it on a heated serving dish and leave to rest for 10-15 minutes in the turned-off oven, with the door open. Keep the bean mixture hot and, when the lamb has rested, add the bean mixture. Garnish with mint sprigs and parsley. Serve with carrots and turnips.

Cook's tips

You will probably have enough left-over meat to make a delicious cold lamb salad on the following day, or try Lamb Parmentier (page 16).

Peach-glazed gammon

• *Preparation: 25 minutes, plus 3 hours soaking*

• *Cooking: 2½ hours, plus cooling* **• *Serves 6***

1.4kg/3lb MIDDLE GAMMON JOINT, soaked for 3 hours
1 CELERY STALK, in pieces
1 CARROT, roughly chopped
1 ONION, halved
BOUQUET GARNI
1 BAY LEAF, plus a few to garnish
1tsp WHOLE CLOVES
1tsp BLACK PEPPERCORNS
TARRAGON SPRIGS, to garnish

For the glaze:
225g/8oz canned PEACH SLICES, drained
1tbls HONEY
2tsp CIDER VINEGAR
pinch of GROUND CLOVES

1 Put the drained gammon into a large saucepan, cover with cold water and bring to the boil; drain and rinse.

2 Return the gammon to the rinsed-out pan with the celery, carrot, onion, bouquet garni, bay leaf, cloves and peppercorns. Cover with cold water.

3 Bring to the boil over medium heat and remove any scum that rises to the surface. Cover and simmer very gently for 1¼ hours, or until just tender when pierced with a fork. Remove the pan from the heat and leave the gammon to cool in the stock in a cool place.

4 Heat the oven to 200C/400F/gas 6. Remove the cold gammon from the stock. Strip off the rind, leaving a thin, uniform layer of fat. Score the fat diagonally to make a diamond pattern.

5 Put the cold joint on a rack in a roasting tin and heat it in the oven for 10 minutes, or until the fat around it begins to look transparent.

6 Meanwhile, make the glaze: mix the honey, vinegar and cloves, stirring well to dissolve the honey. Cut four of the peach slices into thin strips.

7 Remove the gammon from the oven and brush with a thick layer of glaze. Return to the oven for 10 minutes. Baste with glaze again and arrange the peach strips on top. Brush these with glaze and return to the oven for 10 minutes or until they are nicely browned. Serve the gammon hot or cold, garnished with the remaining peach slices, the tarragon sprigs and bay leaves.

Freezer

Freeze the boiled joint, without rind or stock, at the end of step 3, sealed in a bag. Store for up to 1 month. Defrost the joint overnight in the fridge, then complete the recipe.

Lamb Parmentier

• *Preparation: 45 minutes*

• *Cooking: 30 minutes* **• *Serves 4-6***

4-6 POTATOES
50g/2oz BUTTER
4tbls OLIVE OIL
SALT and PEPPER
1 ONION, finely chopped
450-700g/1-1½lb COOKED LAMB, diced
4tbls GRATED PARMESAN CHEESE (optional)

For the tomato sauce:
2tbls OLIVE OIL
1 ONION, finely chopped
800g/1¾lb CANNED CHOPPED TOMATOES
½tsp DRIED BASIL
½tsp SUGAR
SALT and PEPPER

1 For the tomato sauce, heat the olive oil in a saucepan and fry the onion over medium heat for 3-4 minutes or until soft and golden. Add the tomatoes and their juices, basil, sugar and a little salt and pepper. Simmer for 20 minutes or until thickened, stirring occasionally.

2 Meanwhile, cut the potatoes into 5mm/¼in dice and blot well with absorbent paper. Heat half the butter and 2tbls oil in a large, deep frying pan. Add the potatoes and sauté for 12 minutes or until soft and golden brown, shaking the pan and turning constantly with a spatula. Season with salt and pepper to taste and transfer to a plate with a slotted spoon.

3 Add the remaining butter and oil to the frying pan, then fry the remaining onion for 5 minutes or until soft. Add the lamb and cook for a further 5-7 minutes or until golden brown, stirring constantly.

4 Add the cooked potatoes and the tomato sauce to the lamb and bring to a simmer. Adjust the seasoning. Either serve as is or turn into a flameproof serving dish, sprinkle with grated Parmesan and grill until melted.

Cook's tips

This is an economical way of using up meat left over from French-style lamb with haricots (page 15) or another roast joint.

★ Broccoli with cheese sauce

- ***Preparation: 20 minutes***
- ***Cooking: 20 minutes***
- ***Serves 6***

900g/2lb BROCCOLI
SALT and PEPPER
15g/½oz BUTTER
15g/½oz FLOUR
150ml/¼pt MILK
150ml/¼pt DOUBLE CREAM
¼tsp DIJON MUSTARD
¼tsp PAPRIKA
100g/4oz MATURE CHEDDAR CHEESE, grated
MINT SPRIG, to garnish (optional)

1 Place the broccoli in a large pan of boiling, salted water and simmer for 15 minutes or until just tender.

2 Meanwhile, make the sauce: melt the butter in a small saucepan and stir in the flour. Cook over a low heat for 1 minute, stirring constantly, then remove from the heat. Gradually add the milk, stirring well to prevent lumps from forming. Stir in the cream, mustard and paprika. Season with salt and pepper to taste. Return the pan to medium-low heat and stir continuously until the sauce has thickened and is very hot. Stir in the cheese.

3 Drain the broccoli and place in a heated serving dish. Pour the sauce over it and garnish with a mint sprig, if liked. Serve immediately.

Cauliflower castles

- ***Preparation: 40 minutes***
- ***Cooking: 1 hour***
- ***Serves 6***

1 LARGE CAULIFLOWER (about 700-900g/1½-2lb), separated into florets
150ml/¼pt MILK
SALT and PEPPER
175-225g/6-8oz POTATO, quartered
3 LARGE EGGS
2tbls PARMESAN CHEESE, grated
50g/2oz BUTTER, softened, plus extra for greasing
FRESHLY GRATED NUTMEG
PARSLEY, to garnish

1 Heat the oven to 190C/375F/gas 5. In a large pan bring the milk and 1.1L/2pt salted water to the boil. Simmer the florets in this liquid for 10-15 minutes or until they are just tender. Drain well.

2 Meanwhile, cook the potato in boiling salted water for 10-15 minutes. Drain thoroughly and mash.

3 Force the cooked florets through a sieve or purée them in a blender or food processor. Beat in the mashed potato, eggs, Parmesan cheese and softened butter. Season to taste with salt, pepper and nutmeg.

4 Line the base of six 150ml/¼pt dariole moulds with greaseproof paper. Butter the base and sides of the moulds and fill with the cauliflower mixture. Cover with buttered foil.

5 Place in a shallow ovenproof pan containing 2.5cm/1in simmering water, and bake in the oven for 35-40 minutes or until set to the touch, or when a knife inserted into the centre comes out clean. Remove from the oven and leave to stand for a few minutes. Invert the cauliflower castles onto a warm serving dish. Sprinkle with parsley and serve hot.

Cook's tips

You may find it easier to invert the castles onto an individual plate and transfer them to a serving dish with a fish slice.

If you haven't any dariole moulds, 150ml/¼pt ramekins will do, though they won't look so spectacular.

★ Fruity treacle tart

- ***Preparation:* *30 minutes, plus 30 minutes chilling***
- ***Cooking:* *45 minutes*** • ***Serves 6-8***

350g/12oz SHORTCRUST PASTRY (follow method in Cook's tips, below, using 225g/8oz flour and 100g/4oz butter)
450g/1lb GOLDEN SYRUP
100g/4oz FRESH BREADCRUMBS (see Plan ahead, page 87)
GRATED ZEST and JUICE of both 1/2 LEMON and 1/2 ORANGE
1/2 tsp GRATED GINGER
2tbls SOFT BROWN SUGAR
2tbls DOUBLE CREAM
1 APPLE, peeled, cored and grated
15g/1/2 oz BUTTER, diced
1 LARGE EGG YOLK, beaten
CREAM, to serve
FRESH FRUIT, to decorate

1 Roll out the pastry thinly and line a 23cm/9in flan tin, reserving the trimmings to make the lattice. Chill the lined tin for 30 minutes and the trimmings until needed. Line the case with foil or greaseproof paper and beans. Bake blind at 200C/400F/gas 6 for 10 minutes. Reduce the heat to 180C/350F/gas 4, remove the beans and lining and bake for a further 8-10 minutes — do not allow the pastry to colour. Leave in the tin.

2 Meanwhile, in a small saucepan, melt the syrup and stir in the breadcrumbs, ginger, grated zest and juice of the lemon and orange, sugar, cream, grated apple and butter. Blend well and pour the mixture into the half-baked pastry case.

3 Roll out the remaining pastry to an oval 20cm/8in long and cut it into strips about 1cm/½in wide. Arrange these over the tart, weaving them under and over each other to make a lattice over the filling. Brush this lattice with the beaten egg yolk.

4 Bake for 20-25 minutes, or until the pastry lattice is golden brown. Allow the tart to cool before decorating with fresh fruit and serving with cream.

Cook's tips

To make 225g/8oz shortcrust pastry, enough to line a 25cm/10in pastry case, you will need 175g/6oz plain flour, ¼ tsp salt, 75g/3oz butter, cut into small dice, and 4-6tbls cold milk or water. Sift the flour and salt into a mixing bowl and add the butter. Using the tips of your fingers mix the butter into the flour until the contents look like breadcrumbs. Stir in the milk and water and mix to a soft pliable dough. Turn the dough out onto a lightly floured board and knead lightly. Wrap and chill for 15 minutes before rolling out.

Bachelor pudding

- ***Preparation:* *25 minutes***
- ***Cooking:* *2 hours*** • ***Serves 6-8***

BUTTER, for greasing
200g/7oz SELF-RAISING FLOUR
½tsp MIXED SPICE
50g/2oz SULTANAS
50g/2oz RAISINS
75g/3oz CASTER SUGAR, plus extra for dredging
50g/2oz FRESH WHITE BREADCRUMBS
75g/3oz SUET
GRATED ZEST of ½ LEMON or ORANGE
1 EGG, beaten
150ml/¼pt MILK
CUSTARD or CREAM, to serve (optional)

1 Grease a 1.1L/2pt pudding basin. Sift the flour and spice into a bowl. Stir in the sultanas, raisins, sugar, breadcrumbs, suet and lemon or orange zest. Mix in the beaten egg and gradually add the milk to make a mixture with a soft dropping consistency.

2 Turn the mixture into the basin and level the top with the back of a spoon. Cover with a sheet of buttered greaseproof paper, pleated across the middle to allow for expansion. Cover with foil and tie tightly around the rim with string.

3 Put the basin in a large saucepan and pour in boiling water to come halfway up the sides of the basin. Bring the water back to the boil, then simmer, covered for 2 hours, adding more boiling water if needed.

4 Remove the pudding from the saucepan and allow to rest for 5 minutes, then run a knife around the edge and turn out onto a warmed serving dish. Dredge with caster sugar and serve hot, with custard or cream, if wished.

Cook's tips

If you have a plastic pudding basin with a snap-on lid, cook the pudding in this, without bothering with greaseproof paper and string. Be doubly careful to keep the boiling water topped up; plastic melts if it gets overheated.

SUNDAY LUNCH FOR FOUR

Lentil soup with lettuce · Roast pork with dried fruits · Rice moulds with sweetcorn · Steamed peas with ham · Brown bread ice cream

THIS SUNDAY LUNCH menu is perfect for a cold winter's day. Lentil soup with lettuce is warming and filling. The main dish, Roast pork with dried fruits, is a traditional Sunday roast with a difference, cooked with a sweet-and-savoury mixture of prunes, apricots, apples and onions. The roasting is begun at high temperature, to crisp the crackling, then continues slowly to ensure the meat is really tender. This, plus the fruit, produces plenty of pan juices so that there is no need for gravy. The vegetable accompaniments are also unusual: individual rice moulds instead of the usual roast potatoes; and peas with fingers of ham. After all this fairly substantial hot food, serve a light cold dessert: the always-popular Brown bread ice cream. This is a Victorian creation, and is much better than it sounds as the breadcrumbs are mixed with brown sugar and caramelized before being added to the ice cream, giving it a lovely crunchiness.

Table Talk

Take a tip from the Continent and serve a variety of different breads to complement the meal. Start with breadsticks for nibbling with pre-lunch drinks, then serve a peasant-style dark wholemeal bread or granary rolls to go with the hearty soup. Thick slices from a crusty white loaf, or a French stick briefly warmed in the oven, would go well with the main course. Alternatively you could serve thinly sliced rye bread – either with or without caraway seeds – both would go perfectly with roast pork.

If you plan to serve a cheese course, accompany it with a selection of all these different breads, plus plain biscuits or crackers.

Wine Ideas

Red or white wine go equally well with roast pork. If you're having white, either go for something fairly robust such as a Chardonnay, or a sharper and slightly dry Sauvignon Blanc. Remember to serve both these wines chilled to bring out their full flavour.

If you prefer a red wine, go for a medium-bodied one – a Pinot Noir or Cabernet Franc are both delicious with pork. Or why not drink a dry cider for a change?

Countdown

The day before
Make the Brown bread ice cream.
Soak the dried apricots and prunes.

Four hours before
Take the pork out of the fridge.
Make the Lentil soup with lettuce to the end of step 4.
Prepare the orange julienne strips to decorate the ice cream.
Defrost the peas and sweetcorn.

Two hours before
Prepare and start to roast the pork. Add the fruit mixture and return to the oven.
Cook the rice, mix with the sweetcorn and spoon into the prepared moulds.

One hour ten minutes before
Prepare the apples, add to the pork and continue roasting.

Ten minutes before
Combine the soup ingredients and start to reheat.
Bake the Rice moulds with sweetcorn.
Cook the Steamed peas with ham and keep warm.

Before serving the main course
Transfer the ice cream from the freezer to the fridge.

Before serving the dessert
Turn out the ice cream and decorate.

★*Lentil soup with lettuce*

- ***Preparation: 20 minutes***
- ***Cooking: 50 minutes*** • ***Serves 4***

100g/4oz GREEN LENTILS
1.3L/2¼pt CHICKEN STOCK
1 SMALL ONION, stuck with 1 CLOVE
1 BOUQUET GARNI
1tbls TOMATO PURÉE
1 ROUND LETTUCE
50g/2oz BUTTER
3tbls DOUBLE CREAM
1tbls LEMON JUICE
SALT and PEPPER

1 Rinse and drain the lentils, discarding any pieces of grit or discoloured lentils. Put the lentils in a saucepan with the chicken stock, onion, bouquet garni and tomato purée. Bring to the boil, then reduce the heat, cover and simmer for 30-40 minutes or until the lentils are tender. Remove from the heat, discard the onion and bouquet garni and leave to cool a little.

2 Meanwhile, shred the lettuce leaves, and melt half the butter in a saucepan. Add the shredded lettuce, cover and cook over very low heat for 2-3 minutes, or until the lettuce is wilted and softened; be careful not to overcook or it will lose its bright colour.

3 Pour the cooled soup into a blender or food processor and blend until smooth. Alternatively, pass it through a fine sieve or vegetable mill. Return the purée to the rinsed-out pan.

4 Stir in the wilted lettuce, cream and remaining butter. Season with lemon juice and salt and pepper to taste. Reheat gently without allowing to boil, and serve very hot.

Cook's tips

To make your own bouquet garni tie together a bay leaf, a few parsley stalks and a sprig of thyme with kitchen string.

Skewered sausages and bacon

- ***Preparation:* 10 minutes**
- ***Cooking:* 10 minutes** • ***Serves 4***

12 small slices of STREAKY BACON
24 CANNED COCKTAIL SAUSAGES, drained
PEPPER
OIL
TOMATO WEDGES and WATERCRESS SPRIGS, to garnish

1 Heat the grill to high. Cut each slice of bacon in half and wrap each piece around a sausage. Thread six bacon-wrapped sausages onto each of four flat metal skewers. Season with pepper.

2 Brush the grid of the grill pan with a little oil. Arrange the skewers on it and grill 7.5cm/3in from the heat, for 5 minutes on each side or until the bacon is cooked.

3 Arrange the skewers on a heated platter and serve at once, garnished with tomato and watercress.

★ Roast pork with dried fruits

- ***Preparation:* 20 minutes, plus soaking**
- ***Cooking:* 2 hours** • ***Serves 4***

1.1kg/2½lb LEAN LOIN OF PORK, chined, with skin left on
1tbls OIL
SALT and PEPPER
175g/6oz DRIED PRUNES, soaked overnight
100g/4oz DRIED APRICOTS, soaked overnight
1 LARGE ONION, very coarsely chopped
¼tsp DRIED THYME
15g/½oz BUTTER
2 TART, CRISP EATING APPLES

1 Take the pork out of the refrigerator about 2 hours before cooking so that it comes to room temperature.

2 Heat the oven to 230C/450F/gas 8. Using a sharp knife, score the pork skin in parallel slanting lines about 1cm/½in apart in one direction, then further apart in the other direction to make a diamond pattern.

3 Put the pork in a roasting tin. Rub the oil into the skin and season generously with salt and pepper. Roast for 15 minutes.

4 Meanwhile, drain the prunes and apricots, reserving the liquid, and stone the prunes if necessary. Put them in a bowl along with the onion and thyme; season generously and mix well.

5 Remove the pork from the oven and reduce the temperature to 150C/300F/gas 2. Surround the pork with the fruit mixture and dot with the butter, then return the tin to the oven.

6 Quarter, peel and core the apples. When the pork has been back in the oven for 20 minutes, add the apples to the other fruit and mix gently.

7 Continue to roast for 1½ hours or until the pork is cooked through, basting occasionally with the reserved soaking liquid.

8 To serve, transfer the pork to a heated serving dish. Remove the fruit with a slotted spoon and arrange round the joint. Pour the juices over the fruits. Serve at once.

Steak and kidney pie

• ***Preparation: 25 minutes***

• ***Cooking: 35 minutes*** • ***Serves 4***

900g/2lb BRAISING STEAK
350g/12oz LAMB'S KIDNEYS
50g/2oz FLOUR
SALT and PEPPER
50g/2oz BUTTER
4 SHALLOTS, finely chopped
1tsp WORCESTERSHIRE SAUCE
425ml/¾ pt BEEF STOCK
1 BAY LEAF
1tbls CHOPPED PARSLEY
a pinch of DRIED MARJORAM
400g/14oz FROZEN PUFF PASTRY, defrosted
1 EGG, beaten

1 Cut the steak into 4cm/1½in cubes. Cut the kidneys in half horizontally and remove the membrane, fat and any large tubes, then cut into 5mm/¼in thick slices. Season the flour with salt and pepper and toss the meat in it until lightly coated all over.

2 Melt the butter in a heavy saucepan or casserole and fry the shallots over medium heat until golden. Add the steak and kidney, in batches if necessary, and brown quickly but thoroughly all over, stirring constantly.

3 Pour on the Worcestershire sauce and stock. Add the bay leaf, parsley and marjoram. Season well. Stir, cover and simmer over low heat for 1½-2 hours or until the steak is tender.

4 Heat the oven to 230C/450F/gas 8. Place a pie funnel in the centre of 1.5L/2½pt oval dish. Add the meat and gravy and set aside to cool slightly.

5 Meanwhile, roll out the pastry and cut a lid for the pie a little larger than the pie dish. Cut a strip from the pastry trimmings, moisten the edge of the pie dish and fit the strip round it. Then moisten the strip and put on the pastry lid, cutting a cross in the centre for the funnel. Knock up the edge of the pastry with the blade of a knife and crimp it evenly all round with your fingers. Cut leaf-shaped decorations from the remaining trimmings and stick them on with beaten egg. Glaze the pastry with beaten egg.

6 Bake the pie for 10 minutes, then lower the heat to 190C/375F/gas 5. Continue baking for a further 10-15 minutes or until the pastry is golden brown.

★ *Rice moulds with sweetcorn*

• ***Preparation: 10 minutes***

• ***Cooking: 40 minutes*** • ***Serves 4***

SALT and PEPPER
1tsp LEMON JUICE
175g/6oz LONG-GRAIN RICE
75g/3oz FROZEN SWEETCORN, defrosted and drained
MELTED BUTTER, for greasing

1 Bring a large pan of salted water to the boil and add the lemon juice. Slowly trickle in the rice so that the water doesn't go off the boil. Stir once, then boil gently for 13-16 minutes or until the rice is tender but not mushy.

2 Drain the rice, rinse with hot water and drain again thoroughly. Stir in the sweetcorn and season to taste with salt and pepper.

3 Heat the oven to 150C/300F/gas 2. Brush four 150ml/¼pt soufflé dishes or ovenproof ramekins with melted butter. Spoon in the rice and sweetcorn mixture, pressing down gently and making sure that it comes level with the tops, to stop the moulds from collapsing when turned out. Put the dishes on a baking tray, cover each one with foil and cook in the oven for 20 minutes.

4 Protecting your hands with oven gloves, invert each dish in turn onto a heated plate and give the base a little tap. Remove the dishes very carefully and serve the rice moulds immediately.

★ Steamed peas with ham

- ***Preparation: 10 minutes, plus defrosting***
- ***Cooking: 10 minutes*** • ***Serves 4***

450g/1lb FROZEN PEAS, defrosted
2tbls finely chopped SPRING ONION or SHALLOT
50g/2oz BUTTER
1 thick slice of COOKED HAM
1tbls LEMON JUICE
SALT and PEPPER

1 Put the peas, spring onion or shallot and 25g/1oz butter in the top pan of a double boiler, or in a heatproof bowl set over a pan of water. Cover and cook over boiling water for 7 minutes or until tender.

2 Meanwhile, cut the ham into strips about 5cm/2in long by 5mm/¼in wide. Heat the remaining butter in a small frying pan and fry the ham strips for 4 minutes or until golden, tossing occasionally.

3 Combine the peas and ham strips in a heated serving dish. Add the lemon juice and season to taste with salt and pepper. Serve as soon as possible.

Danish cabbage

- ***Preparation: 15 minutes***
- ***Cooking: 25 minutes*** • ***Serves 4***

450g/1lb WHITE CABBAGE
25g/1oz BUTTER
2tbls FLOUR
150ml/¼pt MILK
SALT and PEPPER
FRESHLY GRATED NUTMEG and FLAT-LEAVED PARSLEY, to garnish

1 Remove the coarse outer leaves from the cabbage. Cut the cabbage into quarters and remove the solid central core with a sharp knife. Slice the cabbage very finely with a large, sharp knife.

2 Melt the butter in a small pan and stir in the flour. Cook for 2-3 minutes, stirring, to make a roux. Add the milk, whisking constantly, then cook for 10 minutes or until the mixture thickens, stirring occasionally.

3 Meanwhile, bring a large saucepan of salted water to the boil. Add the cabbage and simmer for 5-7 minutes or until just tender. Drain the cabbage, reserving 150ml/¼pt of the cooking liquid. Keep the cooked cabbage hot.

4 Stir the reserved cooking liquid into the white sauce. Season with salt and pepper to taste and cook for 5 minutes, whisking occasionally.

5 Pour the sauce over the cabbage and mix well. Spoon into a heated serving dish, garnish with a grating of nutmeg and a sprig of parsley and serve at once.

Cook's tips

Save the outer cabbage leaves for use in minestrone or another vegetable soup. Wrap in a polythene bag and store in the fridge for a day or two.

Variations

For an authentic Scandinavian touch, scatter a few crushed dill or caraway seeds over the top of the dish instead of the nutmeg.

★ Brown bread ice cream

- **Preparation: 30 minutes, plus cooling and freezing**
- **Cooking: 30 minutes** • **Serves 4**

100g/4oz BROWN BREADCRUMBS
100g/4oz DEMERARA SUGAR
600ml/1pt DOUBLE CREAM
7-8tbls BRANDY
thin strips of ORANGE ZEST, to decorate

1 Heat the oven to 190C/375F/gas 5. Mix the breadcrumbs with the sugar and spread the mixture evenly on a baking tray. Cook in the oven for 30 minutes or until caramelized, stirring with a fork every 5 minutes. Leave to cool.

2 Whip the cream to soft peaks. Gently fold in the brandy and cold caramelized breadcrumbs. Pour the mixture into a shallow freezer container and freeze until the mixture hardens to a depth of 2.5cm/1in around the sides of the container; this should take about 1 hour. Meanwhile, line an 850ml/1½pt loaf tin with stretch wrap.

3 Remove the ice cream from the freezer and beat vigorously with a fork to break down any ice crystals. Spoon into the lined tin. Press down firmly, cover with stretch wrap and freeze for 5-6 hours or until firm.

4 About 30 minutes before serving, transfer the ice cream to the refrigerator so that it softens slightly. When ready to serve, invert the tin onto a flat serving dish and cover with a cloth wrung out in hot water. Ease off the tin and peel off the stretch wrap. Decorate with the strips of orange zest.

Variations

Decorate the ice cream with orange segments, either instead of or as well as the strips of zest.

Semolina mould with blackcurrant sauce

- **Preparation: 1 hour, plus chilling**
- **Cooking: 20 minutes** • **Serves 4-6**

700ml/1¼pt MILK
75g/3oz SEMOLINA
1½tsp POWDERED GELATINE
2 EGGS, separated
75g/3oz CASTER SUGAR
1-2 drops of VANILLA ESSENCE
JUICE OF ½ LEMON
4tbls DOUBLE CREAM
450g/1lb BLACKCURRANTS, fresh or frozen
100g/4oz ICING SUGAR, sifted

1 Pour the milk into a saucepan and bring to the boil. Stir in the semolina and simmer, stirring frequently, for 15-20 minutes or until the mixture is thick and the semolina cooked. Remove from the heat and cool slightly.

2 Put 2tbls water in a small bowl, sprinkle over the gelatine and leave for 5 minutes to soften. Put the bowl in a pan of boiling water until the gelatine dissolves and the liquid is clear; do not stir. Allow to cool slightly.

3 Combine the egg yolks and caster sugar in a bowl. Whisk until thick and light, then beat in the semolina mixture, vanilla essence and lemon juice. Beat in the dissolved gelatine.

4 Dampen a 1.1L/2pt decorative mould. Whisk the egg whites until stiff but not dry. With a large metal spoon, fold the cream into the semolina mixture. Then fold in the whisked egg whites. Turn the mixture into the prepared mould and chill until set, about 2-3 hours.

5 Meanwhile, strip the stalks from fresh blackcurrants with a fork. Put the fruit in a sieve and rinse quickly in cold running water. Drain well, shaking off as much moisture as possible. If using frozen blackcurrants, defrost and drain well.

6 Purée the blackcurrants in a blender or food processor. Rub the purée through a sieve into a bowl and beat in the icing sugar.

7 To serve, dip the mould briefly in hot water and invert onto a serving plate. Spoon the sauce over the mould and serve.

BUFFET LUNCH FOR FOUR TO SIX

Pepper and mozzarella strips · Turkey salad with oranges ·

Ham and apple salad · Winter salad ·

Apricot upside-down cake

A BUFFET MEAL BASED on salads is a good idea just after Christmas when you may not feel like doing a lot of cooking.

Start with something hot but quickly made: Pepper and mozzarella strips, puff-pastry mini pizzas served straight from the oven. Follow this with a mouth-watering array of salads where guests can help themselves. Turkey salad with oranges is an ideal way to serve leftover roast turkey; similarly Ham and apple salad makes good use of any cold gammon. Accompany these with another salad of your choice: Winter salad, based on red and white cabbage, is quick and easy.

Finish this informal buffet meal with easy-to-eat Apricot upside-down cake, served warm with chilled apricot cream.

Wine Ideas

A buffet lunch calls for wines which are fairly light-bodied. Choose a light Italian red such as Valpolicella, or French Anjou Rouge; plus a medium dry white for those who prefer it – Pinot Grigiot, to stay in Italy; or a Riesling such as Bernkasteler Kurfurstlay or Munsterer Schlosskapelle. If it's a cold day a glass of medium-dry sherry would give guests a warm welcome.

Countdown

The day before
Defrost the pastry for the Pepper and Mozzarella strips, then prepare them ready for baking and chill. Prepare all the ingredients for the Turkey salad with oranges. Make the dressing and marinate the turkey.

In the morning
Make the Winter salad; cover with stretch wrap and store in a cool place.

Two hours before
Prepare the Ham and apple salad.

One hour before
Make the Apricot upside-down cake and chill the apricot cream. When the cake is cooked, raise the oven temperature ready for the Pepper and mozzarella strips.

Thirty-five minutes before
Bake the Pepper and Mozzarella strips.

Thirty minutes before
Finish the Turkey salad with oranges.
Transfer the Winter salad to a serving dish.
Transfer the Ham and apple salad to a serving dish, garnish and decorate with the reserved apple slices.

Before serving the starter
Take the Pepper and mozzarella strips out of the oven, cut into six and garnish with olives.

Pepper and mozzarella strips

● ***Preparation:*** *10 minutes, chilling, then 10 minutes*

● ***Cooking:*** *55 minutes* ● ***Serves*** *4-6*

100g/4oz FROZEN PUFF PASTRY, defrosted
15g/½ oz BUTTER
1tbls OIL
1 RED PEPPER, deseeded and thinly sliced
1 ONION, thinly sliced
SALT and PEPPER
75g/3oz MOZZARELLA CHEESE, thinly sliced
MELTED BUTTER, for brushing
BLACK OLIVES, to garnish

1 Heat the oven to 200C/400F/gas 6. Roll the pastry out into a strip 40cm/16in long by 7.5cm/3in wide. Cut the strip in half crosswise and lay the pieces side by side on a dampened baking tray. Chill for 30 minutes.

2 Meanwhile heat the butter and oil in a large heavy saucepan. Add the sliced onion and cook over low heat for 10-15 minutes until soft and pale golden, stirring frequently. Add the red pepper slices and cook for a further 10 minutes, stirring occasionally. Season with salt and pepper to taste and leave to cool.

3 Spread the onion and pepper mixture over the pastry strips, not quite to the edges. Lay the mozzarella slices over the top.

4 Fold the outer edges of the pastry over so they just touch the mixture. Brush the edges with a little melted butter and press them down firmly to seal. Bake for 20-30 minutes, until the pastry edges are golden.

5 To serve, cut each strip into three pieces and garnish with black olives. Serve hot or make ahead and re-heat for 5 minutes in a hot oven.

Tunnied veal pâté

● *Preparation: 50 minutes, plus cooling and chilling*

● *Cooking: 40 minutes* ● *Serves 6*

350g/12oz PIECE BONELESS VEAL
50g/2oz CANNED ANCHOVY FILLETS
2 GARLIC CLOVES, slivered
1 VEAL KNUCKLE BONE
1 ONION, stuck with 2 CLOVES
SALT and PEPPER
1tbls CHOPPED FRESH BASIL
1tbls LEMON JUICE
100g/4oz CANNED TUNA, drained
1tbls MELTED BUTTER
1tbls FINELY CHOPPED PARSLEY
425ml/15fl oz CANNED BEEF CONSOMME
2tsp POWDERED GELATINE
CANNED PIMIENTO, cut into triangles
LETTUCE LEAVES, to garnish
TOAST and BUTTER, to serve

1 Using a sharp-pointed knife, make small incisions all over the veal. Cut four of the anchovy fillets in half lengthways, then in half again, crossways. Insert a sliver of garlic and anchovy fillet into each incision.

2 Put the veal in a casserole with the veal knuckle and the cloved onion. Season with salt and pepper to taste. Add enough water to come halfway up the meat; bring to the boil and skim. Reduce the heat to low, cover and simmer gently for 25 minutes or until the meat is tender but still slightly pink in the centre. Transfer the veal to a plate, season and leave to cool.

3 Cut the veal into pieces, discarding any fat and gristle, and put it through a food processor or the finest blade of a mincer. Transfer to a bowl and stir in the basil, lemon juice, tuna, melted butter and chopped parsley.

4 Boil the consommé for 10 minutes or until reduced to 300ml/½pt. Leave to cool. Meanwhile put 2tbls cold water in a small bowl, sprinkle over the gelatine and leave for 5 minutes to soften. Put the bowl in a saucepan of simmering water and leave until the gelatine has dissolved. Stir it into the consommé to make an aspic and allow to become cold.

5 Pour a thin layer of aspic into the bottom of an 850ml/1½ pt loaf tin and chill until set. Cut the remaining anchovy fillets into thin strips. Arrange a fine lattice of strips with triangles of pimiento.

6 Pour a little more aspic on top (not too much or then decoration will float away) and chill to set. Pour in another layer of aspic.

7 Spoon half the veal and tuna mixture on top of the set aspic and level with a palette knife. Make sure that the remaining aspic is thick and syrupy, on the point of setting. Spoon it over the veal mixture and chill to set. Finally spoon the remaining veal and tuna into the tin and level. Hold a tea towel wrung out in very hot water around the tin for a few seconds, then invert the tin onto a serving plate.

★ *Turkey salad with oranges*

● *Preparation: 20 minutes, plus marinating* ● *Serves 4*

3kg/6½lb ROASTED TURKEY, cold
4 SHALLOTS, finely chopped
2 CELERY STALKS, sliced
6-9tbls OLIVE OIL
2-3tbls RED WINE VINEGAR
½tsp CHOPPED FRESH ROSEMARY LEAVES (or ¼tsp dried)
SALT and PEPPER
4 SMALL ORANGES, divided into segments
1 LETTUCE
8-10 BLACK OLIVES, stoned
1 ROSEMARY SPRIG, to garnish

1 Carve enough meat from the turkey to serve four (about 700g/1½lb). Dice the meat into 1cm/½in cubes and put them in a large bowl. Sprinkle the shallots and celery over the top.

2 Put the oil, vinegar and rosemary in a small bowl or screwtop jar; season with salt and pepper to taste and beat or shake until emulsified. Pour half this dressing over the diced turkey. Toss well, cover and leave to marinate for at least 2 hours in a cold place.

3 To serve, drained the diced turkey and transfer to a clean bowl. Add the orange segments and the remaining dressing; toss well. Line a salad bowl with lettuce leaves, fill with the turkey salad and top with the olives. Garnish with the rosemary sprig.

★ Ham and apple salad

● *Preparation: 25 minutes* ● *Serves 4*

JUICE OF 1 LEMON
3 RED DESSERT APPLES
125ml/4fl oz MAYONNAISE
3tbls SINGLE CREAM
350g/12oz COOKED HAM, cut into cubes
1 SMALL GREEN PEPPER, deseeded and thinly sliced
SALT and PEPPER
75g/3oz STILTON or other blue cheese, crumbled
3tbls CHOPPED WALNUTS

1 Prepare some acidulated water by putting 2tbls water and the juice of the lemon in a bowl. Core and slice the apples but do not peel them. Turn the slices in the acidulated water to prevent discolouration.

2 Put the mayonnaise and cream into a large bowl and stir to mix. Drain the apple slices and reserve 16 for garnishing.

3 Add the ham, green pepper and apple slices to the mayonnaise mixture. Season with salt and pepper to taste and toss with a fork until the ingredients are evenly coated with mayonnaise.

4 To serve spoon the salad onto a serving platter and sprinkle with the crumbled cheese and chopped walnuts. Garnish attractively with the reserved apple slices.

Green rice salad

● *Preparation: 20 minutes, plus cooling*

● *Cooking: 20 minutes* ● *Serves 4-6*

225g/8oz LONG-GRAIN RICE
SALT and PEPPER
1 LARGE GREEN PEPPER, deseeded and diced
75g/3oz SPRING ONIONS, finely chopped
2tbls WHITE WINE VINEGAR
8tbls OLIVE OIL
1tbls FINELY CHOPPED MINT

For the garnish:
3 SPRING ONIONS, trimmed
1 MINT SPRIG

1 Measure 600ml/1pt water into a saucepan, add 1tsp salt and bring to the boil. Add the rice, return to the boil, then reduce the heat and cover tightly. Leave for 12-15 minutes until the water has been almost completely absorbed by the rice.

2 Stir the green pepper and spring onions into the pan and continue cooking over low heat until all the liquid has been absorbed – about 5 minutes. The rice should be firm, with separate grains, and the vegetables crisp. Allow the rice mixture to become cold.

3 Put the vinegar, oil and finely chopped mint into a small bowl or screwtop jar and season with salt and pepper. Beat or shake until emulsified. Pour over the cold rice and set aside, covered, until ready to serve. Garnish with the spring onions and mint sprig just before serving.

★ Winter salad

• Preparation: 25 minutes **• Serves 4**

225g/8oz WHITE CABBAGE
225g/8oz RED CABBAGE
150ml/¼pt SOURED CREAM
6tbls CHOPPED WALNUTS
1 GARLIC CLOVE, finely chopped
SALT and PEPPER
FLAT-LEAVED PARSLEY or CORIANDER, to garnish

1 Cut the red and white cabbage into quarters with a large sharp knife and remove the cores. Weigh out the specified amounts and slice them finely and evenly.

2 Pour the soured cream into a large bowl, add the walnuts and garlic and season with salt and pepper to taste. Add the prepared cabbage and toss with a fork until it is evenly coated in the dressing. Spoon onto a serving platter and garnish with a sprig of flat-leaved parsley.

Cook's tips

This is an economical way to enjoy a crisp, crunchy salad in the middle of winter. It is similar to coleslaw, but the red cabbage adds colour and the soured cream and garlic add extra flavour.

Red, white and green salad

• Preparation: 20 minutes **• Serves 4**

½ CUCUMBER
100g/4oz COOKED BEETROOT
100g/4oz MOZZARELLA CHEESE
175g/6oz COOKED PEAS
4 GREEN SPRING ONION TOPS, cut into 5mm/¼in segments
4 SMALL TOMATOES, thinly sliced

For the vinaigrette dressing:
½tsp DIJON MUSTARD
2tbls WINE VINEGAR
6tbls OLIVE OIL
1tbls MIXED DRIED HERBS
SALT and PEPPER

1 Peel the cucumber and beetroot; cut the flesh into dice of even size. Dice the mozzarella to the same size. Put the diced vegetables in a bowl with the peas, cover and chill until needed. Keep the cheese in a separate bowl.

2 To make the vinaigrette dressing, put the mustard in a cup with the vinegar, oil and herbs; season with salt and pepper and beat to mix.

3 When ready to serve, remix the dressing and pour it over the vegetables. Toss gently, add the green onion segments and toss again.

4 Arrange a circle of overlapping slices of tomato around the edge of a glass salad bowl. Add the mozzarella cheese to the vegetable mixture, toss to mix and put carefully into the ring of tomatoes. Serve at once.

Cook's tips

This colourful salad makes a good first course as well as an accompaniment to any cold meat meat dish.

★Apricot upside-down cake

• *Preparation: 25 minutes, plus chilling*

• *Cooking: 35 minutes* **• *Serves 4-6***

40g/1½oz BUTTER
6tbls SOFT LIGHT BROWN SUGAR
425g/15oz CANNED APRICOT HALVES
10 WHOLE ALMONDS
2 LARGE EGGS
150g/5oz CASTER SUGAR
100g/4oz FLOUR
PINCH OF SALT
½tsp BAKING POWDER
½tsp ALMOND EXTRACT
7tbls HOT MILK
150ml/¼pt DOUBLE CREAM
1-2tbls BRANDY

1 Heat the oven to 180C/350F/gas 4. Melt the butter in small saucepan over a very low heat. Remove from the heat and stir in the soft light brown sugar.

2 Spread the sugar and butter mixture over the base of an 8cm/7in square cake tin, using a palette knife.

3 Drain 10 apricot halves and pat dry with absorbent paper. Put an almond in each apricot cavity and arrange the halves, almond side down, in the prepared tin, placing one in the centre.

4 Break the eggs into a bowl and whisk with the caster sugar until light and fluffy. Sift in the flour, salt and baking powder. Beat with a wooden spoon until well blended. Stir in the almond extract and hot milk and pour the batter slowly into the cake tin.

5 Bake for 35 minutes, or until the cake is golden brown and springs back when gently pressed with the fingertips.

6 Meanwhile put the remaining apricots in a blender with a little of the liquid and blend until smooth. Discard the remaining liquid or keep to use in another recipe.

7 Whip the cream until soft peaks form, then stir in the apricot purée and add brandy to taste. Stir until well blended and chill until needed.

8 Remove the cake from the oven and loosen the edges with a sharp knife. Leave to cool in the tin for 6 minutes, then invert it onto a heated serving platter. Serve warm with the chilled apricot cream.

Apple mince tarts

• *Preparation: making pastry, then 40 minutes*

• *Cooking: 25 minutes* **• *Makes 12***

225g/8oz SHORTCRUST PASTRY (see Cook's tips, page 18)
175g/6oz SOFT LIGHT BROWN SUGAR
3tbls FLOUR
8 TART DESSERT APPLES, peeled, cored and sliced
450g/1lb BOUGHT MINCEMEAT
2tbls BRANDY
2 LARGE DESSERT APPLES
15g/½oz BUTTER

1 Roll out the pastry and use it to line 12 individual tart tins. Heat the oven to 200C/400F/gas 6.

2 Put the sugar and flour in a bowl and mix well. Sprinkle 2tsp of the mixture in the bottom of each pastry case. Reserve 4tbls of the mixture for the topping. Layer the sliced apples in the pastry cases, sprinkling each layer with some of the reserved flour and sugar mixture.

3 Put three-quarters of the jar of mincemeat into a bowl and stir in the brandy. Spread the brandied mincemeat in a layer in each pastry case.

4 Peel and core the two large dessert apples and cut them into 12 rings, 5mm/¼in thick. Put a ring on top of each filled pastry case. Divide the remaining mincemeat between the tarts, spooning it into the hole in each apple ring. Sprinkle the top with the remaining flour and sugar mixture and dot with butter.

5 Bake for 20-25 minutes or until the apples are tender and the pastry is golden. Allow to cool slightly before removing from the tins. These tarts can be served warm or cold as liked.

TEA FOR EIGHT *Spicy egg sandwiches · English muffins · Ginger fruit cake · Cheesecake biscuits · Iced chocolate brownies*

A TRADITIONAL AFTERNOON tea – one of the great British institutions – conjures up visions of families sitting round the fireside, of home baking and hearty appetites, the room warm and snug to keep out the dark, wet afternoon. These days there isn't time to make a proper tea every day – so offer this scrumptious spread to your family or friends as a special treat. You'll probably find our suggested menu caters for the larger appetite and there won't be much call for dinner afterwards! Serve the Spicy egg sandwiches first, and follow with the hot buttered muffins and squares of chocolate brownies and cheesecake biscuits – sheer indulgence. The fruit cake is a classic but made special with an extra gingery flavour which goes very well with a piping hot cup of tea, so keep a freshly brewed pot ready for pouring.

Setting the Scene

Make the most of the idea of a traditional tea by serving it on your best china plates and providing cake forks if you have them. If you have a cake stand, this is the time to use it. Teatime is a relaxed affair so put all the dishes out on the table, and let your guests help themselves. Naturally, if you have an open fire and it's a cold day, serve tea in front of the fire. When it dies down you can even toast your muffins over the embers.

A Taste of Tea

The obvious drink to have with tea is tea! To make a good cup of tea, always warm the pot first, use loose tea leaves, not tea bags, and pour on boiling (not just hot) water. Leave to brew for 3-5 minutes, then pour out using a strainer. Whether the milk goes in before or after is just a matter of personal preference. Some people may prefer a slice of lemon instead. Offer a choice of sugar or honey for those who like to sweeten their tea. In the summer, if it is very hot, serve iced tea – soak the leaves in cold water overnight, then strain and refrigerate, or make tea normally, allow to cool, then strain and chill. Serve, sweetened to taste, in tall glasses with lots of ice and slices of lemon.

Countdown

Two or three days before
Make the Ginger fruit cake. Wrap in foil and store in an airtight container.

One or two days before
Make the Cheesecake biscuits and store in an airtight container in the refrigerator.

In the morning
Prepare the dough for the muffins and leave to prove.
Prepare the chocolate brownies and bake.
Complete the muffins but do not toast. Store in an airtight container when cool.

1 hour 30 minutes before
Toast the sesame seeds and boil the eggs for the sandwich filling. Allow to cool.

One hour before
Prepare the icing for the brownies, ice and cut into squares.
Complete the sandwich filling.

Thirty minutes before
Cut and butter the bread for the sandwiches. Fill with the spicy egg mixture and cut into quarters.
Toast the muffins and spread with butter.

★ *Spicy egg sandwiches*

- ***Preparation: 10 minutes***
- ***Cooking: 20 minutes, plus cooling***
- ***Makes 16 small sandwiches***

2tbls SESAME SEEDS
4 EGGS
3tbls MAYONNAISE
SALT and PEPPER
pinch of CAYENNE PEPPER
pinch of GROUND CUMIN
2tbls CHOPPED WATERCRESS
BUTTER, for spreading
8 slices of WHOLEMEAL BREAD

1 Heat the oven to 180C/350F/gas 4. Sprinkle the sesame seeds onto a heatproof dish and bake for 15-20 minutes, until toasted, stirring frequently. Meanwhile, boil the eggs for 10 minutes. Leave to cool, then peel and chop.

2 In a small bowl, combine the eggs with the mayonnaise and add salt, pepper, cayenne pepper and cumin to taste. Stir in the sesame seeds and watercress.

3 Butter the slices of bread lightly and divide the filling between four of them. Top with the remaining slices of bread and trim the crusts off, if wished. Cut each sandwich in four to serve.

Chicken almond flower sandwiches

● *Preparation: 10 minutes* ● *Makes 8*

75g/3oz skinned COOKED CHICKEN, thinly sliced
25g/1oz CELERY STALK, thinly sliced
15g/½oz FLAKED ALMONDS, toasted
3tbls MAYONNAISE
SALT and PEPPER
pinch of CAYENNE PEPPER
4 thin slices day-old WHITE BREAD
BUTTER, softened for spreading
SPRIGS OF CRESS, to garnish

1 In a bowl, combine the chicken, celery and almonds. Add the mayonnaise and stir well to blend, using a wooden spoon. Season with salt and pepper to taste, and a pinch of cayenne pepper.

2 Spread the slices of bread with softened butter. Divide the chicken mixture between two slices of bread, and make two sandwiches with the remaining slices of bread.

3 Using 5cm/2in flower-shaped biscuit cutter, cut each sandwich into four flower shapes. Serve as soon as possible, garnished with sprigs of cress, or wrap in stretch wrap and keep chilled until needed.

Variations

To give the sandwiches added flavour and colour, try using different breads, such as black rye or wholemeal, as well as the white.

★ English muffins

● *Preparation: 20 minutes, plus proving*

● *Cooking: 20 minutes. plus toasting* ● *Makes 16*

15g/½oz FRESH YEAST, or 2tsp DRIED YEAST
1tsp SUGAR
300ml/½pt MILK, lukewarm
450g/1lb STRONG WHITE FLOUR
1tsp SALT
1 EGG, lightly beaten
25g/1oz BUTTER, melted, plus extra .for greasing
BUTTER, to serve

1 Put fresh yeast in a small bowl, and cream together with the sugar and 3tbls of the milk until smooth. Add half of the remaining milk and mix well. If using dried yeast, stir the sugar into half the milk, sprinkle the yeast over the top and mix well. Either way, set aside in a warm place for 15-20 minutes until the mixture is frothy.

2 Sift the flour and salt into a bowl, then stir in the yeast mixture, remaining milk, egg and melted butter. Beat until smooth and well combined. Cover and put in a warm place for 45 minutes or until the dough has doubled in size.

3 Gently heat a large heavy frying pan or griddle until a sprinkling of flour on the surface turns brown in 2-3 minutes. Dust off the flour and lightly butter the pan.

4 With lightly floured hands, divide the muffin mixture into 16 pieces. Shape into 7.5cm/3in rounds. Cook, in batches, for 5-6 minutes on one side, then flip the muffins over and cook on the other side for 3-4 minutes until evenly brown. Butter the pan between batches. Cool the muffins on a wire rack.

5 To serve, split the muffins, grill or toast just enough to reheat, and spread with butter.

Cook's tips

If using easy-blend yeast, mix it with the flour and salt, following the packet instructions – do not add to the milk.

Variations

Make savoury muffins by adding 75g/3oz grated Cheddar cheese and 2tsp chopped herbs to the batter. Split the muffins and top with more cheese before toasting under the grill.

★

Ginger fruit cake

● ***Preparation: 30 minutes***

● ***Cooking: 1¼ hours, plus cooling and maturing***

● ***Serves 8-10***

150g/5oz BUTTER, softened, plus extra for greasing
150g/5oz SOFT LIGHT BROWN SUGAR
3 LARGE EGGS, lightly beaten
225g/8oz FLOUR, sifted
1tsp BAKING POWDER
1-2tbls MILK (if needed)
175g/6oz DRIED APRICOTS, chopped
175g/6oz DRIED DATES, chopped
100g/4oz CRYSTALLIZED GINGER, chopped
50g/2oz FLAKED ALMONDS
25g/1oz GROUND ALMONDS
grated zest of 1 LEMON

1 Heat the oven to 170C/325F/gas 3. Grease a 15cm/6in deep cake tin; line with greaseproof paper, then grease again.

2 Put the butter and the sugar into a large mixing bowl. Beat with an electric whisk or wooden spoon until light and fluffy. Beat in the eggs a little at a time, adding a bit of the flour if the mixture looks like curdling.

3 Sift together the flour and baking powder and carefully fold into the creamed mixture using a large metal spoon, adding a little milk if necessary to achieve a soft dropping consistency.

4 Carefully fold in the apricots, dates, ginger, flaked and ground almonds and lemon zest until evenly combined. Spoon the mixture into the prepared tin, smooth the surface and bake in the centre of the oven for 1¼ hours or until a skewer inserted into the centre comes out clean. Cover with foil if necessary to prevent burning.

5 Leave to cool in the tin for 10 minutes, then turn out to cool completely on a wire rack. Wrap the cake in foil and store in an airtight tin for 2-3 days before serving.

Walnut layer cake

● ***Preparation: 30 minutes***

● ***Cooking: 1¼ hours, plus cooling***

● ***Serves 8***

175g/6oz SOFT MARGARINE, plus extra for greasing
175g/6oz SELF-RAISING FLOUR
1½tsp BAKING POWDER
175g/6oz SOFT LIGHT BROWN SUGAR
3 LARGE EGGS, lightly beaten
50g/2oz CHOPPED WALNUTS
few drops of VANILLA ESSENCE

For the filling and topping:

350g/12oz FULL-FAT SOFT CHEESE
2tbls CLEAR HONEY
WALNUT HALVES, to decorate

1 Heat the oven to 170C/325F/gas 3. Grease and line a deep 19cm/7½in round cake tin, and grease the lining paper. Sift the flour with the baking powder into a large bowl. Add the margarine, sugar, eggs, walnut pieces and vanilla essence and beat with a wooden spoon or electric whisk for 2-3 minutes until evenly blended.

2 Turn the mixture into the prepared tin and make a shallow hollow in the centre. Bake the cake for about 1¼ hours, until a fine skewer inserted in the centre comes out clean. Leave the cake to stand in the tin for 5 minutes before turning it out onto a wire rack. Remove the lining paper and allow the cake to cool.

3 Make the filling and topping. Beat the soft cheese with a wooden spoon until smooth and creamy, then gradually beat in the honey. Chill until required. Slice the cold cake horizontally into three equal layers. Use some of the cheese mixture to sandwich the layers together and spread the rest over the top, using a palette knife to make an attractive wheel pattern on the surface. Decorate with walnut halves.

Cook's tips

Eggs for all cooking purposes should be used at room temperature. If they are too cold or used straight from the fridge, they curdle more easily. So take your eggs out of the fridge a couple of hours before beginning baking.

Variations

Coffee is a natural complement to walnut. To make a coffee and walnut cake, just replace the vanilla with 1tbls of instant coffee dissolved in 1tbls hot water and mix into the basic ingredients in step 1.

Butterfly cakes

- *Preparation: 30 minutes*
- *Cooking: 20 minutes*
- *Makes 12-16*

100g/4oz BUTTER, softened
100g/4oz CASTER SUGAR
2 EGGS, lightly beaten
100g/4oz SELF-RAISING FLOUR, sifted

For the butter icing:
50g/2oz BUTTER, softened
few drops of PINK FOOD COLOURING
100g/4oz ICING SUGAR, plus extra for dredging

1 Heat the oven to 190C/375F/gas 5 and position a shelf just below centre. Line a bun tin with paper cake cases.

2 Beat the butter until light and creamy. Beat in the sugar until the mixture is light and fluffy.

3 Add the eggs, a little at a time, beating well after each addition, adding a little flour if necessary to prevent curdling. Fold in the flour using a metal spoon. Divide the mixture among the paper cases or moulds. Bake for 15-20 minutes or until golden brown, then leave on a wire rack until cold.

4 To make the icing, cream the butter with a wooden spoon. Add a few drops of food colouring, sift in the icing sugar and beat until smooth.

5 Cut a thin slice from across the top of each cake. Cut the slices in half, and arrange, cut sides down, on the work top. Dredge with icing sugar.

6 Put a generous swirl of butter icing on the centre of each cake, using a piping nozzle or a teaspoon. Press pairs of cake halves into the icing at an angle to represent butterfly wings.

★ Cheesecake biscuits

- *Preparation: 20 minutes*
- *Cooking: 40 minutes, plus cooling*
- *Makes 16*

150g/5oz SOFT LIGHT BROWN SUGAR
175g/6oz FLOUR
75g/3oz CHOPPED WALNUTS
75g/3oz BUTTER, melted
225g/8oz FULL-FAT SOFT CHEESE
100g/4oz SUGAR
1 EGG, beaten
1tbls LEMON JUICE
2tbls MILK
1tsp VANILLA ESSENCE

1 Heat the oven to 180C/350F/gas 4. Combine the brown sugar, flour and walnuts in a large bowl. Stir in the butter and rub with your fingertips until the mixture is light and crumbly.

2 Reserve one-third of the mixture. Place the remainder in a 20cm/8in square tin and press down firmly, making a layer at the bottom of the tin. Bake for 15 minutes.

3 Meanwhile, beat the soft cheese and sugar together in a large bowl until smooth. Beat in the egg, lemon juice, milk and vanilla essence.

4 Pour the filling over the baked crust, top with the reserved crumbs, return to the oven and bake for 25 minutes.

5 Leave to cool in the tin, then cut into 16 squares and carefully remove from the tin. Store the Cheesecake biscuits in an airtight container in the refrigerator for up to two days.

★ Iced chocolate brownies

• *Preparation: 30 minutes*

• *Cooking: 40 minutes, plus setting* •*Makes 12*

100g/4oz BUTTER, plus extra for greasing
50g/2oz PLAIN CHOCOLATE
100g/4oz FLOUR
½tsp BAKING POWDER
pinch of SALT
225g/8oz SUGAR
2 LARGE EGGS
½tsp VANILLA ESSENCE
50g/2oz CHOPPED WALNUTS

For the icing:
40g/1½oz BUTTER
100g/4oz ICING SUGAR, sifted
25g/1oz COCOA

1 Heat the oven to 180C/350F/gas 4. Butter a 18cm × 18cm/7in × 7in baking tin and line it with greaseproof paper. Melt the plain chocolate in the top of a double saucepan over simmering water.

2 Sift the flour with the baking powder and salt into a bowl. In another, large bowl, beat the butter and sugar together until light and creamy. Beat in the eggs, one at a time, followed by the vanilla essence and melted chocolate.

3 With a large metal spoon, fold the flour mixture and the chopped walnuts into the chocolate mixture. Spoon it into the prepared baking tin and bake in the oven for 35-40 minutes, or until the surface is firm to the touch and a skewer inserted in the centre comes out clean. Cool in the tin for a few minutes, then turn out onto a wire rack and allow to cool. Trim away the crusty edges using a serrated knife.

4 To make the icing, melt the butter in a small pan and stir in the icing sugar and cocoa. Gradually add 2tbls water, beating with a wooden spoon until smooth.

5 Spread the icing over the top of the cake with a palette knife and leave to set, then cut into 12 portions.

Freezer

Iced chocolate brownies, like most chocolate cakes, freeze very well for up to 3 months. Store them in a rigid polythene box, rather than a plastic bag, so that the icing will not be disturbed. They will thaw in about an hour at room temperature.

Scotch shortbread

• *Preparation: 30 minutes*

• *Cooking: 25 minutes* •*Makes 46 biscuits*

225g/8oz FLOUR, plus extra for rolling
225g/8oz GROUND RICE
275g/10oz BUTTER, diced
100g/4oz CASTER SUGAR, plus extra for dusting
1 EGG
3-4tbls DOUBLE CREAM
½tsp VANILLA ESSENCE

1 Heat the oven to 190C/375F/gas 5. Sift the flour into a mixing bowl and add the ground rice, mixing well. Rub in the butter lightly with your fingertips, then stir in the sugar.

2 In a small bowl, beat the egg with cream and vanilla essence using a fork. Pour this over the dry ingredients, mixing to a smooth paste with your hands, adding more cream if necessary.

3 Turn the dough out onto a floured board and knead lightly until the dough is free from cracks. Flour a rolling pin and roll the dough out to about 5mm/¼in thick. Cut out rounds with a 5cm/2in biscuit cutter and place them on baking sheets, re-rolling as necessary until all the dough is used. Prick each biscuit with a fork.

4 Bake the biscuits for 20-25 minutes or until they are lightly coloured. Dust them with caster sugar while they are still hot and transfer them to a wire rack to cool. When cold, pack them in an airtight tin or glass jar.

DINNER IN THE GARDEN FOR SIX *Seafood rice salad · Spiced beef · Cold pea salad · Orange and onion salad · Gateau Esterel*

ENTERTAINING IN THE garden should be a relaxed occasion, not just for the guests but for the hosts as well. So this menu is based on a magnificent cold joint of beef and a rich chocolate gateau, both cooked in advance, plus a selection of original salads easily prepared on the day.

As a starter serve Seafood rice salad, a delicious mixture of cold asparagus, crabmeat and prawns.

The Spiced beef for the main course is a large piece of silverside (salted topside) steeped in a spicy marinade for 10 days before cooking. (Any left over will make superb sandwiches.) Seve this thinly sliced with two kinds of salad: a green salad with a difference, consisting of garden peas, mange tout and lettuce; and colourful Orange and onion salad.

For the finale: Gateau Esterel, made from sweet yeast dough baked in a ring mould, moistened with syrup and liberally spread with Cointreau-flavoured chocolate icing.

Setting the Scene

Tidy the garden and mow the lawn in the days running up to the dinner party so that it looks its best. Check whether you will need to borrow any extra garden chairs. For the evening itself, arrange to have some kind of outdoor lighting: nothing makes a garden look so glamorous. This can take the form of outdoor-grade fairy lights run from the house electrical supply; large candles protected from breezes by glass jars or lanterns; camping gaz lamps; or tall flares which are guaranteed to burn for many hours. Finally, make sure that you have a fall-back plan just in case the worst happens and it rains.

Wine Ideas

A wine cup is the ideal drink to serve throughout the evening, especially if the weather is hot. Spanish sangria is particularly suitable, as it contains almost as much soda water as wine, boosted by a little brandy. This makes it cooling and refreshing, while at the same time pleasantly exhilarating without being too strong. It is easily made at home, provided that you have a large punch bowl to mix it up in, or you can buy it ready-bottled, based on either red or white wine.

Countdown

Eleven days before
Rub the beef with sugar, cover and chill.

Nine days before
Make the dry marinade for the beef. Rub in, cover and chill. Rub in the marinade and turn the beef for the following eight days.

The day before
Cook the Spiced beef and store in the refrigerator.

In the morning
Make the Gateau Esterel and keep cool.

2 hours before
Take the Spiced beef out of the refrigerator.
Prepare the Cold pea salad and leave to marinate.
Cook the rice and asparagus for the Seafood rice salad.

1½ hours before
Finish the Seafood salad and chill.
Make the Orange and onion salad but do not dress it.

30 minutes before
Carve the Spiced beef.
Assemble the Cold pea salad.
Pour the dressing over the Orange and onion salad and garnish it with parsley.

★ *Seafood rice salad*

- ***Preparation: 25 minuttes, plus chilling***
- ***Cooking: 20 minutes, plus cooling*** • ***Serves 6***

175g/6oz LONG-GRAIN RICE
SALT and PEPPER
24 ASPARAGUS SPEARS, scraped and trimmed
275g/10oz CRABMEAT
2-3tbls FINELY SNIPPED CHIVES
4tbls FINELY CHOPPED PARSLEY
275g/10oz COOKED PEELED PRAWNS
1 COS LETTUCE
SNIPPED CHIVES, to garnish

For the dressing:
150ml/¼pt OLIVE OIL
4-5tbls LEMON JUICE

1 Cook the rice in plenty of lightly salted boiling water until just tender. Drain, rinse, shake out excess moisture and leave to cool.

2 Meanwhile, cook the asparagus spears. Tie them into a bundle and stand upright in a tall saucepan of salted boiling water (or in a glass jar filled with salted boiling water to just below the tips, set in a pan of simmering water). Cover the tips loosely with a dome of foil, crimping it round the top of the pan or jar. Return to the boil, then simmer gently for 10-20 minutes. Drain immediately the stalks feel tender when pierced with the tip of a sharp knife. Leave to cool.

3 Shred the crabmeat with a fork, removing any shell or cartilage, and transfer to a bowl. Add the rice, chives and parsley and 175g/6oz of the prawns. Stir to mix.

4 Make the dressing: combine the oil and lemon juice, season with salt and pepper to taste and shake or beat until emulsified. Pour over the seafood salad and toss until well coated. Taste and adjust the seasoning.

5 Arrange the lettuce leaves on a round platter and pile the seafood salad in the centre. Scatter on the remaining prawns and arrange the asparagus spears on top. Chill for at least 30 minutes and garnish with a sprinkling of chives just before serving.

Roquefort cream quiche

● *Preparation: making the pastry case, then 20 minutes*

● *Cooking: 30 minutes* ● *Serves 6*

25cm/10in PASTRY CASE, baked blind (see Fruity treacle tart, p.18)

For the filling:

175g/6oz FULL-FAT SOFT CHEESE
75g/3oz ROQUEFORT CHEESE
25g/1oz BUTTER, softened
3 EGGS, well beaten
300ml/½pt SINGLE CREAM
1tbls FINELY CHOPPED PARSLEY
1tbls FINELY SNIPPED CHIVES
SALT and PEPPER

1 Remove the pastry case from the tin and put it on a baking tray. Heat the oven to 190C/375F/gas 5.

2 Turn the full-fat soft cheese into a mixing bowl, add the Roquefort cheese and butter and beat with a wooden spoon or mash with a fork until smoothly blended. Add the eggs and cream, mix thoroughly, then stir in the parsley and chives. Season with a little salt and plenty of pepper.

3 Turn the cheese filling into the pastry case, smoothing it down evenly. Bake the quiche for 25-30 minutes, until the filling is puffed up and golden brown. Serve hot, lukewarm or cold.

★ Spiced beef

● *Preparation: 10 days, then 20 minutes*

● *Cooking: 3½ hours, plus cooling and chilling* ● *Serves 6*

75g/3oz SOFT LIGHT BROWN SUGAR
1.6kg/3½lb SILVERSIDE OF BEEF
100g/4oz COARSE SALT
2tbls BLACK PEPPERCORNS
2tbls JUNIPER BERRIES
1tbls ALLSPICE BERRIES
150ml/¼pt RED WINE
GHERKIN FANS, to garnish
CHUTNEY and ENGLISH MUSTARD, to serve

1 Rub the sugar all over the beef, then put it in an earthenware casserole just large enough to hold it. Cover and chill for 2 days.

2 Crush or very coarsely grind together the coarse salt, peppercorns, juniper and allspice berries to make a dry marinade. Rub the sugared beef with the mixture. Each day for a further 8 days, rub the marinade into the beef with your fingers and turn it over, then return to the refrigerator.

3 Remove the beef from the casserole and shake off any excess syrup and spices. Heat the oven to 140C/275F/gas 1. Return the beef to a clean casserole and add the wine and an equal quantity of water. Cover the casserole with two layers of greaseproof paper before putting on the lid, to ensure a really tight fit. Put in the oven for 3-3½ hours, or until the beef is very tender. Leave to cool.

4 Transfer the cooked beef to a board (reserve the juices for soup or stock). Wrap the beef in foil and put another board and a heavy weight on top, to give the beef a flat, even shape. Chill for 24 hours.

5 To serve, slice the beef thinly, garnish it with gherkin fans and accompany with chutney and English mustard.

Cold roast pork

- ***Preparation: 30 minutes***
- ***Cooking: 1½ hours, plus cooling*** • ***Serves 6***

1.4kg/3lb LOIN OF PORK, chined
¼-½tsp DRIED OREGANO
¼-½tsp DRIED ROSEMARY
¼-½tsp DRIED THYME
¼-½tsp CRUSHED BAY LEAF
SALT and PEPPER
6 TOMATOES
425ml/¾pt MAYONNAISE
DIJON MUSTARD
WATERCRESS SPRIGS, to garnish

1 Remove the rind and half the thickness of fat from the pork. Cut the meat back to expose 2.5cm/1in of the top of the bones and clean the exposed bones of every scrap of meat by scraping with a knife. Score the fat diagonally in each direction to make diamond markings. Remove the loin from the refrigerator 2 hours before cooking to bring it to room temperature.

2 Heat the oven to 230C/450F/gas 8. Put the herbs into a small bowl, season with salt and pepper to taste, then rub the mixture into the fatty surface of the meat. Put the loin in a roasting tin, herbed side up, so that it is standing on the rib bones, and brown it in the oven for 15 minutes.

3 Reduce the oven setting to 180C/350F/gas 4 and continue to cook the pork for a further 1-1¼ hours or until the juices run clear when it is pierced almost to the bone with a fine skewer.

4 Meanwhile, slice off the tops of the tomatoes and reserve them to make lids. Carefully scoop out the seeds and pulp with a teaspoon. Sprinkle the cavities with salt. Turn the tomatoes upside down and leave to drain for at least 30 minutes. Mix the mayonnaise with Dijon mustard to taste.

5 Leave the loin to cool, herbed side up, resting on a rack standing over a dish so that its juices will be collected.

6 Rinse out the hollowed tomatoes and pat dry. Fill them with mustard mayonnaise and replace the tops. Chill until ready to serve, serving any left-over mayonnaise in a bowl.

7 Just before serving, cut the loin of pork into chops and decorate the exposed bones with paper frills. Arrange them on a serving plate, garnish with watercress and accompany with the tomatoes.

Plan ahead

The loin of pork can be prepared and cooked a day or two before it is to be served. Store in the refrigerator, but make sure to take it out 2 hours before carving to take off the chill.

★ *Cold pea salad*

- ***Preparation: 10 minutes, plus marinating***
- ***Cooking: 15 minutes*** • ***Serves 6***

350g/12oz FROZEN PEAS
SALT and PEPPER
175g/6oz MANGE TOUT
3tbls OLIVE OIL
1½tbls LEMON JUICE
pinch of CAYENNE PEPPER
225ml/8fl oz SOURED CREAM
1 BUTTERHEAD LETTUCE
LEMON WEDGES and HERB SPRIGS, to garnish

1 Cook the frozen peas in lightly salted boiling water for 3-4 minutes. Drain and refresh under cold running water, then drain again. Cook the mange tout in the same way but for 1 minute only, or until just tender. Drain, refresh and drain again.

2 Combine the oil and lemon juice, season with salt and pepper to taste, plus a pinch of cayenne pepper, shake or beat until emulsified. Add both lots of peas, mix well, then leave to marinate in the dressing for at least 1 hour.

3 Drain the peas thoroughly, discarding the marinade. Taste and adjust the seasoning.

4 Arrange clusters of lettuce leaves on six individual serving plates. Spoon the peas into the middle of each cluster and spoon over the soured cream. Garnish with lemon wedges and herb sprigs and serve at once.

★ Orange and onion salad

● *Preparation: 15 minutes* ● *Serves 6*

1 LETTUCE
1 bunch of WATERCRESS
4 LARGE ORANGES
1 SPANISH ONION
FINELY CHOPPED PARSLEY, to garnish

For the dressing:
4tbls OLIVE OIL
2tbls VINEGAR
1 GARLIC CLOVE, crushed
SALT and PEPPER
½tsp MUSTARD POWDER
1tsp SUGAR

1 Arrange the lettuce leaves and watercress in a large salad bowl or smaller individual bowls. Peel the oranges with a sharp knife, carefully removing all the white pith. Slice the oranges thinly into rounds.

2 Slice the onion thinly into rounds and separate them into rings. Arrange the orange slices and onion rings in the salad bowl or bowls.

3 Mix together all the dressing ingredients and pour it over the salad immediately before serving. Garnish the salad with chopped parsley.

Variations

Substitute ¼ head curly endive for the watercress to make a less peppery tasting salad. Spring onions could be used if Spanish ones are unavailable.

Gazpacho salad

● *Preparation: 15 minutes, plus soaking* ● *Serves 6*

1 SPANISH ONION, thinly sliced
ICED WATER
1 LARGE CUCUMBER, thinly sliced
12 TOMATOES, thinly sliced
4-6tbls FINE FRESH BREADCRUMBS
PARSLEY SPRIGS, to garnish

For the dressing:
150ml/¼pt OLIVE OIL
4tbls WINE VINEGAR
2 LARGE GARLIC CLOVES, crushed
SALT and PEPPER

1 Put the onion slices in a bowl of iced water and leave to soak for 1 hour. Drain well. Meanwhile, make the dressing: combine the oil, vinegar and garlic with salt and pepper to taste. Beat or shake until the mixture emulsifies.

2 In a tall glass bowl, layer the cucumber and tomatoes with the onion and breadcrumbs. Season each layer with a little salt and pepper to taste. Repeat until all the ingredients are used up.

3 Just before serving, beat or shake the dressing again and pour it over the salad. Serve at once, garnished with parsley sprigs.

Variations

If you haven't got a suitable large glass bowl, make six individual salads in small glass bowls.

★ Gateau Esterel

• ***Preparation: 1 hour***

• ***Cooking: 40 minutes, plus cooling*** • ***Serves 6***

225g/8oz FLOUR, plus extra
pinch of SALT
1 sachet EASY-BLEND DRIED YEAST
175g/6oz BUTTER
4 EGGS
225g/8oz CASTER SUGAR
4-5tbls ORANGE MARMALADE
225g/8oz PLAIN CHOCOLATE
1tbls GOLDEN SYRUP
1tbls MILK
1tbls COINTREAU
25g/1oz ICING SUGAR
CANDIED ORANGE PEEL, to decorate

For the syrup:
100g/4oz SUGAR
3tbls COINTREAU

1 Heat the oven to 200C/400F/gas 6. Sift the flour and salt into a bowl and stir in the yeast.

2 Melt 150g/5oz butter in a small saucepan over low heat. Lightly grease a 20cm/8in ring mould with a little melted butter, then dust it with flour.

3 Put the eggs and sugar in a large bowl and whisk with an electric whisk until thick and creamy. Fold in the flour mixture with a large metal spoon. Then fold in the remaining melted butter. Spoon into the prepared mould, smooth the surface and bake for 10 minutes.

4 Reduce the oven temperature to 180C/350F/gas 4 and cook the cake for a further 25-30 minutes or until golden. Turn out onto a rack and cool.

5 Meanwhile, make the syrup. Put the sugar in a small saucepan with 225ml/8fl oz water and dissolve over low heat, stirring. Bring to the boil and boil without stirring until the temperature on a sugar thermometer reaches 108C/220F; about 10-15 minutes. Alternatively, test the syrup with two teaspoons – when dipped in, then pulled apart, a short thread should form between them. Remove the pan from the heat immediately, flavour the syrup with the Cointreau and leave to cool.

6 Cut the cake in half horizontally and prick the cut sides of both halves with a fine skewer. Sprinkle with the syrup, then spread the cut sides with the marmalade and re-form the cake.

7 Melt the chocolate in the top pan of a double boiler set over low heat, then beat in the golden syrup, remaining butter, and milk until smooth and glossy. Remove from the heat and stir in the 1tbls Cointreau and the icing sugar. Beat until smooth. Put the cake on a serving platter and cover with the chocolate icing, spreading it on roughly with a palette knife. Decorate with strips of candied orange peel.

Apricot whip with Madeira

• ***Preparation: 30 minutes, plus chilling***

• ***Cooking: 20 minutes, plus cooling*** • ***Serves 6***

225g/8oz NO-SOAK DRIED APRICOTS
100g/4oz CASTER SUGAR
125ml/4fl oz MADEIRA
2 LARGE EGG WHITES
125ml/4fl oz DOUBLE CREAM, whipped
50g/2oz BLANCHED SLIVERED ALMONDS, toasted

For the decoration:
125ml/4fl oz DOUBLE CREAM
4tbls MADEIRA

1 Cover the apricots with cold water. Bring to the boil, cover the pan, then simmer gently for 20 minutes or until tender. Drain and leave to cool.

2 Put the apricots in a blender or food processor with the Madeira and process until smooth, or pass through a vegetable mill. Transfer to a large bowl.

3 Put the egg whites in a clean dry bowl and whisk until stiff peaks form. Whisk in the sugar, a little at a time, then whisk until the mixture is stiff and glossy.

4 Using a large metal spoon, fold the meringue mixture into the apricot purée. Fold in the whipped cream. Pour the mixture into a glass serving dish and sprinkle with the toasted almonds. Chill.

5 To make the decoration, whisk together the cream and Madeira until stiff. Fit a piping bag with a 1cm/½in star nozzle and spoon in the flavoured cream. Pipe a continuous scroll around the edge of the apricot whip. Serve as soon as possible.

PICNIC LUNCH FOR FOUR

Italian courgette soup ·

Cold crisp-fried chicken · Pan bagna · Curried potato salad ·

Petits pots au chocolat

THIS IS PICNIC food in the grand style, ideal for summer days out or for when you are travelling and places to eat are few and far between.

The starter is Italian courgette soup: if you are picnicking as the French do, with a table and chairs, serve it in bowls; otherwise mugs would be better. After that come delicious crispy fried chicken portions, accompanied by Pan bagna: crusty, garlicky bread oozing with a salad, anchovy and olive filling; and Curried potato salad.

The dessert is most elegant, but at the same time extremely portable: Petit pots au chocolat, little pots of melt-in-the-mouth chocolate mousse.

Helpful Hints

A traditional wicker picnic hamper is wonderful for atmosphere, but nothing like as practical as modern insulated bags or boxes. If you have one, use it to carry the crockery, cutlery and glasses. Pack the food and drink in rigid plastic containers or vacuum flasks and then in the bag or box: dairy products and mayonnaise especially must be kept cool. (If you have an ice pack with the bag, remember to put it in the freezer the day before.)

A tablecloth is handy if you aren't using a picnic table; make sure you spread it somewhere flat. Also, pack plenty of paper napkins. If you're not being very grand, paper plates and plastic cutlery save on washing up. If you want to serve coffee, make it just before leaving and pour it into a vacuum flask; carry milk or cream separately in a non-spill plastic container.

Don't forget salt and pepper, a corkscrew for the wine, a bottle opener if needed, and a tube of antihistamine cream in case anyone gets bitten or stung.

Wine Ideas

Champagne springs to mind as the first choice. But vintage champagne is costly, and non-vintage can be disappointingly acid or tasteless, so your best bet would be a sparkling wine. Look for bottles labelled *méthode champenoise*; California and Australia produce some excellent ones. If you like something sweeter, go for a sparkling wine from Piedmont: Asti Spumante or Piedmontello; or save this for the dessert.

Countdown

The day before

Make the Petit pots au chocolat, cover and chill.
Fry the chicken portions and leave to get cold in a cool place, then cover and chill.
Cook the courgettes for the Italian courgette soup (step 1). Prepare the garnish, if using.
Prepare the Curried potato salad, cool, cover and chill.

Before the journey

Prepare the Pan bagna and pack in a chilled container.
Pack the potato salad and chicken in chilled containers.
Decorate and pack the Petit pots au chocolat.
Finish the Italian courgette soup and pour into a vacuum flask.

★ Italian courgette soup

- ***Preparation: 30 minutes***
- ***Cooking: 15 minutes*** • ***Serves 4***

25g/1oz BUTTER
1 ONION, finely chopped
700g/1½lb COURGETTES, sliced
700ml/1¼pt CHICKEN STOCK
1-2tbls FINELY CHOPPED FRESH BASIL
SALT and PEPPER
CAYENNE PEPPER
2 COURGETTES, cut into 2.5cm/1in sticks, to garnish
4tbls SINGLE CREAM

1 Melt the butter in a saucepan. When it is hot, add the onion and fry over low heat until transparent, stirring occasionally. Add the sliced courgettes, stock and basil. Season with salt and pepper to taste, add a pinch of cayenne pepper and simmer for 10 minutes or until the courgettes are soft. Leave to cool a little.

2 To prepare the garnish, bring a saucepan of lightly salted water to the boil, put in the courgette sticks and boil for 1-2 minutes to blanch them. Drain and refresh under cold running water.

3 Purée the cooled courgette and stock mixture in a blender or food processor. Return to the pan; stir in the cream and courgette sticks. Taste and adjust the seasoning, reheat the soup over low heat and serve hot.

Cook's tips

If you are going to serve the soup in mugs, rather than take bowls and spoons on the picnic, omit the garnish.

Devilled gherkin eggs

• *Preparation: boiling the eggs, then 20 minutes* **• *Serves 4***

4 LARGE EGGS, hard-boiled and shelled
2tbls MAYONNAISE
1tsp LEMON JUICE
1tsp DIJON MUSTARD
SALT and PEPPER
CAYENNE PEPPER
4 COCKTAIL GHERKINS, finely diced
50g/2oz CUCUMBER, finely diced
50g/2oz HAM, finely diced

For the garnish:
4 COCKTAIL GHERKINS
PAPRIKA

1 Cut the eggs in half lengthways. Remove the yolks, being careful not to break the whites. Put the yolks in a bowl and mash with the mayonnaise, lemon juice, mustard, salt, pepper and cayenne pepper to taste.

2 Add the diced gherkins, cucumber and ham and mix them in thoroughly. Using a piping bag fitted with a large plain nozzle, refill the egg whites with this mixture, mounding it attractively. Put the eggs cut side up in a sealed box to travel.

3 Make the gherkin fans for the garnish. Cut each one in half crossways, then slice three or four times lengthways, not quite to the stalk end. Cover the fans in stretch wrap. When ready to serve ease the slices apart until they open like a fan.

4 To serve, garnish the serving plate with gherkin fans and sprinkle the eggs with a little paprika.

★ Cold crisp-fried chicken

• *Preparation: 20 minutes*

• *Cooking: 55 minutes, plus cooling* **• *Serves 4***

4 CHICKEN LEGS
6tbls FLOUR
2tbls PAPRIKA
SALT and PEPPER
2 LARGE EGGS
100g/4oz DRY BREADCRUMBS
75g/3oz BUTTER
6tbls OLIVE OIL

1 Blot the chicken legs well with absorbent paper. Put the flour and paprika into a large dish and season generously with salt and pepper. Beat the eggs in a large bowl and sprinkle the breadcrumbs into another large dish.

2 Coat each chicken leg with seasoned flour, shaking off any excess. Dip each portion in the beaten egg and then toss it in the breadcrumbs until well coated on all sides.

3 Heat the butter and oil in a large, heavy frying pan. When the foaming subsides, put in the chicken legs and fry them for 4 minutes on each side. Reduce the heat, cover the pan with a lid or a piece of foil, and continue cooking for about 20 minutes. Then turn the chicken legs over, re-cover and cook for a further 20-25 minutes until tender, removing the lid or foil for the last 10 minutes.

4 Drain each portion carefully on absorbent paper. Leave to cool completely before wrapping or putting in a box.

★

Pan bagna

• *Preparation: 20 minutes, plus chilling* • *Serves 4*

1 GARLIC CLOVE
4tbls OLIVE OIL
1 LARGE FRENCH STICK (BAGUETTE), or 4 LARGE ROLLS
8 LETTUCE LEAVES
4 LARGE RIPE TOMATOES, sliced
185g/6½oz CANNED PIMIENTOES, drained and sliced
2 SMALL GREEN PEPPERS, seeded and sliced
2tbls VINAIGRETTE DRESSING
16 BLACK OLIVES, stoned and coarsely chopped
8 CANNED ANCHOVY FILLETS, coarsely chopped
2tbls LEMON JUICE
SALT and PEPPER

1 Crush the garlic clove in the oil and mix well. Cut the French stick across into four and slice the pieces in half lengthways or halve the rolls through the middle. Pull out most of the crumb from the bread or rolls with your fingers and brush the insides with the garlic-flavoured oil.

2 Put one lettuce leaf on the bottom half of each piece of bread or roll. Cover the lettuce with slices of tomato and pimiento. Toss the green pepper slices in the vinaigrette and arrange them on top. Sprinkle with the chopped olives and anchovies. Season generously with lemon juice and pepper, and sparingly, if at all, with salt. Top with another lettuce leaf and cover with the top pieces of bread or roll.

3 Roll the pieces of bread tightly in foil, or weight the rolls with a plate. Chill for 1-3 hours before serving.

Cook's tips

Pan bagna means soaked bread in Provençal dialect, and can be a little messy to eat, so serve the sandwiches on large paper napkins.

Cold summer kedgeree

• *Preparation: 20 minutes*

• *Cooking: 50 minutes, plus cooling* • *Serves 4*

225g/8oz LONG-GRAIN RICE
450g/1lb SMOKED HADDOCK FILLETS
SALT and PEPPER
about 300ml/½pt MILK
25g/1oz BUTTER
3 LARGE HARD-BOILED EGGS
100g/4oz COOKED, PEELED SHRIMPS or PRAWNS
2tbls COARSELY CHOPPED PARSLEY
4 ANCHOVY FILLETS, finely chopped
JUICE AND GRATED ZEST OF 1 LEMON
150ml/¼pt DOUBLE CREAM

For the garnish:
3 TOMATOES, skinned, seeded and diced
6 ANCHOVY FILLETS, cut into thin strips
2tbls FINELY CHOPPED PARSLEY

1 Boil the rice for 15-18 minutes or until just cooked. Drain, rinse in a sieve under cold running water and drain well. Spread the rice on a baking sheet lined with a tea-towel to dry it out and finish cooling. Heat the oven to 170C/325F/gas 3.

2 Season the smoked haddock fillets with a little salt and pepper. Lay them in an ovenproof dish large enough to take them in one layer. Cover with equal quantities of milk and water, dot with butter and cover with foil. Put in the oven for 20-30 minutes or until the fish flakes easily when tested with a fork.

3 Drain the fish well. Strip off the skin and flake the fillets coarsely. Leave until cold.

4 Chop the hard-boiled eggs coarsely. Put them in a bowl and mix with the cold rice, shrimps or prawns, parsley, anchovy fillets, lemon juice, lemon zest and the fish. Season with salt and pepper to taste. Stir in the cream; taste and adjust the seasoning.

5 To serve, spoon the kedgeree onto a serving platter. Sprinkle with diced tomato. Lay the anchovy strips across in rows and sprinkle with parsley.

Picnic meatloaf

● ***Preparation:* 30 minutes**

● ***Cooking:* 1 hour, plus cooling** ● ***Serves 4***

100g/4oz LEAN BEEF
100g/4oz LEAN PORK
50g/2oz STREAKY BACON
1 LARGE EGG YOLK
½ SLICE OF BREAD, soaked in 1tbls CHICKEN STOCK
2tbls FINELY CHOPPED ONION
1tbls FINELY CHOPPED PARSLEY
2tsp GERMAN MUSTARD
2tsp WORCESTERSHIRE SAUCE
¼tsp DRIED BASIL
¼tsp DRIED MARJORAM
CAYENNE PEPPER
CELERY SALT
SALT and PEPPER
BUTTER, for greasing
6 RASHERS OF STREAKY BACON
STUFFED GREEN OLIVES, sliced, to garnish

1 Heat the oven to 170C/325F/gas 3. Put the beef, pork and 50g/2oz streaky bacon through the finest blade of a mincer three times or chop finely in a food processor. Put the mixture in a bowl and mix in the egg yolk, soaked bread, onion, parsley, mustard, Worcestershire sauce, basil and marjoram. Season with a large pinch each of cayenne pepper and celery salt, and salt and pepper to taste.

2 Butter a 425ml/¾pt rectangular dish or tin. Lay the rashers of bacon across the base and up the sides, letting them hang over the edges. Press the meatloaf mixture into the dish, levelling the top with a palette knife. Fold the bacon over to seal the top.

3 Cover with foil and bake for 1 hour, or until the meatloaf is cooked through: when a skewer is inserted into the centre of the loaf the juices should run clear.

4 Drain off and discard the cooking juices. Turn the meatloaf out onto a flat plate and leave until cold. Wrap in foil and a plastic bag for travelling. Serve sliced, garnished with olives.

★ Curried potato salad

● ***Preparation:* 20 minutes, plus cooling and chilling**

● ***Cooking:* 20 minutes** ● ***Serves 4***

450g/1lb NEW POTATOES
2tsp CIDER or WHITE WINE VINEGAR
SALT and PEPPER
150ml/¼pt SOURED CREAM
6tbls MAYONNAISE
1-2tsp CURRY POWDER
2tsp LEMON JUICE
2 APPLES, cored and diced
2 CELERY STALKS, sliced
2 BACON RASHERS, cooked and chopped
CELERY STALKS and APPLE SLICES, to garnish (optional)

1 Boil the potatoes in their skins for 15-20 minutes or until just tender. Drain and leave until cool enough to handle. Peel, then slice them thickly.

2 Put the warm potatoes into a large bowl, pour on the vinegar and season generously with salt and pepper. Toss gently to mix and leave to cool.

3 Put the soured cream, mayonnaise, curry powder and lemon juice in a bowl and mix well. Pour the mixture over the potatoes and add the apples, celery and bacon. Use two large spoons to toss the salad gently until all the potato is well coated, taking care not to break it up. Spoon the salad into a serving dish or plastic container. Chill for at least 1 hour before serving, garnished with celery and apple, if wished.

Cook's tips

Do not try to make this salad with floury potatoes: they will break up and spoil its appearance.

★ Petit pots au chocolat

- ***Preparation: 15 minutes, plus 2-3 hours chilling***
- ***Cooking: 5 minutes*** • ***Serves 4***

175g/6oz PLAIN CHOCOLATE
25g/1oz BUTTER
4tbls STRONG BLACK COFFEE
1tbls RUM
3 LARGE EGGS, separated
1 SLICE OF CRYSTALLIZED ORANGE or 4 CHOCOLATE LEAVES, to decorate

1 Break the chocolate into the top pan of a double boiler, or a bowl set over simmering water. Add the butter and coffee. Heat gently, stirring occasionally, until the chocolate has melted and the ingredients are well mixed. Remove the pan from the heat, then add the rum and beat until the mixture is smooth.

2 Beat the egg yolks thoroughly, then beat them into the chocolate mixture. Strain the egg and chocolate mixture through a fine sieve into another bowl and leave until cold.

3 Whisk the egg whites in a large, clean, dry bowl until stiff but not dry. Fold them very gently into the cold chocolate mixture and blend thoroughly. Pour the mixture into individual soufflé dishes or ramekins. Chill until set; about 2-3 hours.

4 Just before serving, decorate with a quarter slice of crystallized orange or a chocolate leaf on each pot.

Cook's tips

To make chocolate leaves, wash and dry some rose leaves. Holding a leaf with fine tweezers, dip the underside in melted cooking chocolate. Leave to dry chocolate side up. When the chocolate has set, carefully peel away the leaves.

Late summer fruit flan

- ***Preparation: 25 minutes, plus chilling***
- ***Cooking: 15 minutes, plus cooling*** • ***Serves 4***

175g/6oz DIGESTIVE BISCUITS
GRATED ZEST OF 1 ORANGE
75g/3oz BUTTER, plus extra for greasing
25g/1oz CASTER SUGAR
225g/8oz APRICOTS, halved and stoned
100g/4oz BLACKBERRIES
9 WHITE GRAPES, halved and seeded
For the glaze:
4tbls APRICOT JAM
2tbls KIRSCH

1 Heat the oven to 180C/350F/gas 4. Put the digestive biscuits in a strong polythene bag and crush them with a rolling pin. Press the crumbs through a sieve into a bowl. Add the orange zest.

2 Put the butter in a saucepan and melt it over very low heat. Add the sugar, pour in the biscuit crumbs and mix until they cling together.

3 Lightly butter an 18cm/7in fluted flan tin. Press the biscuit crust evenly over the base and sides with your fingers. Bake for 10 minutes, then leave until cold.

4 Arrange the apricots, cut side down, round the edges of the cold flan case. Put the blackberries in concentric circles in the centre. Decorate with the grapes.

5 To make the glaze, put the apricot jam in a small saucepan with 2tbls water. Heat gently until the jam melts, then sieve. Stir in the kirsch, leave to cool, then brush evenly over the fruit. Chill until set.

Cook's tips

To take the flan on your picnic, leave it in the tin, wrap in foil, then place in a rigid container.

Variations

When apricots and blackberries aren't in season, substitute 200g/7oz well-drained canned apricots and 100g/4oz defrosted frozen blackberries for the fresh fruits.

DINNER IN THE GARDEN FOR FOUR

Tuna with anchovies · French beef casserole · Marinated pepper salad · Green peppercorn tomato salad · Minted potatoes · Tarte aux figues

SERVE THIS STYLISH dinner with a French touch on a summer evening when your garden looks at its best. The extra effort involved in bringing the food out into the garden will be well rewarded – your guests will appreciate the idyllic setting and remember the meal as a special treat.

Start the meal with a typical hors d'oeuvre from the south of France: tuna with anchovies and fennel.

The French influence is continued in the main course: an earthy, traditional beef casserole with onion, bacon, garlic and herbs. Accompany it with minted new potatoes and two colourful salads: one made from a medley of peppers; the other from ripe red tomatoes with a tangy dressing. Finish with the deliciously rich and fruity Tarte aux figues, to show off your baking talents.

Setting the Scene

Make your guests feel even more special and choose an elegant tablecloth, white and lacy or flower-embroidered linen, complemented by stylish traditional china. A seasonal flower arrangement will make a suitable and attractive centrepiece.

Before the meal, serve a light refreshing aperitif like Kir, dry white wine with a little cassis, accompanied by pre-dinner nibbles French style, such as green and black olives and roasted, salted almonds. The ideal digestif to be served with or just after the dessert is kirsch.

Wine Ideas

Choose a light dry French white wine to go with the salad starter and – if the aperitif was Kir – stick to the same grape variety. Muscadet from near Nantes, Chardonnay, Chablis and Pinot Blanc from Alsace all fall into this category. A smooth full red wine, rich in flavour and warmth, will go well with the beef casserole. Châteauneuf-du-Pape, from the southern Rhône vineyards near Avignon, is the ideal candidate, but Médoc, Pommard and Moulin-a-Vent are equally good choices and are all medium-priced.

Countdown

The day before
Make the pastry for the Tarte aux figues, wrap in polythene and chill.

In the morning
Cut the beef and bacon for the French beef casserole into pieces, cover and chill.
Prepare and marinate the peppers for the Marinated pepper salad.
Prepare the Tarte aux figues to the end of step 6.

Three and a half hours before
Cook the French beef casserole. Keep warm.
Prepare the Tuna with anchovies to the end of step 2; chill, covered.

Forty minutes before
Scrub the new potatoes.
Prepare and chill the Green peppercorn tomato salad and make the vinaigrette.

Twenty minutes before
Cook the Minted potatoes and keep warm.
Whip the cream and pipe it round the edge of the fig tart. Keep cool.
Garnish the tuna and fennel salad.

Before serving the main course
Dress the Green peppercorn tomato salad.
Garnish the beef casserole, potatoes and pepper salad.

★ *Tuna with anchovies*

• *Preparation: 15 minutes* **• *Serves 4***

400g/14oz CANNED TUNA, drained
8tbls MAYONNAISE
2 SPRING ONIONS, thinly sliced
SALT and PEPPER
5 sprigs of FENNEL
6 CANNED ANCHOVY FILLETS, drained

1 In a bowl, mix the tuna with the mayonnaise and thinly sliced spring onions. Season with salt and pepper to taste.

2 Break the fennel sprigs into wispy stalks and reserve two-thirds for decoration. Cut the remainder in half and stir them into the tuna and spring onion mixture. Spoon the mixture into a serving bowl and chill, covered, until ready to serve.

3 Carefully arrange the reserved fennel stalks around the edge of the tuna, in a circle. Cut the drained anchovy fillets into thin strips. Arrange them in a delicate lattice over the tuna. Garnish the centre with a fennel frond, if wished. Serve as soon as possible.

Asparagus moulds

● *Preparation: 45 minutes, plus chilling*

● *Cooking: 5 minutes* ● *Serves 4*

450g/1lb COOKED ASPARAGUS
3tbls MAYONNAISE
3tbls CHICKEN STOCK
15g/½oz POWDERED GELATINE (1 sachet)
CRUSHED ICE
4tbls DOUBLE CREAM, whipped
SALT and PEPPER
OIL, for greasing
2tbls FINELY CHOPPED RADISH
2tbls FINELY CHOPPED COOKED BEETROOT
FLAT-LEAVED PARSLEY, to garnish

1 Put the asparagus in a blender with the mayonnaise and purée until smooth. Pour the mixture into a bowl.

2 Pour the cold chicken stock into a small bowl or cup. Sprinkle the gelatine onto the liquid and leave to soften for 5 minutes. Then place the bowl or cup in a pan of hot water over very low heat until the gelatine is dissolved and the liquid quite clear; do not stir. Stir the dissolved gelatine into the asparagus purée. Set the bowl over a large bowl of crushed ice and stir until the mixture is on the point of setting.

3 With a large metal spoon, fold in the whipped cream. Season to taste with salt and pepper. Grease four 150ml/¼pt ramekins with a little oil, then divide the asparagus mixture between the moulds and chill for 2-3 hours or until set.

4 Dip the moulds in hot water for a few seconds and turn the moulds out onto individual serving plates. Decorate each plate with little mounds of finely chopped radish and beetroot and garnish each mould with a sprig of parsley. Serve immediately.

Cook's tips

To cook fresh asparagus, grade the washed and trimmed stalks into bundles of even thickness. Stand the bundles upright in a tall saucepan and pour in boiling water to come just under the tips. Salt the water. Bring back to the boil and cover the tips loosely with a cap of foil, crimping this round the top of the saucepan. Simmer gently for 10-15 minutes from the time the water comes to the boil again. Drain as soon as the stalks feel tender when pierced with the tip of a sharp knife.

★ French beef casserole

● *Preparation: 30 minutes*

● *Cooking: 3½ hours* ● *Serves 4*

2tbls FLOUR
PEPPER
900g/2lb SHIN OF BEEF, cut into 5cm/2in squares, 1cm/½in thick
350g/12oz UNSMOKED BACON, cut into 4cm/1½in cubes
25g/1oz BUTTER
2tbls OLIVE OIL
1 SPANISH ONION, thinly sliced
2 GARLIC CLOVES, unpeeled
2 strips of ORANGE ZEST
1 BOUQUET GARNI
300ml/½pt BEEF STOCK, more if needed
150ml/¼pt RED WINE
FRESH THYME, to garnish (optional)

1 Heat the oven to 140C/275F/gas 1. Sprinkle the flour onto a plate and season generously with pepper. Toss the pieces of beef and bacon in the flour to coat, then shake off the excess.

2 In a large, flameproof casserole, heat the butter and oil. When the foaming subsides, fry the beef and bacon for 3 minutes each side or until evenly browned, turning with a spatula. Using a slotted spoon, transfer the beef and bacon pieces to a plate. Do this in several batches.

3 Add the thinly sliced onion to the casserole and cook over moderate heat for 7 minutes or until just soft, stirring occasionally.

4 Return the browned beef and bacon to the casserole. Add the garlic cloves, the strips of orange zest, the bouquet garni and the stock. Season with pepper to taste. Cover and cook in the oven for 2½-3 hours or until tender, checking occasionally that it is not drying out; add a small amount of stock if necessary.

5 Meanwhile, put the wine in a small saucepan and boil over a high heat until reduced to 4tbls. Remove the garlic, orange zest and bouquet garni from the casserole. Pour in the reduced wine. Scrape the sides and bottom of the casserole with a wooden spoon and blend in well.

6 Transfer to a heated serving dish and serve immediately, garnished with fresh thyme, if wished.

Spaghetti loaf

● ***Preparation: 30 minutes***

● ***Cooking: 2 hours*** ● ***Serves 4-6***

25g/1oz SOFTENED BUTTER, plus extra for greasing
SALT and PEPPER
225g/8oz SPAGHETTI
300ml/½pt MILK
½ CHICKEN STOCK CUBE
3 LARGE EGGS, beaten
150g/5oz CHEDDAR CHEESE, grated
1 GREEN PEPPER, seeded and chopped
1 CANNED PIMIENTO, chopped
50g/2oz COOKED HAM or CHICKEN, chopped
4tbls FINELY CHOPPED PARSLEY
1tbls FINELY SNIPPED CHIVES
TOMATO WEDGES and BLACK OLIVES, to garnish

1 Heat the oven to 150C/300F/gas 2. Butter a 1.5L/2½pt loaf tin. Bring a large pan with at least 1.7L/3pt of salted water to the boil and add the spaghetti. Cook for about 10 minutes or until *al dente* – tender but still firm. Do not overcook. Drain well in a colander.

2 Meanwhile, heat the milk and dissolve the stock cube in it. Then, in a large bowl, mix the butter with the beaten eggs. Stir in the flavoured milk, cheese, green pepper, pimiento, ham or chicken, parsley and chives. Season generously.

3 Toss the spaghetti thoroughly with the cheese mixture, distributing the green pepper and pimiento evenly. Pour into the loaf tin and cover tightly with a piece of lightly buttered foil. Bake in the oven for 1½-1¾ hours or until set and firm.

4 Turn the loaf out onto a serving dish; if any butter runs out wipe away with absorbent paper. Garnish with tomato wedges and olives. Serve the loaf hot.

Variations

Alternatively, you can serve the spaghetti loaf cold, with mustard-flavoured mayonnaise, made by adding ready-made mustard to mayonnaise.

★ *Marinated pepper salad*

● ***Preparation: 20 minutes, plus marinating***

● ***Cooking: 10 minutes*** ● ***Serves 6-8***

2 GREEN PEPPERS
2 RED PEPPERS
2 YELLOW PEPPERS
OLIVE OIL
FRESH ROSEMARY, to garnish (optional)

For the garlic vinaigrette:
¼tsp DIJON MUSTARD
1tbls WINE VINEGAR
SALT and PEPPER
3tbls OLIVE OIL
1 GARLIC CLOVE, finely chopped

1 Heat the grill to high. Halve each pepper, core and seed. Brush the grid with a little oil and lay the halved peppers on it side by side, skin sides up. Brush the peppers lightly with oil.

2 Grill 12.5cm/5in away from the heat for 7-8 minutes or until the pepper skins are brown and blistered, turning as necessary. Leave until cool enough to handle.

3 Meanwhile, make the garlic vinaigrette. Put the mustard in a small cup and add the wine vinegar. Add salt and pepper to taste, and the olive oil. Beat vigorously with a fork or whisk until the mixture emulsifies.

4 Peel the blistered skin from each pepper half. Cut the peppers lengthways into thin slices. Arrange the strips on a long or oval serving dish in rows of green, red and yellow.

5 Stir the finely chopped garlic into the vinaigrette and pour it over the pepper strips. Leave to marinate in the refrigerator for at least 2 hours before serving. Garnish with fresh rosemary, if wished, and serve chilled.

★ Green peppercorn tomato salad

● Preparation: 20 minutes **● Serves 4**

450g/1lb TOMATOES
SALT and PEPPER
1tsp GREEN PEPPERCORNS, drained
2 SPRING ONIONS, thinly sliced
1tbls FINELY CHOPPED PARSLEY
50ml/2fl oz VINAIGRETTE (see Red, white and green salad, page 29)

1 Cut the tomatoes into thin slices and arrange in overlapping rows in a round or oval serving dish, seasoning each layer with salt and pepper to taste.

2 Sprinkle the tomato slices with the green peppercorns, spring onions and parsley. Cover and chill until needed.

3 Just before serving, pour over the vinaigrette, making sure that all the tomato slices get an even coating of the dressing.

Cook's tips

Green peppercorns are unripe peppercorns sold dried or pickled in vinegar or brine. They are less pungent and more fruity than black ones. Use the pickled ones for this salad.

★ Minted potatoes

● Preparation: 15 minutes

● Cooking: 20 minutes **● Serves 4**

700g/1½lb NEW POTATOES
75g/3oz BUTTER
SALT and PEPPER
3tbls CHOPPED FRESH MINT
MINT SPRIGS, to garnish

1 Place the potatoes in a large pan of boiling salted water. Cover and boil for 20 minutes or until tender when pierced with a knife. Drain well and return to the pan off the heat.

2 Add the butter, salt and pepper to taste and the chopped mint to the warm pan and stir until the butter has melted and coated all the potatoes.

3 Transfer the potatoes to a heated serving bowl and garnish with sprigs of mint. Serve at once.

★ *Tarte aux figues*

● ***Preparation: making pastry case, then 40 minutes***

● ***Cooking: 1¼ hours, plus cooling and chilling*** ● ***Serves 6***

25cm/10in PASTRY CASE, baked blind (see Fruity treacle tart, p.18)
1 EGG WHITE, beaten
For the crème pâtissière:
100g/4oz CASTER SUGAR
3tbls CORNFLOUR
600ml/1pt MILK
4 LARGE EGG YOLKS
50g/2oz BUTTER, diced
¼-½tsp VANILLA ESSENCE
For the topping:
850g/1lb 14oz CANNED FIGS in syrup
2tbls ICING SUGAR
2tbls KIRSCH (optional)
150ml/¼pt DOUBLE CREAM

1 Place the fully baked pastry case on a baking sheet. Brush the inside with the beaten egg white.

2 Prepare the crème pâtissière filling. Combine the sugar and cornflour in a saucepan. Add the milk, stirring with a wooden spoon and making sure there are no lumps left. Slowly bring to the boil over medium heat, stirring constantly. Simmer for 3-4 minutes, stirring frequently, until the mixture has thickened. Remove from the heat.

3 In a large bowl, beat the egg yolks lightly with a whisk until well blended. Add the hot sauce to the beaten yolks in a thin stream, beating vigorously. Strain the custard through a fine sieve into a large bowl. Beat in the diced butter piece by piece until completely melted and incorporated into the custard. Leave to cool until lukewarm. Meanwhile, heat the oven to 170C/325F/gas 3.

4 Flavour the cooled custard with vanilla essence. Pour the filling into the pastry case, then bake for 50 minutes–1 hour or until the custard is set. Remove from the oven and leave to cool.

5 Make the topping. Drain the figs and reserve the syrup. Cut the figs in half lengthways and drain well on absorbent paper. Arrange the halved figs over the tart, leaving a narrow border around the outer edge.

6 In a small saucepan, combine 75ml/3fl oz of the reserved fig syrup with the icing sugar, beating vigorously until the sugar has dissolved. Place the pan over a medium heat and boil until the syrup has reduced to half its original quantity. Remove from the heat and stir in the kirsch, if wished. Spoon over the figs until they are coated. Allow to cool, then chill.

7 Close to serving time, whip the cream until thick. Spoon the whipped cream into a piping bag fitted with a star nozzle and pipe it round the outer edge of the tart.

French fruit cup

● ***Preparation: 2 hours, plus marinating***

● ***Cooking: 10 minutes*** ● ***Serves 4***

1 LARGE APPLE
1 LARGE PEAR
200g/7oz CANNED PINEAPPLE RINGS
100g/4oz BLACK GRAPES
4tbls ARMAGNAC or BRANDY
sprigs of MINT, to garnish
For the crème chantilly:
150ml/¼pt DOUBLE CREAM
1tbls CASTER SUGAR
1tbls ICED WATER
few drops of VANILLA ESSENCE
For the crème pâtissière:
425ml/¾pt MILK
5cm/2in piece of VANILLA POD, split
100g/4oz CASTER SUGAR
2tbls FLOUR
1tbls CORNFLOUR
5 LARGE EGG YOLKS
BUTTER

1 Core and dice the apple and pear and place in a bowl. Drain the pineapple, reserving 4tbls syrup. Cut the pineapple rings into wedges and add to the bowl with the reserved syrup. Halve the grapes and remove the pips. Add the grapes to the bowl, reserving four halves for decoration. Sprinkle with armagnac or brandy and marinate for 2-4 hours.

2 Meanwhile, make the crème chantilly and crème pâtissière. For the crème chantilly, whip the cream and sugar until stiff. Add the iced water and vanilla essence and whip again until soft and fluffy. Chill until needed.

3 For the crème pâtissière, heat the milk in a heavy saucepan with the split vanilla pod until scalding. Remove from the heat. Cover and leave to infuse for 10-15 minutes.

4 In a large bowl, combine the sugar, flour and cornflour until well blended. Add the egg yolks and whisk together until pale and thick. Remove the vanilla pod from the milk. Pour the milk in a thin stream into the egg and sugar mixture, whisking until well blended. Return the mixture to the saucepan. Bring to the boil over moderate heat, stirring constantly with a wooden spoon. Reduce the heat and simmer for 3 minutes, beating vigorously with the spoon to disperse the thickened parts of the mixture.

5 Remove the pan from the heat and beat in 25g/1oz butter. Continue beating for 1-2 minutes. Pour into a bowl and cover with a piece of lightly buttered greaseproof paper to prevent a skin forming. Leave to cool.

6 To serve, spoon the cold crème pâtissière into four small glass dishes. Spoon the fruits and marinade over the top. Using a piping bag fitted with a star nozzle, pipe a swirl of crème chantilly on top of the fruit. Decorate with mint sprigs and grape halves and serve immediately.

PATIO BARBECUE FOR FOUR

Côte d'Azur seafood salad ·

Pork and green pepper brochettes · Courgette and tomato pilaff ·

Strawberries in orange juice

A GLAMOROUS BARBECUE dinner party on the patio is a delightfully different way to entertain your friends. Easy to prepare and fun to cook, this menu is a marvellous idea for a summer's day.

Start the meal with the spectacular Côte d'Azur seafood salad. You'll find the flavour improves if the ingredients are left to marinate, so toss the prepared seafood with the dressing the night before and chill in separate bowls until serving time.

Follow this with sizzling Pork and green pepper brochettes and the Courgette and tomato pilaff. You can also serve a refreshing, simple green salad with herbs.

Finish off with strawberries lightly tossed in orange juice, which helps bring out the flavour, served with or without cream.

Setting the Scene

Sweep and tidy the patio before the dinner party and water tubs of flowers and plants. Create a magical atmosphere with strategically placed lanterns, garden flares or large candles in glass jars. Make the table look really special with crisp linen and flowers and have some table candles ready for when it gets dark. If the weather turns cold, you can always barbecue on the patio and move the table indoors.

Wine Ideas

It's a good idea to serve something chilled with an outdoor meal – red wine could be too heavy, particularly if the weather is hot. However, the menu needs a wine with a strongish flavour so try offering a white Rhône such as a rich, golden Hermitage, or a fruity provençal rosé.

Countdown

Two or three days before
Check the barbecue equipment and buy fuel.

The day before
Prepare the seafood, make the dressing and marinate overnight.
Prepare the pork and green peppers for the brochettes and marinate overnight.

Two hours before
Remove the pork and peppers from the refrigerator and thread onto skewers. Cover and allow to come to room temperature.
Prepare the strawberries and chill.
Prepare the remaining ingredients for the seafood salad.

One hour before
Set up the barbecue and light the charcoal.
Prepare and cook the Courgette and tomato pilaff and keep warm.

Twenty minutes before
Barbecue the brochettes.
Assemble the seafood salad.

Before serving the dessert
Transfer the strawberries to individual bowls and add cream, if using.

★ *Côte d'Azur seafood salad*

● ***Preparation:*** *cooking fish, then 20 minutes plus marinating* ● ***Serves 4-6***

225g/8oz COOKED LOBSTER MEAT
225g/8oz COOKED HALIBUT or SOLE
225g/8oz COOKED CRABMEAT
225g/8oz COOKED PEELED PRAWNS, defrosted if frozen
1 ROUND LETTUCE, chilled
1 COS LETTUCE, chilled
4 TOMATOES, cut into wedges
8 LARGE BLACK OLIVES
FINELY CHOPPED PARSLEY

For the dressing:
2tsp DIJON MUSTARD
150ml/¼pt WINE VINEGAR
425ml/¾pt OLIVE OIL
2 GARLIC CLOVES, crushed
2tbls FINELY CHOPPED PARSLEY
SALT and PEPPER

1 Dice the lobster meat and halibut or sole and flake the crabmeat. Place the lobster meat, halibut, crabmeat and prawns in separate bowls. Using a fork, whisk together all the ingredients for the dressing. Divide the dressing between the bowls and leave the fish in the refrigerator to marinate, preferably overnight but for a minimum of 5 hours.

2 When ready to serve, line a serving dish with the inner leaves of the lettuces. Arrange the lobster meat, halibut, crabmeat and prawns separately on the bed of salad greens. Garnish with wedges of tomato, olives and finely chopped parsley.

French leek flan

● ***Preparation: making pastry case, then 30 minutes***

● ***Cooking: 1 hour 5 minutes*** ● ***Serves 4-6***

23cm/9in PASTRY CASE, baked blind (see Fruity treacle tart, p.18)
1 SMALL EGG, beaten
75g/3oz GRUYERE or EMMENTAL CHEESE, grated
250g/9oz WHITES of LEEKS (about 4-5 medium-sized leeks)
40g/1½oz BUTTER
150ml/¼pt CHICKEN STOCK
MILK, if needed
1tbls FLOUR
150ml/¼pt SINGLE CREAM
2 EGG YOLKS
SALT and PEPPER

1 Heat the oven to 180C/350F/gas 4. Leaving the pastry case in its container on a baking sheet, brush it with beaten egg and sprinkle with 25g/1oz of the grated cheese.

2 Slice the leeks into 5mm/¼in thick rounds. In a heavy saucepan, sauté the leeks in 25g/1oz butter for 5 minutes or until just coloured. Add the stock, cover and simmer for 10 minutes or until softened.

3 Drain the leeks in a sieve over a bowl to catch the cooking liquid, pressing them gently against the sides of the sieve with a spoon to extract as much liquid as possible, but without crushing them toc much. Pour 150ml/¼pt of the cooking liquid into a measuring jug, adding milk to make up the quantity if necessary.

4 Melt the remaining butter in the top pan of a double boiler over direct heat. Blend in the flour and cook over low heat, stirring constantly, to make a pale roux. Remove from the heat and gradually add the leek cooking liquid, stirring briskly to prevent lumps forming. Return to the heat and bring to the boil. Simmer for 1-2 minutes, stirring frequently.

5 In a small bowl, beat the cream and egg yolks together with a fork until well mixed. Pour into the sauce gradually, stirring vigorously. Over simmering water, cook the sauce for 10 minutes or until slightly thickened, stirring frequently. Do not allow the mixture to boil or the egg yolks will curdle. Remove from the heat and beat in 25g/1oz grated cheese. When melted, season with salt and pepper to taste.

6 To assemble the flan, spoon in the leeks in an even layer. Spoon the sauce over the top and sprinkle evenly with the remaining cheese. Bake for 30-35 minutes or until the filling has set and the surface is golden. Serve hot or lukewarm.

★ *Pork and green pepper brochettes*

● ***Preparation: 30 minutes, plus overnight marinating***

● ***Cooking: 20 minutes*** ● ***Serves 4***

1kg/2¼lb PORK, cut from the leg
2 LARGE GREEN PEPPERS
1 SPANISH ONION, finely chopped
SALT and PEPPER
6-8tbls OLIVE OIL

1 Trim the fat from the pork and cut the pork into 24 x 2.5cm/1in cubes. Core and seed the peppers, then cut into 24 x 2.5cm/1in squares.

2 Place the pork cubes, green pepper squares and chopped onion in a bowl with salt and pepper to taste and the olive oil. Toss well, cover and chill overnight. Remove from the refrigerator 1-2 hours before cooking to allow the meat to come to room temperature. Arrange the meat and green peppers alternately on four flat skewers, reserving the marinade.

3 When ready to cook, brush with the marinade and season with salt and pepper to taste. Place on a grill over hot coals and cook for about 20 minutes or until tender and no longer pink, turning the skewers frequently and basting several times.

Variations

To serve these brochettes as a light first course in the Polynesian manner, simply cut the pork and peppers into 1cm/½in cubes and thread onto small skewers. Reduce the grilling time by about half. Served this way, these tiny brochettes will feed eight people.

Cape Malay lamb kebabs

• ***Preparation: 30 minutes, plus 2-3 days marinating***

• ***Cooking: 20 minutes*** • ***Serves 4***

1kg/2¼lb LEG of LAMB
4 SMALL ONIONS
LEMON SLICES and MINT SPRIGS, to garnish

For the marinade:
100ml/3½fl oz RED WINE VINEGAR
3tbls OIL
2tsp GROUND TURMERIC
½tsp SALT
4 PEPPERCORNS, crushed
3 ALLSPICE BERRIES, crushed
2 CLOVES, crushed
4cm/1½in CINNAMON STICK
2 BAY LEAVES, crumbled
½tsp GRATED LEMON ZEST
3tbls APRICOT JAM

1 Remove the meat from the bone and cut it into 24 cubes. Combine all the marinade ingredients in a large bowl and mix well. Add the cubed lamb, stirring well to cover, and marinate in the refrigerator for 2-3 days, turning occasionally.

2 When ready to cook the lamb, poach the onions in water for 2-3 minutes and drain. Slice each poached onion into five pieces and skewer six pieces of lamb and five onion slices alternately on each skewer.

3 Brush the lamb and onions with some of the marinade and place on a grill over hot coals, 7.5cm/3in from the heat, for 10-15 minutes, turning and basting the kebabs halfway through the cooking time. Serve hot, garnished with lemon slices and mint sprigs.

Barbecued corn on the cob

• ***Preparation: 10 minutes***

• ***Cooking: 20 minutes*** • ***Serves 4***

4 young, unhusked COBS of SWEETCORN
SALT and PEPPER
pinch of CAYENNE PEPPER
4tbls SOFTENED BUTTER

1 Strip off the outer husks and the silks from each cob of corn. Season each generously with pepper and a little cayenne pepper, then spread each one with 1tbls softened butter. Wrap tightly in foil.

2 Lay the cobs on the grid over hot coals and cook for 15-20 minutes, depending on size, turning frequently until tender. Open the foil packets, season the cobs with salt and serve immediately.

Cook's tips

When cooking corn, either boiled or barbecued, always remember that overcooking will make it tough and hard.

Courgette and tomato pilaff

- ***Preparation: 20 minutes***
- ***Cooking: 45 minutes*** • ***Serves 4-6***

350g/12oz LONG-GRAIN RICE
½ SPANISH ONION, finely chopped
75g/3oz BUTTER
425ml/¾pt HOT BEEF STOCK
½tsp DRIED THYME
SALT and PEPPER
3 SMALL COURGETTES, thinly sliced
2 SMALL TOMATOES, skinned, seeded and diced

1 Heat the oven to 180C/350F/gas 4. Wash the rice; drain and dry by wrapping it up in a cloth.

2 In a flameproof casserole, sauté the onion in 25g/1oz butter until pale golden. Add the rice and continue to cook, stirring constantly, until it begins to colour. Pour in the hot stock, add the thyme and salt and pepper to taste. Cover the casserole and place in the oven for 25-30 minutes or until the liquid has been absorbed and the rice is tender but not mushy.

3 Fry the sliced courgettes in 25g/1oz butter, stirring constantly, until the courgettes are just tender. Add the diced tomatoes and continue to cook until the tomatoes are warmed through. Season generously with salt and pepper.

4 Just before serving, toss the cooked vegetables into the cooked rice and top with the remaining butter.

Cook's tips

For the best results, wash the rice in several changes of water. This removes the starchy powder left over from the milling process and helps prevent the grains from sticking together.

Variations

If you prefer to serve this cold as a salad, substitute 4tbls olive oil for the butter. Use 2tbls to sauté the onion in step 2 and the rest to cook the courgettes and tomato in step 3. Finish the dish by tossing the courgette mixture into the rice.

Celeriac salad with mustard mayonnaise

- ***Preparation: 20 minutes***
- ***Cooking: 10 minutes*** • ***Serves 4***

350-400g/12-14oz CELERIAC, peeled
SALT and PEPPER
2tsp DIJON MUSTARD
300ml/½pt MAYONNAISE
CELERY LEAVES, to garnish (optional)

1 Using a sharp knife, cut the celeriac into 4cm/1½in lengths, then cut the lengths into 3mm/⅛in thick matchstick strips. Place the strips in a saucepan and cover with cold water. Season with a good pinch of salt and bring to the boil. Simmer for 3-5 minutes or until cooked but still firm. Drain well and transfer to a bowl. Leave to cool to lukewarm.

2 Stir the mustard into the mayonnaise. Correct the seasoning, adding more salt and pepper if necessary. Using a large metal spoon, fold the mayonnaise into the celeriac matchsticks.

3 Transfer to a serving dish and garnish with celery leaves, if wished. Serve as soon as possible.

Strawberries in orange juice

• Preparation: 10 minutes, plus chilling **• Serves 4**

450g/1lb SMALL STRAWBERRIES
JUICE OF 2 ORANGES, strained
SIFTED ICING SUGAR
DOUBLE CREAM (optional)

1 Hull the strawberries and place them in a bowl with the strained orange juice. Add sifted icing sugar to taste and toss lightly. Cover and chill for at least 1 hour.

2 Serve the strawberries in individual bowls with a little double cream poured over them, if wished.

Cook's tips

In this simple recipe, macerating in orange juice and sugar brings out all the summery flavour of the strawberries.

Sticky filo squares

• Preparation: 40 minutes, plus 24 hours standing

• Cooking: 45 minutes **• Makes 9**

250g/9oz MELTED BUTTER
8 sheets FILO PASTRY, defrosted if frozen
225g/8oz GROUND ALMONDS
250g/9oz SUGAR
2tsp LEMON JUICE

1 Heat the oven to 180C/350F/gas 4. Brush an 18cm x 18cm/7in x 7in square tin with melted butter. Cut eight squares of filo pastry to fit the tin.

2 Line the dish with one square of filo and brush generously with melted butter. Sprinkle evenly with a little of the ground almonds. Layer up the remaining squares of filo in the same way, using about 100g/4oz butter and all the ground almonds, and ending with a layer of pastry. Pour 50g/2oz melted butter over the top; reserve the remaining butter. With a very sharp knife, cut through the layers to make nine squares. Bake for 35-40 minutes or until puffed and golden brown.

3 Meanwhile, prepare the syrup. In a heavy-based saucepan, combine the sugar and lemon juice with 225ml/8fl oz water. Stir over low heat until the sugar is dissolved, then boil for 10-12 minutes or until slightly reduced. Leave to cool slightly.

4 Pour the remaining butter over the cooked pastry. Leave for 10 minutes, then pour the warm syrup over it. Leave in a cool place for 24 hours before serving. Cut into pieces along the original lines when serving.

Cook's tips

Frozen filo pastry is available from large supermarkets. Only take the sheets of filo out of the packet when you are ready to use them as they tend to dry out very quickly.

PICNIC FOR EIGHT

Ginger beer · Cornish pasties ·

Mustard potato salad · Provençal beetroot salad ·

Peanut butter cookies

HERE'S A PICNIC to enjoy at any time of day, beginning with a refreshing drink of homemade Ginger beer which can be enjoyed by all picnickers, whatever their age.

What could be better for the main item on the menu than Cornish pasties, originally made by tin miners' wives for men with hearty appetites, and designed for ease of transport. Accompany these by two tangy-tasting vegetable dishes; filling Mustard potato salad, and Provençal beetroot salad, mixed with raw onion and dressed with an onion- and anchovy-flavoured vinaigrette.

Finish the meal with Peanut butter cookies, washed down with more ginger beer if the thirsty picnickers have left any!

Wine Ideas

The Ginger beer recipe makes about 5L/8pts; make sure it is well chilled before the day and if possible transfer at least some of it into vacuum flasks to keep it cool on the journey. (Otherwise use an old camper's trick – set your picnic out by a stream or lake and suspend the bottles in the water, which will be cold however hot the day.)

Ginger beer is barely alcoholic – grownups might prefer Evesham shandy, a mixture of half-and-half ginger beer and chilled sweet cider. Or serve Bucks Fizz – refreshing, easy to make and not too strong. Just take a chilled box or bottle of white wine in a cooler bag, plus cartons of orange juice, and mix together in roughly equal proportions or to taste.

Helpful Hints

Remember to put ice packs for insulated bags and boxes in the freezer the night before the picnic. There are relatively inexpensive plastic insulated bags now made for bottles which leave much more space in the other bags for the food. Pack crockery, plates and lots of paper napkins in a basket. Remember to take a plastic bag with a couple of damp sponges as well as a roll of absorbent paper as there is nothing worse than sticky fingers!

If you are taking wine, beer or soft drinks do remember to pack the corkscrew and bottle opener.

Countdown

Two weeks before
Start making the Ginger beer.

One week before
Bottle and store the Ginger beer.

The day before
Make the Cornish pasties.
Prepare the Mustard potato salad and chill; mix the dressing and keep it separate in a screwtop jar.
Make the Provençal beetroot salad to the end of step 3.
Make the Peanut butter cookies.

The night before
Chill the Ginger beer and any other cold drinks.
If using an insulated bag or box with ice packs to carry the food, put ice packs in the freezer.

Before the journey
Pack the food in plastic boxes.

★

Ginger beer

- ***Preparation:** 10 minutes for 8 days, then 1 week storage*
- ***Cooking:** 15 minutes*
- ***Makes** 5L/8pt*

25g/1oz FRESH YEAST or 15g/½ oz DRIED YEAST
1kg/2¼lb SUGAR
8tsp GROUND GINGER
JUICE OF 2 LEMONS

1 Put the yeast into a large clean jar. Pour in 300ml/½pt water and stir well. Stir in 2tsp sugar and 2tsp ground ginger, then cover the jar and leave to stand for 24 hours.

2 On each of the following six days, stir in 1tsp sugar and 1tsp ground ginger; re-cover the jar each time. After the last addition, leave the solution to stand, covered, for another 24 hours.

3 Line a sieve with muslin. Strain the solution, reserving both the liquid and the sediment. Put 900g/2lb sugar into a large saucepan and pour in 600ml/1pt water. Stir over low heat to dissolve the sugar, then bring to the boil and boil for 5 minutes.

4 Pour the syrup into a large bowl and stir in the lemon juice, ginger liquid and 3.5L/6pt water. Stir well. Pour the ginger beer into clean rinsed-out bottles. Secure the bottles with corks (do not use screw tops because fermentation sometimes causes bottles to explode). Store for 1 week before drinking. Serve well chilled.

Cook's tips

Use the reserved sediment to start the next batch of ginger beer instead of the yeast. Half will be enough for this quantity, so the rest can be given to friends to make their own brew.

Variations

For an extra-refreshing thirst quencher, pour 3tbls lime cordial into a tumbler, then add lots of crushed ice and top up with the ginger beer.

Devilled drumsticks

● *Preparation: 15 minutes, plus marinating*

● *Cooking: 40 minutes* **● *Serves 8 or more***

16 CHICKEN DRUMSTICKS
1 LARGE ONION, finely chopped
6tbls LEMON JUICE
6tbls SOY SAUCE
½tsp SALT
pinch BLACK PEPPER
2tsp GROUND CORIANDER
4tbls SOFT BROWN SUGAR
4tbls PLUM JAM
4tbls OIL
LIME SLICES and CELERY LEAVES, to garnish

1 Make 2-3 slashes in each drumstick with a sharp knife. Put the drumsticks in a shallow ovenproof dish. Mix together the remaining ingredients to make a marinade.

2 Pour the marinade over the drumsticks. Cover the dish with foil and leave to stand for 1 hour, turning the drumsticks occasionally.

3 Heat the oven to 180C/350F/gas 4. Uncover the dish and put it in the oven for 40 minutes, turning and basting the drumsticks once with the sauce in the dish.

4 Put the drumsticks on a serving plate, garnish with lime slices and celery leaves and serve. For a picnic allow to cool and pack in a plastic box.

Cook's tips

The drumsticks will come to no harm if the serving dish is covered with foil and put in a low oven to keep warm for 30 minutes or so if required for a picnic in the garden.

★ *Cornish pasties*

● *Preparation: making pastry, then 1 hour*

● *Cooking: 45 minutes* **● *Serves 8***

450g/1lb SHORTCRUST PASTRY (see Cook's tips, p.18, and make double the quantity)
1 LARGE EGG YOLK, beaten with 1tbls water, to glaze

For the filling:
225g/8oz RAW LEAN LAMB, finely chopped
1 LAMB'S KIDNEY, skinned and chopped
1 SMALL ONION, finely chopped
1 SMALL CARROT, finely chopped
100g/4oz POTATOES, finely diced
2tsp FRESH ROSEMARY, chopped, or 1tsp dried
1tbsl FINELY CHOPPED PARSLEY
SALT and PEPPER

1 Roll out the pastry to 3mm/⅛in thick. Using a 15cm/6in cutter, cut the dough into eight rounds. Combine all the filling ingredients in a large bowl and season generously with salt and pepper.

2 Put a heap of filling in the centre of each round of pastry. Brush the edge of the pastry with egg glaze. Bring the pastry up to meet on the top of the stuffing and seal the edges together firmly with your fingers. Crimp the edges lightly. Put the pasties on a baking tray and leave in the refrigerator to relax for 45 minutes.

3 Heat the oven to 200C/400F/gas 6. Brush the pasties with egg glaze. Bake for 15 minutes, then reduce the heat to 180C/350F/gas 4 and bake for a further 30 minutes or until the pasties are a deep golden colour. Serve hot or cold. Before packing pasties for a picnic, allow to cool on a wire tray.

Sausage parcels

● ***Preparation: 20 minutes***

● ***Cooking: 25 minutes*** ● ***Serves 4-6***

450g/1lb CHIPOLATA SAUSAGES
225g/8oz FROZEN PUFF PASTRY, defrosted
FLOUR
1-2tbls TARRAGON or DIJON MUSTARD
BEATEN EGG
WATERCRESS, to garnish (optional)

1 Heat the oven to 200C/400F/gas 6. Heat the grill. Prick the sausages, place them side by side in the grill pan and cook under a moderate heat for 10 minutes or until an even golden brown, turning them frequently. Transfer the sausages to a plate, using absorbent paper to mop up excess fat. Allow the sausages to cool.

2 Lightly flour a board and roll out the pastry 5mm/¼in thick to make a strip just a little wider than the sausages. Cut the strip into rectangles large enough to fold over each sausage.

3 Spread each rectangle of pastry with a little tarragon or Dijon mustard with a palette knife, leaving the edge free. Place a cold sausage on each rectangle and brush the edges with a little milk or water.

4 Roll up the pastry like a little package, sealing the edges firmly together. Brush the top of each with a little beaten egg and transfer to a baking tray. Bake in the oven for about 15 minutes or until the pastry is golden brown. Allow to cool on a wire tray and pack in a plastic container. Take along some extra mustard.

Picnic sandwiches

● ***Preparation: cooking chicken and eggs, then 1 hour***

● ***Cooking: 10 minutes*** ● ***Serves 8***

For chicken salad sandwiches:
1 BAGUETTE (French stick)
SOFTENED BUTTER, for spreading
225g/8oz COOKED CHICKEN MEAT, chopped
2 AVOCADOS, peeled, stoned and sliced
50g/2oz WALNUT PIECES
3tbls SOURED CREAM
1tbls LEMON JUICE
SALT and PEPPER
16 LETTUCE LEAVES

For devilled egg sandwiches:
8 HARD-BOILED EGGS
8 SMALL RASHERS STREAKY BACON
16 SLICES BROWN BREAD, crusts removed if wished
SOFTENED BUTTER, for spreading
150ml/¼pt MAYONNAISE
2tsp WORCESTERSHIRE SAUCE
4tsp GERMAN MUSTARD
1tsp CURRY PASTE
HOT PEPPER SAUCE
CAYENNE PEPPER
BLACK PEPPER
3 BANANAS
MUSTARD AND CRESS, to garnish

1 Chicken salad sandwiches: cut the baguette into eight equal lengths, then cut each length in half horizontally. Spread with butter.

2 Put the chicken in a bowl and mix with the avocado and walnut pieces. Moisten with soured cream, season with lemon juice, salt and pepper.

3 Put two lettuce leaves on one half of each length of bread. Spoon the chicken mixture on top and cap with the other bread half. Arrange on a serving platter and cover with stretch wrap.

4 Devilled egg sandwiches: chop the eggs roughly and put in a bowl. Dry-fry the bacon until crisp and golden, then drain on absorbent paper and chop finely. Butter the bread.

5 Mix the egg and bacon together and add the mayonnaise, Worcestershire sauce, mustard, curry paste, a dash of hot pepper sauce, pinch of cayenne and pepper to taste. Mix well.

6 Divide the mixture between 8 slices of bread. Slice the bananas thinly and arrange on top. Cover with the remaining bread and cut each sandwich into triangles. Arrange on a serving platter, sprinkle with mustard and cress and cover with stretch wrap.

★ Mustard potato salad

● *Preparation: 25 minutes, plus chilling*

● *Cooking: 20 minutes* ● *Serves 8*

1.1-1.4kg/2½-3lb WAXY POTATOES
SALT and PEPPER
12 LARGE RADISHES, sliced
12 SPRING ONIONS
300ml/½pt SOURED CREAM
4-6tbls DIJON MUSTARD
1tbls LEMON JUICE
6 BLACK OLIVES, stoned and quartered

1 Cook the potatoes in boiling salted water for 20 minutes or until just cooked. Be careful not to overcook or they will be impossible to cut up neatly. Drain and cool.

2 Cut the potatoes into 2cm/¾in cubes. Reserve five or six radish slices to garnish and add the rest to the potatoes. Finely chop the white part of the spring onion, and cut the green part into 5mm/¼in lengths. Add both to the potatoes and chill for about 30 minutes.

3 Combine the soured cream, mustard and lemon juice in a screwtop jar and season with salt and pepper to taste. Spoon the dressing over the salad and toss just before serving; otherwise the mustard tends to dry out, giving the salad a dull look. Garnish with the olives and radish slices.

Cook's tips

For a picnic, make the dressing in a plastic jar and transport it separately from the salad. Omit the garnish and mix the olives into the salad.

★ Provençal beetroot salad

● *Preparation: 30 minutes* ● *Serves 6*

450g/1lb COOKED BEETROOT
2 SPANISH ONIONS
50g/2oz CANNED ANCHOVY FILLETS
4tbls OLIVE OIL
1tsp WINE VINEGAR
½tsp DIJON MUSTARD
BLACK PEPPER
1 SMALL LETTUCE

1 Slice the beetroot thinly. Grate or process 1/½ of the onions to make onion juice. Chop the remaining half finely and reserve.

2 Pound the anchovies and their oil, adding the onion juice, oil, vinegar, mustard and pepper to taste to make a pungent sauce.

3 Separate the lettuce leaves and chill. Toss the beetroot slices in the anchovy dressing until well coated; chill.

4 Line a salad bowl with the lettuce leaves and arrange the beetroot slices on top. Sprinkle with the reserved chopped onion.

Cook's tips

As this salad contains raw onion and has a strongly flavoured dressing, it will not appeal to everyone, so enough to serve six should be sufficient.

For a picnic mix the beetroot with the onion, pack in a plastic box. Take the washed lettuce in a plastic bag, separately.

Toll-house cookies

● ***Preparation: 30 minutes, plus cooling***

● ***Cooking 10 minutes*** ● ***Makes about 60***

100g/4oz BUTTER, softened, plus extra for greasing
100g/4oz SOFT LIGHT BROWN SUGAR
100g/4oz CASTER SUGAR
1 LARGE EGG
¼tsp BICARBONATE OF SODA
100g/4oz FLOUR, sifted
1tbls CORNFLOUR, sifted
½tsp SALT
50g/2oz WALNUTS, chopped
75g/3oz TINY PLAIN CHOCOLATE DROPS
1tsp VANILLA EXTRACT

1 Heat the oven to 190C/375F/gas 5. Butter two large baking trays generously. Put the butter in a bowl with the sugars and cream together. Whisk the egg with a wire whisk and gradually beat it into the butter and sugar mixture.

2 Combine the bicarbonate of soda with ¼tsp hot water and beat into the creamed mixture. Using a metal spoon, fold the flour, cornflour and salt into the mixture, along with the walnuts, chocolate drops and vanilla extract.

3 Put teaspoonfuls of the mixture on the baking trays, spaced well apart to allow it to spread while cooking. Bake for 6-8 minutes, depending on whether you prefer them golden or brown.

4 Remove the cookies from the oven. Very carefully transfer the cookies to wire racks, using a palette knife, and leave until cold and hardened. Store in an air-tight container until needed.

Cook's tips

These American biscuits date from the days when a toll-house keeper collected dues from passing travellers to pay for the upkeep of the road. While resting and paying the toll, the travellers were offered this type of biscuit.

★ *Peanut butter cookies*

● ***Preparation: 20 minutes***

● ***Cooking 35 minutes*** ● ***Makes 18***

100g/4oz BUTTER, plus extra for greasing
100g/4oz CRUNCHY PEANUT BUTTER
100g/4oz SOFT BROWN SUGAR
175g/6oz WHOLEMEAL FLOUR, plus extra for rolling
½tsp BICARBONATE OF SODA
1 LARGE EGG
50g/2oz UNSALTED PEANUTS, skinned

1 Heat the oven to 180C/350F/gas 4. Grease a large baking tray. Put the butter in a large bowl with the peanut butter and sugar and cream together until light and fluffy.

2 Sift the flour and bicarbonate of soda into a separate bowl. Tip the bran back into the bowl and shake to blend it in. The bran content of the flour will remain in the sieve.

3 Add egg to the creamed mixture, then stir in the flour until well mixed. Alternatively mix in a food processor.

4 Shape the mixture into a ball. Break off small even-sized pieces and roll them into balls, using floured hands. Put the balls on the baking tray and flatten them slightly with the palm of the hand. Sprinkle each cookie with a few peanuts.

5 Bake for 30-35 minutes or until cooked through and golden brown. Transfer to a wire rack with a palette knife and leave to get cold.

SPECIAL DINNER PARTY FOR FOUR

Avocado and crab starter · Plum-glazed beef · Scalloped potato bake · Herbed mustard carrots · Caramel fruit salad

When you're inviting some close friends to eat with you on a special occasion, it's nice to have a special menu to offer them, and this dinner for four fits the bill perfectly. Avocado and crab starter is very easy to make and always well received, but a little care with the presentation makes it eye-catching. Roast beef is more of a treat than ever nowadays, and a tasty plum glaze and sauce make this dish quite unusual. Serve with a cheesy potato bake and herbed carrots for a satisfying combination of flavours. Fruit salad always makes a refreshing dessert and again a little extra effort in the presentation – the crushed caramel topping – makes it just that extra bit special.

Setting the Scene

Add a French flavour to your meal by serving a traditional aperitif from southern France. Kir is a deliciously fruity combination of white wine with just a splash of the black-currant liqueur *crème de cassis*. Use a medium or dry wine and serve it well chilled. (If you haven't got *crème de cassis*, blackcurrant syrup will do at a pinch.) On very special occasions mix the *crème de cassis* with chilled champagne for a Kir Royale.

Wine Ideas

The fruity flavour of the glazed beef calls for a fruity red wine to accompany it. A Beaujolais is a good choice; they vary in price and quality but a Beaujolais Villages will be affordable and have a very pleasant flavour — particularly with this meal. Other alternatives could be a light, fresh Spanish Rioja such as Artardi Tinto or, from the Burgundy region of France, a Bourgogne Rouge, very fruity and full of flavour.

Countdown

In the morning
Prepare the fruit salad, coating all the fruit well with syrup, cover and chill.
Prepare the caramel and store in an airtight container.
Cut the carrots into matchsticks and chill in a polythene bag.

Two hours before
Assemble the potato bake but do not add the milk and cream; cover lightly.
Prepare the beef and glaze but do not start to cook.

1 hour 20 minutes before
Heat the oven.

About 1 hour before
Finish assembling the beef and potatoes; put both into the oven.

Twenty minutes before
Assemble the Avocado and crab starter.
Uncover the potatoes and continue cooking.
Cook the carrots and keep warm.

Before serving the main course
Garnish the carrots.
Remove the beef to a serving platter and keep warm while you make the sauce.

Before serving the dessert
Sprinkle the caramel over the fruit salad.

MINIMUM EFFORT

★ Avocado and crab starter

• Preparation: 15 minutes **• Serves 4**

2 LARGE RIPE AVOCADOS, halved and stoned
1tbls plus 1-2tsp LEMON JUICE
6tbls YOGHURT
2tbls OLIVE OIL
SALT and PEPPER
175g/6oz CRABMEAT, fresh, frozen or canned and drained
1 LEMON, cut into wedges, to garnish
LETTUCE LEAVES, shredded, to garnish

1 Peel three of the avocado halves and slice the flesh thinly. Brush with 1tbls lemon juice and arrange the slices in fan shapes on four individual plates.

2 Scoop the flesh from the remaining avocado half and blend to a smooth purée in a food processor or blender with the yoghurt, oil, remaining lemon juice and salt and pepper to taste.

3 Spoon the sauce onto the plates next to the avocado slices and arrange the crabmeat on top.

4 Garnish the plates with the lemon wedges and shredded lettuce. Serve the starter as soon as possible with thinly sliced brown bread and butter, or bread rolls.

Microwave hints

To defrost 175g/6oz frozen crabmeat, microwave at 20–30% (defrost) for 2½–3½ minutes. Break up with a fork halfway through, then leave to stand for 10–15 minutes to complete defrosting.

Creamy celery soup

● *Preparation: 20 minutes*

● *Cooking: 35 minutes* ● *Serves 4*

25g/1oz BUTTER
1 HEAD CELERY, chopped
1 BACK BACON RASHER, diced
1 LARGE ONION, chopped
300ml/½pt MILK
425ml/¾pt HOT CHICKEN STOCK
100g/4oz FULL-FAT SOFT CHEESE
PEPPER
4tbls SINGLE CREAM
few drops of GREEN FOOD COLOURING (optional)
TOASTED FLAKED ALMONDS, to garnish

1 Melt the butter in a large saucepan over low heat. Add the celery, bacon and onion and stir well. Cover and cook for 5 minutes or until softened, stirring occasionally.

2 Add the milk, stock, cheese and pepper to taste. Stir until the cheese melts, then simmer very gently for 15–20 minutes or until the celery softens; do not boil. Stir occasionally.

3 Blend the soup in a food processor or blender until smooth, then strain through a sieve into a clean saucepan, pressing with the back of a spoon.

4 Stir in the cream, and colouring, if using, then reheat very gently for 5 minutes, stirring constantly and taking great care that the soup does not boil. Garnish with toasted flaked almonds and serve.

Variations

To add extra flavour to the soup, use full-fat soft cheese with added chives, and sprinkle with snipped chives instead of toasted almonds to garnish.

★ Plum-glazed beef

● *Preparation: 20 minutes*

● *Cooking: 1 hour 20 minutes* ● *Serves 4–6*

1.4kg/3lb TOPSIDE or SIRLOIN OF BEEF, trimmed of all fat
2 GARLIC CLOVES, cut into slivers
SALT AND PEPPER
4tsp CORNFLOUR
WATERCRESS, to garnish

For the glaze:
5tbls PLUM JAM, sieved
2tbls TOMATO KETCHUP
1tsp RED WINE VINEGAR
1tsp WORCESTERSHIRE SAUCE
1 GARLIC CLOVE, crushed

1 Heat the oven to 220C/425F/gas 7. Pierce the meat in several places with a sharp knife to a depth of about 2.5cm/1in and push in the slivers of garlic. Season the joint with salt and pepper and place in a roasting tin.

2 Make the glaze: mix together all the ingredients in a small bowl, then brush half of the glaze over the meat. Place in the oven and cook until done to your liking (medium-rare beef will take about 1 hour, medium about 1¼ hours). Brush occasionally with some of the remaining glaze.

3 Transfer the meat to a serving platter and keep warm. Scrape any juices and sediment from the roasting tin into a saucepan; add the remaining glaze and 300ml/½pt water. In a small bowl, blend the cornflour with a little of this liquid, then return to the saucepan.

4 Place over medium heat and boil, stirring constantly, until thickened and bubbling. Garnish the meat with watercress sprigs and serve at once, with the plum sauce.

Microwave hints

To make the sauce, place the meat juices and sediment, remaining glaze, water and cornflour in a medium-sized bowl and microwave at 100% (high) for 6–7 minutes or until thickened and bubbling, stirring frequently.

Cook's tips

For really perfect results when cooking a joint of beef, a meat thermometer is a good investment. Insert the thermometer into the thickest part of the joint, so the tip is near the centre. For rare beef the temperature should be 60C/140F, for medium 70C/160F and for well done, 80C/180F.

Pork and chickpea casserole

- ***Preparation: 50 minutes, plus overnight marinating***
- ***Cooking: 2¼ hours*** • ***Serves 4***

800g/1¾lb SHOULDER OF PORK, cut into 2.5cm/1in cubes (boned weight)
OLIVE OIL
2 ONIONS, thinly sliced
100ml/3½fl oz RED WINE
3 TOMATOES, skinned, seeded and chopped
150ml/¼pt RICH BEEF STOCK
1 BAY LEAF
1 LARGE RED PEPPER, seeded and sliced
400g/14oz CANNED CHICKPEAS, drained
RED PEPPER RINGS and FLAT-LEAVED PARSLEY, to garnish

For the marinade:
1½tsp SALT
PEPPER
large pinch of GROUND ALLSPICE
¼tsp DRIED MARJORAM
2 GARLIC CLOVES, crushed

1 Mix together the pork and marinade ingredients in a bowl. Cover and chill overnight, stirring once or twice if possible.

2 Heat 1tbls oil in a frying pan over medium heat. Fry the pork in batches, stirring, until it changes colour, adding more oil if necessary. Transfer to a flameproof casserole with a slotted spoon. Add more oil if needed, then add the onions and cook until softened. Transfer to the casserole. Add the wine to the frying pan and boil, scraping the sediment from the bottom of the pan; add to the casserole with the tomatoes, stock and bay leaf.

3 Bring the contents of the casserole to simmering point, then lower the heat, cover and simmer gently for 30 minutes, stirring occcasionally. Add the sliced pepper and chickpeas, partially cover and simmer gently for 1–1½ hours or until the meat is very tender. Stir occasionally.

4 Transfer the meat and vegetables to a heated serving platter with a slotted spoon. Boil the remaining juices quickly until they thicken slightly. Season and pour over the pork, sprinkle with parsley and serve.

Serving ideas

Try serving this with fried aubergines: thinly slice 1-2 aubergines, sprinkle generously with salt and leave to degorge in a colander for at least 30 minutes, then rinse, pat dry and shallow-fry in olive oil until tender and lightly browned. Drain on absorbent paper before serving.

★ Scalloped potato bake

- ***Preparation: 30 minutes***
- ***Cooking: 1¼ hours*** • ***Serves 4***

700g/1½lb LARGE, WAXY POTATOES, thinly sliced
BUTTER, for greasing
SALT and PEPPER
100g/4oz CHEDDAR CHEESE, grated
½ SPANISH ONION, finely chopped
2 tbls FINELY CHOPPED PARSLEY
½tsp PAPRIKA
200ml/7fl oz MILK
75ml/3fl oz DOUBLE CREAM
PARSLEY SPRIG, to garnish

1 Heat the oven to 220C/425F/gas 7. Put the potatoes in a saucepan, cover with cold water and bring to the boil. Boil for 2 minutes, then drain thoroughly and pat dry with absorbent paper.

2 Butter a medium-sized gratin dish generously. Use a third of the potatoes to make an overlapping layer in the bottom of the dish. Season with a little salt and pepper.

3 Reserve 4tbls Cheddar cheese for the topping. Sprinkle half the remainder over the potatoes, then sprinkle with half the onion, parsley and paprika. Cover with half the remaining slices of potato, season, then sprinkle with the remaining cheese, onion, parsley and paprika. Cover with the remaining slices of potato and season. Mix together the milk and cream and pour over the potatoes. Sprinkle the reserved 4tbls cheese over the potatoes, cover and bake for 30 minutes.

4 Remove the cover and cook for a further 30–40 minutes, or until the potatoes are tender and the topping is golden brown. Garnish with a sprig of parsley and serve.

★ Herbed mustard carrots

- **Preparation: 20 minutes**
- **Cooking: 25 minutes**
- **Serves 4**

25g/1oz BUTTER
450g/1lb CARROTS, cut into 6.5cm/2½in matchsticks
6tbls DRY WHITE WINE
150ml/¼pt CHICKEN STOCK
1tbls FINELY CHOPPED FRESH THYME
1tsp WHOLEGRAIN MUSTARD
SALT AND PEPPER
pinch of CAYENNE PEPPER
2tsp LEMON JUICE
CHOPPED THYME, to garnish

1 Melt the butter over medium heat in a heavy saucepan. Add the carrots and stir to coat.

2 Add the wine and chicken stock and bring to the boil. Reduce to a simmer and stir in the thyme, mustard and salt and pepper to taste. Cover and simmer gently for 10 minutes, shaking the pan occasionally.

3 Uncover and simmer for 5 more minutes, or until the liquid has reduced to a glaze and the carrots are tender.

4 Add the cayenne pepper and lemon juice, adjust the seasoning and transfer to a warmed serving dish. Garnish with sprigs of thyme and serve hot.

Serving ideas

Delicious with a roast or casserole, these herby carrots are also very tasty served with grilled meat or poultry. Made with vegetable instead of chicken stock, they make a special and colourful accompaniment to a vegetarian meal.

Green salad with egg vinaigrette

- **Preparation: 20 minutes, plus chilling**
- **Serves 4**

2 LETTUCES, separated into leaves
For the vinaigrette:
1 LARGE HARD-BOILED EGG
6–8tbls OLIVE OIL
2tbls WINE VINEGAR
½–1tsp DIJON MUSTARD
SALT AND PEPPER
2tsp LEMON JUICE
2tbls CHOPPED PARSLEY
4tbls CHOPPED SPRING ONION TOPS

1 To make the vinaigrette, chop the hard-boiled egg and put it in a bowl with the rest of the dressing ingredients. Whisk well with a fork.

2 Just before serving, arrange the lettuce leaves in a bowl, whisk the dressing again, then add to the lettuce and toss the salad.

Cook's tips

Always dry lettuce leaves well before dressing a salad, using a salad spinner or patting them dry with a clean tea-towel. Wet leaves would dilute the dressing too much.

★ *Caramel fruit salad*

• ***Preparation: 30 minutes, plus chilling***

• ***Cooking: 15 minutes*** • ***Serves 4***

175g/6oz KUMQUATS, halved
40g/1½oz SUGAR
1 SMALL PINEAPPLE
1 GREEN APPLE
100g/4oz BLACK GRAPES, halved and seeded

For the caramel:
OIL, for greasing
75g/3oz SUGAR

1 Place the kumquats, sugar and 300ml/½pt water in a saucepan. Bring to the boil, then reduce the heat and simmer for 10 minutes or until the kumquats have softened slightly. Leave to cool, then transfer the kumquats and syrup to a serving bowl.

2 Cut the top and base from the pineapple and cut away the skin. Slice the pineapple into 1cm/½in thick slices, then cut each slice into eight wedges and cut away the woody core.

3 Core and thinly slice the apple. Add the pineapple, grapes and apple to the kumquats. Stir well, then cover and chill for 2–3 hours.

4 Make the caramel. Line a baking sheet with foil and oil the foil well. Put the sugar in a medium-sized saucepan over medium heat for 2–3 minutes, stirring constantly, until the sugar melts and changes to a dark brown colour. If patches begin to overcook, remove from the heat and stir constantly to cool, then return to the heat. Pour onto the lined baking sheet and leave until cold.

5 When the caramel is quite cold, remove from the foil and place in a polythene bag. Use a rolling pin or meat bat to crush it into small pieces. Store in an airtight container for a few hours if not serving immediately. Just before serving, sprinkle the caramel over the fruit salad.

Microwave hints

If you have a microwave it is easy to cook the kumquats and syrup in the serving bowl (as long as it's microwave-safe). Combine the kumquats, 300ml/½pt water and sugar and microwave at 100% (high) for 5–6 minutes or until the kumquats are tender, stirring once.

Chocolate orange pudding cake

• ***Preparation: 1 hour, plus cooling and setting***

• ***Cooking: 1 hour 40 minutes*** • ***Serves 8–10***

225g/8oz BUTTER, softened, plus extra for greasing
200g/7oz PLAIN CHOCOLATE, broken up
3tbls STRONG BLACK COFFEE
225g/8oz CASTER SUGAR
GRATED ZEST of 1 ORANGE
5 LARGE EGGS, separated
100g/4oz FRESH WHITE BREADCRUMBS
100g/4oz GROUND ALMONDS
2 LARGE ORANGES, peeled and segmented, to garnish

For the icing:
200g/7oz PLAIN CHOCOLATE, broken up
5tbls DARK RUM or COINTREAU
50g/2oz BUTTER, diced

1 Heat the oven to 190C/375F/gas 5. Grease a 19cm/7½in round cake tin, 7.5cm/3in deep. Line the base with a circle of non-stick baking paper.

2 Melt the chocolate with the coffee over a low heat, stirring constantly. Leave to cool but do not allow to harden.

3 In a large mixing bowl, cream the butter until soft. Add the sugar and zest and continue beating until light and fluffy. Add the egg yolks one at a time, beating constantly. Stir in the cooled chocolate, then the breadcrumbs and ground almonds and continue stirring until well blended. Whisk the egg whites until they form soft peaks. Stir a spoonful into the chocolate mixture, then carefully fold in the remainder using a metal spoon.

4 Spoon the mixture into the tin and bake for 40 minutes. Cover the top with foil and continue baking for 40–45 minutes or until a skewer inserted into the centre of the cake comes out clean. Remove from the oven, cool in the tin for 5 minutes, then turn out onto a wire rack to cool completely.

5 When the cake is cold make the icing. Place the chocolate and rum or Cointreau in a small saucepan and melt over low heat, stirring constantly. When the mixture is the consistency of thick cream, remove from the heat and whisk in the butter, piece by piece, waiting for one piece of butter to melt before incorporating the next, and whisking constantly.

6 Place the cold cake on a serving dish. Pour the icing over the cake and spread it all over with a metal spatula, working quickly. Leave to set. Garnish with orange segments just before serving.

MIDWEEK DINNER FOR FOUR

Salmon and cheese roll ·

Chicken scaloppine with lemon · Bean and onion salad ·

Pear and brandy sorbet

DOES THE THOUGHT of entertaining in the middle of the week make you throw up your hands in horror? It needn't, if you plan carefully and do most of the preparation beforehand. Start with a salmon roll which not only looks great but tastes delicious too. Made the night before, then finished off on the evening of the dinner, it is simplicity itself. Follow with quick to do – but nevertheless impressive – chicken breasts in a creamy lemon and Madeira sauce, served with noodles and a crunchy bean and onion salad (also prepared the night before) for a lovely contrast of textures and flavours. Finally, a light and refreshing sorbet makes the perfect ending to a trouble-free dinner party.

Setting the Scene

Start off the evening as you mean to carry on – in a relaxed, informal way. Instead of serving the starter at the table as you would for a more formal dinner party, hand round the salmon roll and Melba toast while your guests are having pre-dinner drinks.

Wine Ideas

With salmon and chicken, the obvious choice for most people is a white wine. A New Zealand Sauvignon Blanc with its zingy, almost gooseberry flavour, is very drinkable and would go well with both the starter and main course. A good alternative would be the clean and slightly appley taste of an Italian Soave. For those who prefer red, Valpolicella would be a good choice since it is light and enhances, rather than masks, the delicate flavours of the food. From Italy, the ever-popular Valpolicella is a very approachable wine which is light and not too dry.

Countdown

Up to one month before
Make the Pear and brandy sorbet; freeze.

The night before
Prepare the Salmon and cheese roll; chill.
Cook the beans for the salad, cool, cover and chill.
Make the herb dressing, cover and chill.
Toast the almonds and chop the pistachio nuts; reserve separately, covered.

One hour before
Soak the onion rings.
Make the Melba toast.
Whisk the herb dressing, then toss the beans and onions in it and leave to marinate.
Roll the Salmon and cheese roll in parsley and slice.
Prepare the Chicken scaloppine to end of step 2.
Put a pan of water on to boil for the noodles.

Before the main course
Assemble the salad.
Finish cooking the chicken.
Cook the noodles.

★ Salmon and cheese roll

- ***Preparation: 30 minutes, plus overnight chilling***
- ***Serves 4-6***

450g/1lb CANNED SALMON, drained
100g/4oz FULL-FAT SOFT CHEESE
½ SMALL ONION, grated
2tbls LEMON JUICE
2tbls READY-PREPARED HORSERADISH
SALT and PEPPER
2tbls FINELY CHOPPED PARSLEY
MELBA TOAST, to serve

1 Put the salmon, cheese, grated onion, lemon juice and horseradish in a bowl and mash with a fork until smooth. Season to taste with salt and pepper.

2 Screw up a 30cm/1ft square sheet of greaseproof paper in your hand and run it under the cold tap. Squeeze out the excess, then unfold the paper and spread onto a work surface. Place the salmon mixture in the centre of the sheet and wrap the paper around it, making a sausage shape. Twist the ends of the paper in opposite directions like a Christmas cracker, taking care not to twist too hard or the paper will split. The roll should be about 20cm/8in long.

3 Carefully place the roll on a plate and refrigerate overnight. Unwrap and roll in chopped parsley. Cut into eight 2.5cm/1in thick slices and serve with Melba toast.

Cook's tips

Be sure you use plain horseradish for this recipe, rather than ready-prepared horseradish sauce, which is usually a mixture of grated horseradish, vinegar, cream and salt.

Serving ideas

To make Melba toast, lightly toast slices of bread about 5mm/¼in thick on both sides. Remove the crusts, hold the toast firmly with one hand and slice through it horizontally. Grill the uncooked surfaces for about 1 minute until the bread is dry and crisp.

Raw vegetable appetizer with two dips

● ***Preparation: 35 minutes*** ● ***Serves 4***

½ GREEN PEPPER, seeded
½ RED PEPPER, seeded
2 LARGE RADISHES
2 CARROTS
1 HEAD of CHICORY
7.5cm/3in CUCUMBER
12 BUTTON MUSHROOMS
WATERCRESS SPRIG, to garnish

For the herbed cheese dip:
175g/6oz COTTAGE CHEESE
4tbls SOURED CREAM
1tbls LEMON JUICE
4tbls FINELY SNIPPED CHIVES
SALT and PEPPER

For the anchovy dip:
50g/2oz CANNED ANCHOVY FILLETS, drained
1 GARLIC CLOVE, crushed
3tbls OLIVE OIL
1tsp LEMON JUICE
3tbls MAYONNAISE
3tbls DOUBLE CREAM
PAPRIKA

1 To make the herbed cheese dip, blend the cottage cheese, soured cream and lemon juice in a food processor or electric blender until smooth. Reserve some chives to garnish, stir the rest into the mixture and season to taste with salt and pepper. Transfer to a serving bowl and sprinkle the remaining chives over the top. Cover and chill until ready to serve.

2 To make the anchovy dip, place the drained anchovy fillets and the garlic in a small bowl or mortar and pound to a pulp. Add the olive oil, lemon juice, mayonnaise and cream, mix well and season with pepper to taste. Transfer to a serving bowl and sprinkle with paprika. Cover and chill until ready to serve.

3 Cut the green and red pepper halves into strips. Cut the radishes into wedges, and cut each carrot into strips. Separate the chicory leaves. Slice the piece of cucumber.

4 Just before serving, group all the vegetables around the outside of a serving platter, and place the two bowls of dips in the centre. Place a sprig of watercress between the two bowls and serve. Alternatively, place the vegetables in colourful clumps in a basket, and serve the two bowls of dip beside it.

Plan ahead

The two dips can be prepared the day before serving and kept in the refrigerator in well-covered containers; the vegetables can also be prepared an stored in polythene bags in the salad compartment of the fridge.

★ Chicken scaloppine with lemon

● ***Preparation: 25 minutes***

● ***Cooking: 25 minutes*** ● ***Serves 4***

600g/1¼lb SKINNED AND BONED CHICKEN BREASTS
SALT and PEPPER
50g/2oz BUTTER
2tbls OLIVE OIL
1 LARGE SPANISH ONION, coarsely chopped
1 GARLIC CLOVE, finely chopped
4tbls MADEIRA
juice of ½ LEMON
300ml/½pt DOUBLE CREAM
6-8 THIN LEMON SLICES, cut in half
4tbls CHOPPED BLANCHED ALMONDS, lightly toasted
NOODLES, to serve

1 Cut the chicken breasts diagonally across the grain into slices about 5mm/¼in thick. Season generously with salt and pepper.

2 Heat the butter and oil in a large frying pan over medium heat. Add the chopped onion and garlic to the pan and cook, stirring, until soft but not coloured.

3 Add the chicken slices and fry, stirring constantly, for 5 minutes or until cooked through. Add the Madeira and cook over high heat, stirring all the time, until the Madeira and the cooking juices have reduced to half their original quantity, about 10 minutes. Turn the heat to low, add the lemon juice, stir once, and add the cream. Cook for a few minutes longer, stirring, until the sauce is heated through. Add the lemon slices. Scatter over the lightly toasted almonds and serve at once, accompanied by noodles.

Steak au poivre

● ***Preparation: 15 minutes, plus 3 hours or more marinating***

● ***Cooking: 10 minutes*** ● ***Serves 4***

2tbls BLACK PEPPERCORNS
150ml/¼pt BRANDY
4 x 175g/6oz RUMP STEAKS
OIL, for greasing
SALT
WATERCRESS SPRIGS, to garnish

1 Crush the peppercorns coarsely, using a pestle and mortar. Alternatively, place them in a strong polythene bag and crush with a rolling pin. Put the crushed peppercorns in a bowl and sprinkle with 2tbls brandy. Cover and leave to marinate for at least 3 hours or overnight.

2 Take the steaks from the refrigerator to allow them to come to room temperature. Nick the fat in several places to prevent the steaks curling as they cook, then press generous amounts of marinated crushed peppercorns onto both sides of the steaks.

3 Heat a large, heavy frying pan until a sprinkling of water sizzles and evaporates on contact. Rub a thick wad of absorbent paper dipped in oil all over the base and sides of the hot pan; the grease should start smoking almost immediately.

4 Slap the steaks into the pan. Turn them quickly to sear on both sides, then reduce the heat to medium and continue to cook until the meat is done to your taste (2 minutes each side for blue; 2½ minutes for rare; 3-3½ minutes for medium and 4½-5 minutes for well done).

5 Transfer the steaks to a hot serving plate. Sprinkle with salt to taste and keep hot. Add the remaining brandy to the pan. Reduce by half over high heat, scraping the bottom and sides of the pan with a wooden spoon. Quickly pour the hot brandy over the steaks. Garnish with sprigs of watercress and serve immediately.

★ *Bean and onion salad*

● ***Preparation: 20 minutes, plus 30 minutes marinating***

● ***Cooking: 10 minutes*** ● ***Serves 4***

½ SMALL SPANISH ONION, thinly sliced and separated into rings
700g/1½lb COOKED GREEN BEANS
LETTUCE LEAVES
For the herb dressing:
6tbls OLIVE OIL
2tbls WINE VINEGAR or LEMON JUICE
1tsp FINELY CHOPPED FRESH MARJORAM or ½tsp dried
1tsp FINELY CHOPPED FRESH BASIL or ½tsp dried
2tsp FINELY CHOPPED PARSLEY
1 GARLIC CLOVE, finely chopped (optional)
SALT and PEPPER

1 Place the onion rings in a bowl of cold water and leave to soak for 10 minutes.

2 Make the herb dressing by placing the olive oil, wine vinegar or lemon juice, herbs, garlic, if using, and seasoning in a bowl. Whisk with a balloon whisk or fork until well mixed.

3 Drain the onion rings and blot them well with absorbent paper. Add them to the cooked green beans. Toss the beans and onions in the herb dressing and leave to marinate for 30-60 minutes.

4 Line a serving dish with a few lettuce leaves and place the beans and onions on top, then serve at once.

Cook's tips

To cook green beans conventionally, top and tail them, then wash and drain. Place in a large saucepan of boiling salted water, return to the boil, then cook for 6-10 minutes or until just tender. Drain and rinse in cold water to cool completely.

Microwave hints

You can use your microwave cooker to cook the green beans. After topping and tailing them, rinse and drain. Place them in a large bowl with 3tbls water. Cover and microwave at 100% (high) for 22-25 minutes or until just tender, stirring twice. Drain and cool.

Grilled potato slices

● *Preparation: 20 minutes*

● *Cooking: 20 minutes* ● *Serves 4*

SALT and PEPPER
700g/1½lb WAXY POTATOES, thinly sliced
40g/1½oz MELTED BUTTER
FINELY SNIPPED CHIVES, to garnish

1 Bring a saucepan of salted water to the boil, add the potatoes and simmer for 5 minutes, or until just tender but not disintegrating. Drain well and pat dry with absorbent paper.

2 While the potatoes are cooking, heat the grill to high. Lay a piece of foil over the grid of the grill pan and place the sliced potatoes side by side on the foil. Season to taste with salt and pepper and brush with some of the melted butter.

3 Place under the hot grill and grill for 8 minutes or until golden brown on one side, then turn over, using tongs or a fork, season and brush with the remaining butter. Grill for 5-6 minutes or until golden brown. Sprinkle the potatoes with finely snipped chives and serve immediately.

Plan ahead

Slice the potatoes and place in a bowl of cold water. Cover and refrigerate overnight. Drain, then cook.

Microwave hints

To melt 40g/1½oz butter, place it in a small bowl and microwave at 100% (high) for 50-60 seconds, stirring twice.

★ Pear and brandy sorbet

● *Preparation: 20 minutes*

● *Cooking: 10 minutes* ● *Serves 4-6*

800g/1¾lb CANNED PEAR HALVES IN FRUIT JUICE, drained and juice reserved
125ml/4fl oz BRANDY
2tbls LEMON JUICE
175g/6oz SUGAR
1 EGG WHITE
FINELY CHOPPED PISTACHIO NUTS, to decorate

1 Set the freezer to its coldest setting. Make up the reserved pear juice to 600ml/1pt with water. Stir in the brandy and lemon juice. Pour into a heavy-based saucepan, add the sugar and heat gently until the sugar has dissolved, stirring occasionally. Allow to cool.

2 Purée the pears in a blender or food processor and whisk in the cooled syrup until smooth. Transfer to a shallow freezerproof container and freeze for 1½-2 hours or until frozen to a depth of 2.5cm/1in all around the edges.

3 Transfer to a chilled bowl and whisk the mixture until smooth. Return to the freezer container and freeze for a further 30-40 minutes, or until slushy. Whisk again, then return to the freezer for 30-40 minutes.

4 Lightly whisk the egg white until it forms soft peaks. Whisk the pear mixture, then fold in the egg white. Return to the freezer container, cover and freeze for 2-3 hours or until solid.

5 To serve, arrange three small scoops of sorbet on individual serving plates. Sprinkle with the finely chopped pistachio nuts and serve the sorbet at once.

Variations

Replace the brandy with the same amount of calvados and omit the egg white. Timings and method remain the same.

Peach and almond pie

• Preparation: 1 hour, plus 30 minutes chilling

• Cooking: 1 hour **• Serves 4-6**

11 LARGE, ALMOST-RIPE PEACHES, halved, stoned and peeled
75g/3oz CASTER SUGAR
1tsp GROUND CINNAMON
1tsp GROUND MIXED SPICE
225g/8oz SHORTCRUST PASTRY (see Cook's tips, page 18)
FLOUR, for sprinkling
1tbls CORNFLOUR
75g/3oz FLAKED ALMONDS, toasted
1 SMALL EGG, beaten
CREAM, to serve (optional)

1 Heat the oven to 200C/400F/gas 6. Place the peaches, 250ml/9fl oz water, sugar, cinnamon and spice in a large saucepan. Cover and cook over medium heat for 15-20 minutes, stirring occasionally, until the peaches are softened.

2 Roll out the pastry to 2.5cm/1in larger than the top of a 1.7L/3pt pie dish. Sprinkle the pastry with flour and gently fold in half, placing it on a plate. Refrigerate for 30 minutes.

3 Drain the peaches, reserving the cooking liquid. Place them in the pie dish and return the liquid to the saucepan. In a small bowl, combine the cornflour with enough of the cooking liquid to mix to a smooth paste. Then stir the paste into the remaining liquid in the saucepan. Heat gently, stirring constantly, until thickened. Sprinkle the almonds over the peaches, reserving 1tbls for the decoration. Pour the liquid over.

4 Place the pastry lid on the pie and trim the edges. Use the trimmings to make a decorative pattern on top of the pie. Crimp the edges of the pie and brush the pastry well with the beaten egg. Place on the middle shelf of the oven and cook for 30-35 minutes or until golden. Sprinkle with remaining almonds. Serve the pie warm, or leave to cool and serve cold. Accompany with cream, if you wish.

Plan ahead

The pie filling can be prepared a day in advance: turn into the pie dish, add the almonds and cooking liquid, then cover and chill. Home-made pastry can be stored in the fridge for a day or two or frozen. If frozen, defrost overnight in the fridge. Then roll out the pastry and complete the pie on the day.

Chocolate hazelnut truffles

• Preparation: 30 minutes, plus 12-24 hours resting

• Cooking: 10 minutes **• Makes about 20**

100g/4oz PLAIN CHOCOLATE, coarsely grated
75g/3oz BUTTER
2tbls DOUBLE CREAM
50g/2oz ICING SUGAR, sifted
2tbls VERY FINELY CHOPPED HAZELNUTS
1tbls DARK RUM

For the coatings:
1-2tbls CHOCOLATE VERMICELLI
3tbls COCOA POWDER
2tbls CHOPPED HAZELNUTS

1 Combine the grated chocolate and the butter in a small saucepan. Heat gently, stirring, until melted, then remove from the heat and stir in the cream.

2 Gradually stir in the sifted icing sugar, finely chopped hazelnuts and rum. Stir until the mixture is free of lumps, then cover the saucepan and allow the mixture to rest in a cool, not cold, place for 12-24 hours.

3 Using slightly wet hands, make small balls of the chocolate mixture, about 2cm/¾in in diameter. Place each of the coating ingredients in a small shallow dish. Roll each ball in one of the coating ingredients.

4 Put each truffle in a paper sweet case, if wished, and chill until serving time.

Plan ahead

These delicious chocolate truffles can be made one to two days in advance and kept in a covered container in the refrigerator. They can also be frozen for up to 1 month. Defrost overnight in the fridge.

Microwave hints

You can make these truffles in the microwave: place the grated chocolate and butter in a medium-sized bowl and microwave at 50% (medium) for 1½-2 minutes or until melted, stirring twice. Stir in the cream and proceed with the rest of the recipe.

DINNER PARTY FOR FOUR

Country vegetable soup ·

Lager-glazed duck · Potato cake with celery · Creamed spinach ·

Apricot crêpes

ROAST DUCK IS a wonderfully rich and succulent meat, but serving it at a dinner party can be a problem as even the biggest bird available may not have enough meat on it to serve four. The recipe in this menu uses a herby sausagemeat and apple stuffing to make the meat go further, plus a lager-based glaze to give the skin an irresistible crispy brown finish. Creamed spinach and Potato cake with celery make this a menu to satisfy even the heartiest eaters. Start the meal with tasty Country vegetable soup, which will take the chill off any cold day, and finish with Apricot crêpes – sweet triangles with hot apricot filling. An impressive dessert; ideal to prepare the day before.

Setting the Scene

Serve nibbles to go with pre-dinner drinks in four small bowls, one for each guest. Fill each with a selection of items — crisps, savoury biscuits, nuts and olives — so that each guest has a choice within reach. Concentrate on the lighter, less filling nibbles — not too many nuts or olives — so that appetites aren't spoiled.

Wine Ideas

Although duck is classed as poultry, it is too strongly flavoured to serve with a white wine. Choose a medium- to full-bodied red – a Médoc or any ready-to-drink claret. A good alternative would be a Cabernet Sauvignon, whether from France, Eastern Europe, Australia or California.

Countdown

The day before
Make the crêpes, stack between sheets of greaseproof paper, wrap in a polythene bag and chill.
Make the apricot filling for the crêpes, turn into a bowl, cool, cover and chill.

In the early afternoon
Fill and fold the crêpes and arrange in a greased dish. Cover and chill.
Prepare the stuffing for the duck and chill, covered.
Prepare the vegetables for the soup and refrigerate, covered.

Two hours 15 minutes before
Heat the oven while preparing and stuffing the duck. Make the glaze and start cooking the duck.

1 hour before
Prepare the Potato cake with celery to the end of step 1.
Prepare the spinach to the end of step 2.

30 minutes before
Cook the Greek vegetable soup and keep warm.
Make the sauce for the Creamed spinach and keep warm.
Fry the potato cake; keep warm.

Before serving the soup
Remove the duck from the oven and leave in a warm place, lightly covered with foil.
Leave the oven on.

Before serving the main course
Finish cooking the spinach.
Transfer the duck to a serving platter and keep warm. Skim the fat from the pan juices and pour the juices into a heated sauceboat.
Sprinkle the crêpes with orange juice and sugar and place in the oven.

★ Country vegetable soup

● ***Preparation: 40 minutes***

● ***Cooking: 30 minutes*** ● ***Serves 4***

¼ GREEN PEPPER
1 LEEK
1 CELERY STALK
½ SPANISH ONION
225g/8oz POTATOES
3 CARROTS
¼ HEAD FENNEL
850ml/1½pt BEEF STOCK
SALT and PEPPER
3 LARGE MUSHROOMS, sliced
3 TOMATOES, skinned, seeded and chopped
2tbls OLIVE OIL (optional)
2tbls COARSELY CHOPPED PARSLEY

1 Thinly slice the first seven vegetables. Put them in a saucepan with the stock and season to taste with pepper, and salt if needed.

2 Bring slowly to the boil, skim if necessary, then lower the heat and simmer for 15-20 minutes, depending on whether you like your vegetables crisp or more tender. Add the mushrooms and tomatoes for the last 5 minutes of the cooking time.

3 Just before serving, stir in the olive oil, if wished, and sprinkle with chopped parsley.

Stuffed tomato soufflés

• Preparation: 30 minutes **• Serves 4**

• Cooking: 40 minutes

8 FIRM TOMATOES
25g/1oz BUTTER, plus extra for greasing
25g/1oz FLOUR
175ml/6fl oz MILK
1 LARGE EGG, separated
75g/3oz GRUYERE CHEESE, grated
SALT and PEPPER
GRATED NUTMEG
2tbls PARMESAN CHEESE, grated
PARSLEY SPRIGS, to garnish

1 Cut the stalk end off each tomato, a quarter of the way down. Using a sharp teaspoon, remove the central core and seeds. Discard or reserve for use in another recipe. Turn the prepared tomatoes upside down and leave to drain.

2 Meanwhile, make the sauce: melt the butter in a small saucepan over low heat, add the flour and cook, stirring constantly, for 3-4 minutes without allowing it to brown. Gradually add the milk, stirring constantly to a make a smooth thick sauce. Whisk in the egg yolk and Gruyère cheese. Season to taste with salt, pepper and nutmeg.

3 Heat the oven to 220C/425F/gas 7 and grease a shallow ovenproof dish. In a clean, dry bowl, whisk the egg white with a pinch of salt until soft peaks form. Fold into the sauce with a metal spoon. Put the tomatoes in the prepared dish and carefully spoon the sauce mixture into the cavities. Sprinkle with Parmesan and bake for 20-30 minutes or until the soufflés have risen and are golden brown.

4 Transfer the tomatoes to individual serving dishes, peeling off the skins, which will be split and loose, as you do so, and garnish with parsley sprigs. Serve the soufflés at once.

★ Lager-glazed duck

• Preparation: 30 minutes

• Cooking: 2½ hours **• Serves 4**

2-2.5kg/4½-5½lb OVEN-READY DUCK
SALT and PEPPER
100g/4oz FRESH WHITE BREADCRUMBS
275g/10oz SAUSAGEMEAT
1 ONION, finely chopped
½tsp DRIED THYME
½tsp DRIED ROSEMARY
1 DESSERT APPLE, peeled, cored and diced
ROSEMARY SPRIGS and APPLE SLICES, to garnish

For the basting sauce:
600ml/1pt LAGER
75g/3oz SOFT LIGHT BROWN SUGAR
¼tsp GROUND CLOVES
2tbls RED WINE VINEGAR
1tsp DRY MUSTARD

1 Heat the oven to 180C/350F/gas 4. Wipe the duck inside and out with absorbent paper and season inside generously with salt and pepper. Prick the skin all over with a fork.

2 Combine the breadcrumbs, sausagemeat, onion, thyme, rosemary and apple. Season to taste with salt and pepper. Stir to mix thoroughly. Stuff the duck with the sausagemeat mixture through the vent and stitch the vent up firmly with fine kitchen string to make sure that the stuffing does not spill out during cooking. Tie the wings and legs closely to the body and place the duck on a rack in a roasting tin.

3 In a bowl, combine the lager, sugar, cloves, vinegar and mustard. Stir until the sugar has dissolved. Pour the basting sauce over the duck in the tin.

4 Roast, basting with the pan juices and pricking the duck every 30 minutes, for 2-2½ hours or until the duck is tender and the stuffing has cooked through. To test that the duck is cooked, push a skewer through the thickest part of the leg, near the breast. The juices should run clear. Remove the string and pull out the stitching.

5 Transfer the duck to a heated serving dish. Skim the fat from the pan juices and serve the juices separately in a heated sauceboat. Garnish the duck with rosemary sprigs and apple slices.

Variations

To serve this dish cold, reduce the sauce to a glaze over high heat, skimming the fat constantly, and spoon it over the duck. Leave to cool, then chill.

Sole with lemon

● *Preparation: 25 minutes*

● *Cooking: 30 minutes* **● *Serves 4***

700g/1½lb POTATOES
SALT and PEPPER
4 × 225g/8oz LEMON SOLE
FLOUR, for coating
1 LARGE EGG
75g/3oz FRESH WHITE BREADCRUMBS
100g/4oz CLARIFIED BUTTER (see Cook's tips)
2tbls CHOPPED PARSLEY
1 LEMON, thinly sliced, to garnish

1 Cut the potatoes into fairly thick, even-sized slices. Cook in a saucepan of boiling salted water for 20 minutes or until tender. Meanwhile, remove the dark skin from each lemon sole and then trim the fins with a pair of kitchen scissors.

2 Place the flour on a flat plate and season with salt and pepper to taste. Break the egg into a shallow dish and beat it lightly. Put the breadcrumbs on a flat plate.

3 Coat each sole with the seasoned flour, then dip in beaten egg and finally coat with breadcrumbs, patting them on firmly.

4 Divide 65g/2½oz of the butter in half and put one half into a large frying pan. Heat the butter and fry two sole at a time over medium heat for 3 minutes. Turn the fish over carefully with a spatula or fish slice and cook for a further 2 minutes, or until the fish flakes easily when tested with a fork. Drain on absorbent paper, then arrange on a heated serving dish and keep warm. Before frying the next two fish, add the other half of the butter for frying. If you have two large frying pans, divide the 65g/2½oz butter between them and fry all four fish simultaneously.

5 Drain the potatoes and transfer to a bowl. Pour the remaining clarified butter over them. Season with salt and pepper to taste and sprinkle with the parsley. Toss gently until the potatoes are evenly coated with butter, seasonings and parsley. Arrange the potatoes at the tail end of the sole, garnish the fish with the lemon slices and serve immediately.

Cook's tips

To clarify butter, melt it very slowly in a small heavy-based saucepan. The butter will foam and the foam will fall gently to the bottom of the pan, leaving the clarified butter as clear as oil. Pour into a bowl carefully, without disturbing the sediment. Keep the clarified butter in a covered jar in the refrigerator and use as needed.

★ *Potato cake with celery*

● *Preparation: 20 minutes*

● *Cooking: 30 minutes* **● *Serves 4***

75g/3oz BUTTER
3 CELERY STALKS, very finely diced
700g/1½lb POTATOES, mashed (see Cook's tips, below)
SALT and PEPPER

1 Melt 25g/1oz of the butter in a frying pan and fry the celery for 1-2 minutes. Mix the celery with the mashed potatoes and season generously with salt and pepper.

2 Melt another 25g/1oz butter in the pan and, when it is sizzling, pile in the potato and celery mixture. Spread into a flat cake with a palette knife and cook gently until golden brown underneath; about 15 minutes. Turn the potato cake out onto a flat dish and then slip it back into the pan on the uncooked side. Add the remaining butter to the pan and cook for 10 minutes, or until golden brown. Turn out onto a heated plate and serve the potato cake at once, cut in wedges.

Cook's tips

When you are making the mashed potato, do not put milk or butter in it — you need a purée of a firm consistency to make effective cakes.

Variations

This delicious potato cake can be flavoured with a number of other ingredients besides celery — try onions, mushrooms or crisply fried bacon.

★ Creamed spinach

● *Preparation: 15 minutes*

● *Cooking: 15 minutes* ● *Serves 4-6*

1kg/2¼lb FRESH SPINACH
15g/½oz BUTTER
1tbls FLOUR
150ml/¼pt MILK
3-4tbls SINGLE CREAM
PINCH of NUTMEG
SALT and PEPPER
ORANGE SLICE, QUARTERED and ORANGE ZEST, to garnish

1 Wash the spinach meticulously, leaf by leaf, to remove every possible speck of dirt. Discard any yellowed, pale or blemished leaves, and pull away the stems. If they are tender, they will snap off at the base of the leaf; but if tough, the stem will probably rip away along the whole length of the leaf. Shake the leaves — not too energetically — to get rid of excess moisture, and pack them into a large saucepan. Cover tightly, place over medium heat and allow to cook in the water left clinging to the leaves for 2-3 minutes. Do not add salt at this stage.

2 Turn the leaves over with a fork, so that the uncooked layer on top takes the place of the cooked leaves underneath, and continue cooking for 2-3 minutes. Remove from the heat and drain in a colander, pressing firmly to extract any remaining moisture. Chop up the drained spinach.

3 Melt the butter in a pan. Stir in the flour to make a roux. Gradually add the milk, stirring constantly. Leave the sauce to simmer for 1-2 minutes over very low heat, stirring constantly until thickened. Add the spinach to the sauce with the cream, nutmeg, and salt and pepper to taste. Place over low heat for 2-3 minutes to reheat. Transfer the spinach mixture to a serving dish and serve at once, garnished with orange pieces and zest.

Turnip gratin

● *Preparation: 30 minutes*

● *Cooking: 1 hour 50 minutes* ● *Serves 4-6*

700g/1½lb TURNIPS, very thinly sliced
25g/1oz BUTTER, plus a knob for greasing
300ml/½pt SINGLE CREAM
2 LARGE EGGS
SALT and PEPPER
100g/4oz GRUYERE CHEESE, grated
4tbls GRATED PARMESAN CHEESE

1 Heat the oven to 170C/325F/gas 3. Put the thinly sliced turnips in a large bowl of cold water and leave to stand for 10-15 minutes, then dry thoroughly on absorbent paper.

2 Use the knob of butter to grease a gratin dish measuring about 23cm × 15cm/9in × 6in. In a large bowl, whisk together the cream and eggs. Season with salt and pepper to taste.

3 Arrange a quarter of the turnip slices in overlapping rows in the dish. Pour over a quarter of the cream mixture. Sprinkle with a quarter of the Gruyère cheese and 1tbls Parmesan cheese. Dot with a quarter of the butter. Repeat to make three more layers, ending with a sprinkling of cheese.

4 Cover the dish with foil and bake for 1 hour. Remove the foil and bake for a further 45-50 minutes, until the turnips are cooked and the top layer is golden brown in colour.

Cook's tips

The turnips will not go completely soft. They should hold their shape but be tender. For a richer dish, substitute double cream for single.

Apricot crêpes

● ***Preparation: 25 minutes, plus cooling***

● ***Cooking: 1 hour 10 minutes*** ● ***Serves 4***

175g/6oz DRIED APRICOTS
50g/2oz SOFT LIGHT BROWN SUGAR
1 LARGE COOKING APPLE, peeled, cored and chopped
15g/½oz BUTTER, plus extra for greasing
4tbls ORANGE JUICE
2tbls ICING SUGAR, sifted
SINGLE CREAM, to serve (optional)

For the crêpes:
40g/1½oz FLOUR
40g/1½oz WHOLEMEAL FLOUR
¼tsp SALT
2 EGGS
2tbls MELTED BUTTER
150ml/¼pt MILK
OIL, for greasing

1 To make the crêpes, place the flours and salt in a bowl. Make a well in the centre and pour in the eggs and melted butter. Gradually draw in the flour to the centre to blend evenly. Slowly add the milk and 2tbls water, beating well after each addition.

2 Heat an 18cm/7in frying pan and grease lightly. Spoon 3tbls of the batter into the pan, tilting the pan so that the batter coats the surface thinly. Cook over medium heat for 1 minute or until lightly golden underneath, then turn with a palette knife. Continue cooking the other side for 1 minute or until lightly golden.

3 Repeat until all the batter is used up (you should have eight or nine crêpes), greasing the pan lightly between crêpes if necessary. Stack the crêpes between pieces of greaseproof paper to prevent them sticking together.

4 To make the filling, place the apricots, sugar, apple, butter and 5tbls water in a saucepan and bring to the boil. Cover and simmer gently for 20-25 minutes, stirring occasionally. Purée the mixture in a blender or food processor until smooth.

5 Heat the oven to 180C/350F/gas 4. Lay the crêpes flat on a board and spread the apricot mixture evenly over them. Fold the crêpes into quarters to form triangular shapes. Arrange them, slightly overlapping, in a lightly greased, shallow ovenproof dish. Sprinkle with the orange juice and icing sugar. Bake for 15-20 minutes, and serve hot with cream, if wished.

Variations

Omit the wholemeal flour and make the crêpes using 75g/3oz plain white flour, if preferred.

Apple towers

● ***Preparation: 40 minutes***

● ***Cooking: 50 minutes*** ● ***Serves 4***

4 LARGE TART DESSERT APPLES
16 slices of WHITE BREAD
about 50g/2oz BUTTER, softened
65g/2½oz CASTER SUGAR
1tsp GROUND CINNAMON
200ml/7fl oz DOUBLE CREAM
2tbls RUM

1 Heat the oven to 150C/300F/gas 2. Peel the apples and remove the cores with an apple corer. Slice each apple into four rings horizontally, then reassemble.

2 With a pastry cutter cut 16 circles, the same diameter as the apples, from the bread. Spread with softened butter on both sides. Use a little of the butter to grease a baking sheet large enough to take the circles of bread in one layer. Lay the bread circles side by side.

3 Combine 50g/2oz sugar and the cinnamon. Coat each apple slice with this mixture and place it on top of a buttered bread circle, keeping the apple slices in order so that you will be able to reassemble them.

4 Bake for 45-50 minutes or until the apples are tender and the bread is crisp. Meanwhile, whisk the cream, rum and remaining sugar together until they form soft peaks. Chill.

5 Remove the apples and bread from the oven and reassemble the apple slices, with the bread in between. Place them on four individual warmed serving plates. Spoon a little of the chilled rum cream over the top of each apple tower and serve at once, with the remaining rum cream handed round separately.

NO-FUSS DINNER FOR FOUR

Potted prawns •

Crispy-topped beef • Turnip and carrot strips •

Chilled coffee and walnut soufflé

If the thought of giving a dinner party makes you nervous this is the menu for you, as it's planned for easy cooking. Potted prawns is a classic starter which couldn't be easier to make, and which can be left in the refrigerator until just before serving. The main dish, Crispy-topped beef, is finished in the oven and therefore will come to no harm if you are late sitting down to the meal, or if guests linger over their starter. Accompany it with a simple mixed vegetable dish: Turnip and carrot strips. Finish up with delicious and spectacular-looking Coffee and walnut soufflé. This is not the temperamental oven-baked type which has to be eaten immediately or it flops, but is set in the refrigerator so, like the starter, it can be prepared the day before.

Setting the Scene

Plan your table setting to emphasize the robust qualities of the main dish, beef casserole. Have a cheerful checked, patchwork or flowered tablecloth; or put rush place mats on a pine table. Bring the beef to the table in the casserole in which it was cooked, and serve it onto earthenware plates. Carry the theme through with café-style cutlery, rather than silver, and plain Paris goblets, or even small tumblers, for serving the wine.

Wine Ideas

There's little doubt about what to serve with the beef casserole: a fairly dry, robustly flavoured red wine. But the choice is enormous. You could choose a Barolo from Italy; Rioja from Spain; Bandol or Cahors from France; or Cabernet Sauvignon from Eastern Europe or Australia. Whatever the country of origin, pick a wine which is described as full-bodied, and make sure to open it an hour or so before serving, and to serve it at room temperature.

Countdown

The day before
Prepare the Potted prawns and chill.
Prepare the chilled Coffee and walnut soufflé to the end of step 5 and leave to set in the refrigerator.

In the morning
Grate the cheese and prepare the breadcrumbs for the Crispy-topped beef. Store these in plastic bags in the refrigerator. Peel the turnips and carrots and cut into julienne strips. Snip the chives. Store in plastic bags in the refrigerator. Chop the walnuts for the soufflé and store in an airtight container.

2 hours 30 minutes before
Prepare and cook the beef casserole up to the end of step 1. Defrost the sweetcorn.

One hour before
Add the sweetcorn and celery to the beef casserole. Heat the oven and prepare the cheese topping.

Thirty minutes before
Continue cooking the casserole in the oven. Remove the soufflé from the fridge and decorate with walnuts.

Fifteen minutes before
Remove the Potted prawns from their ramekins and garnish. Make the toast.
Cook the vegetables and keep warm.

Before serving the main course
Garnish the beef casserole and the vegetables.

★ *Potted prawns*

- ***Preparation:* 15 minutes**
- ***Cooking:* 15 minutes, plus cooling**
- ***Serves 4***

350g/12oz COOKED, PEELED PRAWNS
225g/8oz BUTTER
CAYENNE PEPPER
GROUND MACE OR GRATED NUTMEG
PEPPER
HOT TOAST, to serve
For the garnish:
CRISP LETTUCE LEAVES
LEMON WEDGES
WATERCRESS SPRIGS

1 Pat the prawns dry with absorbent paper to remove as much excess moisture as possible.

2 Melt half the butter in a saucepan, add the prawns and heat them through slowly over low heat, tossing the pan occasionally. Season with a large pinch of cayenne pepper, and mace or nutmeg, and pepper to taste. The prawns should be highly flavoured. Divide the buttered prawns between four ramekins and leave to become quite cold.

3 Gently melt the remaining butter and pour just enough over each ramekin to cover the prawns. Cool and store in the fridge until needed.

4 Line four serving plates with lettuce leaves, run a sharp knife around the edge of the ramekins and turn out on top. Garnish with lemon wedges and sprigs of watercress. Serve with triangles of hot toast.

Cook's tips

If you plan to keep the potted prawns for more than a day or two, use clarified butter to cover the tops. If preferred, the prawns can be left in the ramekins to serve.

Mushroom beignets

● ***Preparation: 15 minutes***

● ***Cooking: 30 minutes, plus 30 minutes resting*** ● ***Serves 4***

450g/1lb BUTTON MUSHROOMS, halved if large
4tbls DRY WHITE WINE
3tbls LEMON JUICE
SALT and PEPPER
OIL, for deep frying
TOMATO SAUCE (see Cook's tips)

For the batter:
150g/5oz FLOUR
2tbls OLIVE OIL
200ml/7fl oz LIGHT BEER
1 LARGE EGG WHITE

1 First make the batter: sift the flour and a pinch of salt into a mixing bowl and make a well in the centre. Pour in the oil and gradually stir in the beer, incorporating the flour from the sides. Leave to rest for 30 minutes.

2 Put the mushrooms in a saucepan with the wine, lemon juice and salt and pepper to taste. Cover and simmer for about 10-12 minutes until tender but still firm. Drain well and leave until cold. Dry with absorbent paper, then season generously.

3 Heat the oil in a deep-fat fryer or deep pan to 190C/375F or until a 1cm/½in cube of day-old white bread turns golden brown in 50 seconds.

4 Whisk the egg white until stiff, then fold lightly into the batter. Dip the mushrooms into the batter a few at a time. Shake off excess batter and deep-fry for 3-4 minutes or until a rich golden colour. Drain well on absorbent paper and serve at once, with the tomato sauce handed separately.

Cook's tips

To make a basic tomato sauce, fry a finely chopped onion with 2 crushed garlic cloves in 2tbls olive oil in a heavy pan for about 10 minutes, until soft and golden. Add 400g/14oz canned chopped tomatoes, 3tbls tomato purée, 2 bay leaves, 3tbls chopped parsley and ¼tsp dried oregano. Stir well, season to taste and bring to the boil, stirring. Cover and simmer gently for 20-25 minutes or until reduced to a thick sauce.

★ Crispy-topped beef

● ***Preparation: 40 minutes***

● ***Cooking: 2 hours*** ● ***Serves 4***

OIL
700g/1½lb BRAISING STEAK, cut into 3cm/1¼in cubes
2 ONIONS, thinly sliced
1 GARLIC CLOVE, crushed
2tbls FLOUR
200ml/7fl oz RED WINE
2 BAY LEAVES
about 600ml/1pt HOT BEEF STOCK
100g/4oz FROZEN SWEETCORN, defrosted
3 CELERY STALKS, cut into 1cm/½in slices
SALT and PEPPER
CELERY LEAVES, to garnish

For the topping:
100g/4oz BUTTER
225g/8oz FRESH BREADCRUMBS
175g/6oz CHEDDAR CHEESE, grated

1 Heat 2tbls oil in a large, flameproof casserole and fry the beef in batches until golden brown on all sides, adding more oil as needed. Remove the meat and keep warm. Add the onions and garlic to the casserole and fry for 3-4 minutes until the onions are just beginning to colour. Remove from the heat, stir in the flour and cook slowly for a few minutes. Add the beef, wine, bay leaves and enough stock to just cover the meat. Season, bring to the boil, cover and simmer very gently for about 1 hour.

2 Then add the sweetcorn and celery to the casserole and continue to simmer very gently while making the topping. Heat the oven to 180C/350F/gas 4.

3 To make the topping, melt the butter in a large frying pan, add the breadcrumbs and stir over medium heat until golden brown and all the butter has been absorbed. Mix the breadcrumbs with the grated cheese and spread evenly over the beef. Bake for 30-40 minutes or until the top is golden brown and crusty and the cheese has melted. Garnish with celery leaves and serve at once.

Plan ahead

Breadcrumbs are always useful to have ready prepared and stored in the fridge or freezer, so it is worth making a large amount at a time. To make fresh white breadcrumbs, remove the crusts from sliced white bread which is at least one day old. Rub the bread through a fine wire sieve or grate it. Alternatively, tear into pieces and blend, a little at a time, in a blender or food processor.

Calf's liver with vermouth

● ***Preparation: 15 minutes***

● ***Cooking: 10 minutes*** ● ***Serves 4***

2tbls FLOUR
½tsp each SALT and PEPPER
450g/1lb CALF'S LIVER, thinly sliced
50g/2oz BUTTER
2tsp CORNFLOUR
150ml/¼pt HOT CHICKEN STOCK
4tbls DRY VERMOUTH
1tbls CHOPPED PARSLEY
ORANGE SEGMENTS and PARSLEY SPRIGS, to garnish (optional)

1 Mix together the flour, salt and pepper and use to dust the liver slices. Melt the butter in a large frying pan and fry the liver gently for 3-5 minutes, turning frequently, until just cooked. Transfer the liver to a heated serving dish, using a slotted spoon, and keep warm.

2 Put the cornflour in a small bowl and stir in enough stock to dissolve it. Pour into the frying pan and stir well into the fat.

3 Add the remaining stock and the vermouth to the pan and blend into the cornflour mixture. Bring to the boil, then simmer until thickened, stirring constantly. Add the chopped parsley and pour over the liver. Garnish with orange segments and parsley sprigs, if wished, and serve at once.

★*Turnip and carrot strips*

● ***Preparation: 15 minutes***

● ***Cooking: 15 minutes*** ● ***Serves 4***

225g/8oz TURNIPS
225g/8oz CARROTS
SALT and PEPPER
100ml/3½fl oz CHICKEN STOCK
25g/1oz BUTTER
FINELY SNIPPED CHIVES, to garnish

1 Cut the vegetables into thin julienne strips, about 5cm/2in long. Season generously with salt and pepper.

2 In a wide, heavy-based saucepan with a tightly fitting lid, heat the stock to boiling point. Add the butter and reduce the heat to a simmer. Add the carrots, cover the pan and cook for 1 minute.

3 Add the turnips and continue cooking for 9 minutes or until both vegetables are tender, shaking the pan occasionally.

4 Turn the vegetables into a heated serving dish, garnish with the snipped chives and serve at once.

Cook's tips

This is a low-calorie dish, by virtue of the fact that there is very little fat used. Turnips and carrots, like most vegetables, have low calorie counts. If, however, you want to reduce this calorific value still further, you can cut down the amount of butter used, or even omit it completely, if you wish.

Variations

For a change, add a different root vegetable such as celeriac or kohlrabi. Use 175g/6oz of each of the three vegetables, cut into julienne strips. Add the celeriac or kohlrabi strips when you add the turnips.

Chinese courgettes

● *Preparation: 10 minutes*

● *Cooking: 5 minutes* ● *Serves 4*

450g/1lb SMALL COURGETTES
2tbls OIL
SALT and PEPPER
1tbls SOY SAUCE
1tbls DRY SHERRY
CARROT FLOWERS and CHIVES, to garnish

1 Wipe the courgettes with a clean damp cloth. Cut off the ends and slice the courgettes thinly, without peeling them.

2 Heat the oil in a large frying pan. When hot, add the courgette slices and stir-fry over medium heat for 3-5 minutes or until just cooked, turning constantly with a spatula or fish slice. Season to taste with salt and pepper.

3 Add 100ml/3½fl oz cold water, the soy sauce and sherry. Bring to the boil, taste and adjust the seasoning. Transfer the courgettes to a heated serving dish and serve hot, garnished with carrot flowers and chives.

Crunchy apple and celery salad

● *Preparation: 25 minutes*

● *Serves 4*

100g/4oz WATERCRESS
75g/3oz RADISHES
4 CELERY STALKS
2 TART DESSERT APPLES
50g/2oz RAISINS
CELERY LEAVES, to garnish (optional)

For the dressing:
4tbls OIL
2tbls CIDER VINEGAR
1tsp DIJON MUSTARD
1 GARLIC CLOVE, crushed
SALT and PEPPER

1 First, prepare the vegetables: chop the watercress, thinly slice the radishes, and slice the celery stalks and put them all in a salad bowl. Core and thinly slice the apple and add to the salad bowl with the raisins. Mix together gently with a metal spoon.

2 To make the dressing, beat together the oil, vinegar, mustard, garlic and salt and pepper to taste. Stir the dressing into the salad, garnish with celery leaves if liked and serve at once.

Plan ahead

This salad can be prepared well in advance: prepare the vegetables as described in step 1, and store them in a plastic bag, tightly sealed, in the salad drawer of the refrigerator. The apple, however, will brown quickly after slicing, so add the apple just before serving, or brush the slices with lemon juice to help prevent discolouring. The dressing can be made ahead of time and stored, covered, in the refrigerator for a day or two. Whisk it again before dressing the salad.

Serving ideas

This salad is very good served with cheese, cold poultry, or oily fish such as mackerel or trout, as the vibrant colours and crisp textures of the watercress and radishes complement the softer tones and texture of lighter food.

★ Chilled coffee and walnut soufflé

● ***Preparation: 40 minutes, plus chilling***

● ***Serves 4-6***

3 LARGE EGGS, separated
75g/3oz CASTER SUGAR
75ml/3fl oz STRONG BLACK COFFEE
15g/½oz POWDERED GELATINE (1 sachet)
300ml/½pt DOUBLE CREAM
25g/1oz FINELY CHOPPED WALNUTS
WHIPPED CREAM and CANDIED VIOLETS, to decorate

1 Fit a double thickness of greaseproof paper around the outside of an 850ml/1½pt soufflé dish so that it stands 6.5cm/2½in above the rim. Secure with an elastic band or paper clip.

2 In a mixing bowl, combine the egg yolks, sugar and coffee. Put the bowl over a pan of simmering water and whisk for 6-7 minutes or until the mixture is thick. Remove from the heat and whisk until cool.

3 In a cup, sprinkle the gelatine over 3tbls of cold water and leave to soften for 5 minutes. Put the cup in a pan of simmering water and leave until the gelatine has dissolved and the liquid is clear. Allow to cool slightly, then pour the gelatine over the coffee and egg mixture, stirring it in evenly with a large metal spoon.

4 When the mixture is on the point of setting, lightly whip the cream and use a large metal spoon to fold it in.

5 In a clean, dry bowl, whisk the egg whites until soft peaks form. Using a large metal spoon, fold the egg whites into the soufflé mixture, working as lightly and quickly as possible. Pour into the prepared dish and put in the refrigerator until set, about 2-3 hours.

6 About 20 minutes before serving, remove the soufflé from the refrigerator. Run a sharp knife round the soufflé inside the greaseproof paper, then ease the paper off. With a palette knife, press the walnuts around the edge above the rim. Decorate with whipped cream and candied violets.

Plan ahead

Soufflés freeze extremely well for up to 2 months. Use foil rather than greaseproof paper to make the collar for the soufflé dish, securing it firmly with freezer tape. Open-freeze the soufflé on a flat tray until hard, then place the soufflé dish in a polythene bag, seal and return to the freezer. Remove the collar and decorate the soufflé once thawed.

Apricot popovers

● ***Preparation: 20 minutes, plus standing***

● ***Cooking: 30 minutes*** ● ***Serves 4***

16 NO-SOAK DRIED APRICOTS (about 100g/ 4oz)
3tbls MINCEMEAT
BUTTER, for greasing
CREAM, to serve (optional)

For the batter:
40g/1½oz FLOUR
pinch of SALT
20g/¾oz CASTER SUGAR
1 EGG
125ml/4fl oz MILK
1tbls MELTED BUTTER

1 Put the apricots in a small pan with enough water to cover them. Bring to the boil, reduce the heat, cover and simmer for 20-30 minutes or until tender. Drain, reserving the liquid, and leave to cool.

2 Lightly butter eight holes of a bun tin with deep, 6.5cm/2½in wide moulds. Make the batter. Sift the flour and salt into a bowl, stir in the sugar and make a well in the centre. Break in the egg and add a few spoonfuls of milk. Beat with a wooden spoon, drawing in the flour and mixing to a smooth batter. Gradually beat in the remaining milk, then the melted butter. Leave to stand for 30 minutes.

3 Heat the oven to 200C/400F/gas 6. Beat the batter lightly, then spoon a little into each mould of the prepared bun tin. Divide the mincemeat evenly into eight. Sandwich each portion of mincemeat between two apricots and place in the centre of the bun tin moulds, in the batter.

4 Pour in more batter over the apricots to almost fill each mould. Bake for 25-30 minutes or until the batter is risen and golden brown.

5 To serve, remove the popovers from the moulds and arrange them on a large, warmed serving plate, brown tops uppermost so that the apricots show. Serve immediately, with cream, if wished.

BUDGET DINNER FOR FOUR

Potato and carrot soup · Sweet and sour chicken · Raisin rice with pine nuts · Radish flower salad · Lemon clouds

YOU DON'T HAVE to be Scrooge to want value for money and recipes that don't cost a king's ransom. There are plenty of occasions when a costly, sumptuous spread would seem out of place, when you want to offer a tasty, informal dinner to old friends or family that you know *you* will enjoy, relaxed in the knowledge that you have kept to a sensible budget. By buying fruit and vegetables that are in season, and cooking inexpensive cuts of meat or poultry in spicy or piquant sauces you can combine cost-consciousness with taste and style. In our menu, two humble vegetables, the potato and the carrot, are prepared simply with specially chosen herbs and seasonings to make a really handsome soup. For the main course, serve Chinese-style Sweet and sour chicken. Raisin rice with pine nuts would be perfect with the chicken, and Radish flower salad will bring a delightful splash of colour to the meal. For dessert, brighten everyone up with Lemon clouds, made with creamy yoghurt and the zest of lemons.

Setting the Scene

Whether you are giving a dinner party or just cooking for your evening meal, laying the table beforehand always makes a favourable impression. You don't need special skills in napkin-folding to make the table look attractive, or lavish, expensive-looking dinner sets – indeed, a simple setting of plain crockery often looks more inviting. As this is a budget dinner, if you can't pick your own fresh flowers, keep your costs down by investing in some very reasonably priced dried flowers, which not only look lovely but will last forever as well.

Wine Ideas

You may wonder which wine to serve with Sweet and sour chicken, as you don't want the wine to clash with the meal, or indeed swamp the delicacy of the taste of the chicken. For an excellent accompaniment to this meal, try a dryish German white: look out for the words 'Trocken' or 'Halbtrocken' on the label. For a good bargain, look out for a 'wine of the week' on special offer in supermarkets or off-licences.

Countdown

In the morning
Make the Potato and carrot soup, cool and store, covered, in the refrigerator. Cut the bread for the croûtons into cubes and store in an airtight container.
Soak the raisins for the rice.

2 hours 30 minutes before
Drain the raisins and store in a plastic bag.
Prepare the Lemon clouds and chill.
Prepare the vegetables for the salad and chill.

Fifty minutes before
Heat the oven, then fry the rice and transfer to the oven to finish cooking.
Fry the chicken.

Thirty minutes before
Make the salad dressing.
Fry the croûtons and bacon for the soup and keep warm.

Fifteen minutes before
Reheat the soup and garnish.
Drain the cooked chicken and keep warm. Make the sauce. Return the chicken to the casserole and keep warm.
Sauté the pine nuts and add to the rice with the raisins.
Cover and keep warm.
Decorate the Lemon clouds with shreds of lemon zest.

Before serving the main course
Drain the chilled vegetables well. Whisk the dressing again, then complete the salad.

★ Potato and carrot soup

● ***Preparation: 15 minutes***

● ***Cooking: 1 hour 20 minutes*** ● ***Serves 4-6***

225g/8oz POTATOES, thickly sliced
2 LARGE CARROTS, thickly sliced
1 CELERY STALK, thickly sliced
700ml/1¼pt BEEF STOCK
15g/½oz BUTTER
1 SMALL ONION, very finely chopped
PINCH OF DRIED MARJORAM
SALT and PEPPER

For the garnish:
4 STREAKY BACON RASHERS, finely chopped
2 SLICES OF WHITE BREAD, crusts removed
1tbls OLIVE OIL

1 Put the potatoes, carrots and celery in a large saucepan, pour in the stock and bring to the boil. Partially cover the pan and simmer for 40-50 minutes, until the vegetables are falling apart. Purée the soup in a food processor or blender until smooth. Then rub through a fine sieve into a bowl.

2 Melt the butter in the rinsed-out saucepan and fry the onion for 6-8 minutes, until softened and richly coloured. Return the blended soup to the pan and season with the marjoram, salt and pepper to taste. Simmer for 5-10 minutes, stirring occasionally.

3 Meanwhile, prepare the garnish: fry the finely chopped bacon in its own fat in a pan over low heat, stirring, for 3-4 minutes until crisp. Remove with a slotted spoon and drain on absorbent paper. Cut the bread into small dice and fry in the bacon fat left in the pan, adding 1tbls oil if necessary. When golden brown all over, remove and drain on absorbent paper.

4 Serve the soup hot, in heated soup bowls, garnished with the croûtons and crispy bacon.

Cook's tips

The best type of potato to use in this recipe is one of the floury, rather than waxy, varieties. King Edward, Kerrs Pink or Maris Piper are all excellent and widely available.

Variations

The croûtons and the bacon make for a tasty but fairly high-calorie garnish. For a lighter, less-fattening topping, try sprinkling some freshly snipped chives or chopped parsley over each bowl of soup just before serving.

Egg and onion appetizer

● ***Preparation: 20 minutes, plus chilling*** ● ***Serves 4-6***

6 LARGE EGGS, hard-boiled
6 SPRING ONIONS, finely chopped
4-6tbls MELTED BUTTER or RENDERED CHICKEN FAT
SALT and PEPPER
LETTUCE
SPRING ONION TASSELS, to garnish
SLICES OF TOAST, to serve

1 Finely chop the hard-boiled eggs and mix with the spring onion and butter or chicken fat. If using chicken fat, it should be cool but fairly liquid. Season with salt and pepper to taste and chill the mixture for at least 2 hours.

2 Serve the chopped egg on a bed of lettuce, either in individual portions or mounded up on a serving dish, garnished with spring onion tassels and accompanied by toast cut into decorative shapes, if wished.

Cook's tips

Using chicken fat in this Jewish-style recipe makes the eggs very tasty. Rendered chicken fat is made from the two lumps of fat found on either side of the entrance to the cavity of an uncooked chicken. Remove them and fry gently in an ungreased pan, pressing them firmly with a fork or fish slice against the bottom of the pan to extract as much fat as possible. Pour off the fat into a small bowl, cover tightly and refrigerate. Use as required in place of butter or oil. Stored in the refrigerator, it will keep for up to 2 weeks.

★ *Sweet and sour chicken*

● ***Preparation: 20 minutes***

● ***Cooking: 50 minutes*** ● ***Serves: 4-6***

1.5kg/3¼lb CHICKEN PIECES, skinned if wished
SALT
75ml/3fl oz OIL
4cm/1½in CUBE FRESH ROOT GINGER, peeled and finely chopped
1 GARLIC CLOVE, crushed
1 GREEN PEPPER, seeded and thinly sliced (optional)
3 SPRING ONIONS, green part only, thinly sliced on the slant
4tbls LIGHT SOY SAUCE
4tbls WHITE WINE VINEGAR
2 ORANGES, peel and pith removed
225g/8oz CANNED PINEAPPLE CHUNKS
4tbls ORANGE JUICE
2tbls TOMATO PURÉE
3-4tsp CORNFLOUR
PARSLEY or ORANGE SLICES, to garnish (optional)

1 Rub the chicken joints with salt. Heat the oil in a large flameproof casserole, add the chicken pieces, cover and cook over low heat for 30-35 minutes, until cooked and lightly browned, turning and basting the pieces occasionally. You can tell when the chicken is cooked by piercing the thickest part with a skewer – the juices should run clear with no trace of pinkness. Remove the chicken, drain on absorbent paper and keep warm.

2 Drain off all but 1tbls oil and return the casserole to medium heat. Add the ginger, garlic, green pepper and half the spring onions. Stir-fry for 3-4 minutes. Add the soy sauce and vinegar and stir-fry for 1-2 minutes.

3 Slice the oranges and cut each slice in half. Add to the casserole together with the pineapple chunks and 4tbls of their juice, the orange juice and tomato purée. Cook for 3-4 minutes, stirring constantly.

4 Dissolve the cornflour in 2tbls water, then add to the casserole and continue cooking, stirring until the sauce thickens and looks glossy.

5 Return the chicken pieces to the casserole and turn them over in the sauce until well coated. Sprinkle over the remaining spring onions and garnish with parsley or orange slices. Serve immediately.

Cook's tips

As you need to heat the oil to a fairly high temperature in this recipe, you should use an oil with a 'high smoking temperature', meaning that it can get very hot before it starts to smoke. Peanut, sunflower or any good vegetable oil are all fine for this recipe.

Spicy tomato meatballs

● ***Preparation: 10 minutes***

● ***Cooking: 1 hour 20 minutes*** ● ***Serves 4-6***

4tbls OLIVE OIL
2 ONIONS, finely chopped
2 GARLIC CLOVES, crushed
450g/1lb TOMATOES, skinned and chopped
2tbls TOMATO PURÉE
1tsp SUGAR
1tbls CORIANDER SEEDS, crushed
CHOPPED PARSLEY, to garnish

For the meatballs:
450g/1lb MINCED BEEF
250g/9oz MINCED PORK
2.5cm/1in thick SLICE OF WHITE BREAD, crusts removed, soaked in cold water and squeezed dry
1 LARGE EGG, lightly beaten
½tsp DRIED MINT
SALT and PEPPER

1 To make the sauce, heat 2tbls oil in a saucepan. Fry the onion and garlic over medium heat for 10 minutes, until softened and lightly browned. Stir the tomatoes, tomato purée, sugar and coriander in with the onions and garlic. Cover the pan and simmer gently for 20-25 minutes, stirring occasionally.

2 To make the meatballs, mix together the beef, pork, bread, egg, mint and salt and pepper to taste. Using your hands, shape the mixture into about 20 balls.

3 Heat the remaining oil in a large, heavy frying pan. Fry the meatballs for 5-8 minutes, turning frequently until browned all over. Pour off and discard any excess oil. Pour the sauce over, cover and simmer for 30 minutes, stirring occasionally. Adjust the seasoning. Spoon the meatballs and sauce into a warmed serving dish. Sprinkle with parsley and serve hot.

Freezer

Freeze the cooked meatballs and sauce in a rigid container for up to 6 months. Defrost in the refrigerator overnight, then reheat gently in a saucepan for 30 minutes or until thoroughly heated through. If the sauce is too thick, add up to 150ml/¼pt water.

Macaroni and kidney beans

● ***Preparation: 15 minutes, plus overnight soaking***

● ***Cooking: 2 hours*** ● ***Serves 4-6***

175g/6oz DRIED RED KIDNEY BEANS, soaked overnight
1 BEEF MARROW BONE, about 10cm/4in long (optional)
4tbls TOMATO PURÉE
25g/1oz BUTTER
1tbls OLIVE OIL
2 ONIONS, finely chopped
1 GARLIC CLOVE, crushed
2tbls CHOPPED PARSLEY
¼tsp CAYENNE PEPPER
2tsp DRIED OREGANO
175g/6oz MACARONI
425ml/¾pt BOILING WATER
SALT and PEPPER
GRATED PARMESAN CHEESE, to serve

1 Drain the beans and place them in a large heavy-based saucepan with the marrow bone (if using) and the tomato purée. Cover with 1.1L/2pt cold water and bring to the boil. Boil hard for 10 minutes, stirring occasionally with a wooden spoon, then reduce the heat, cover and simmer gently for 45-60 minutes or until tender, stirring occasionally.

2 Heat the butter and oil in a small saucepan. Add the onion and garlic and cook over moderate heat for about 7 minutes or until tender, stirring occasionally.

3 Add the onion and garlic to the kidney beans, with the chopped parsley, cayenne pepper, oregano and macaroni. Add the water, cover and cook for a further 15-20 minutes or until the macaroni is just tender, stirring frequently. Discard the bone and season to taste.

4 Transfer the pasta and beans and their liquid to a heated serving dish. Sprinkle generously with Parmesan cheese and serve immediately, with an accompanying bowl of extra Parmesan cheese.

Cook's tips

This Italian dish, *pasta e fagioli*, is a popular Italian appetizer but it also makes a delicious and economical main course for supper or lunch. The beef marrow bone gives this dish its delicious flavour – just ask your butcher for the length you require.

Raisin rice with pine nuts

● *Preparation: 10 minutes*

● *Cooking: 50 minutes* ● *Serves 4*

50g/2oz SEEDLESS RAISINS
BOILING WATER
50g/2oz BUTTER
1 ONION, finely chopped
225g/8oz LONG-GRAIN RICE
425ml/¾pt CHICKEN STOCK
SALT and PEPPER
25g/1oz PINE NUTS
FLAT-LEAVED PARSLEY, to garnish (optional)

1 Cover the raisins with boiling water to soak. Heat the oven to 180C/350F/ gas 4. Heat 40g/1½oz butter in a heavy flameproof casserole. When the foaming subsides, add the onion and fry for about 5 minutes or until soft but not coloured, stirring frequently.

2 Add the rice and stir over moderate heat for 2-3 minutes or until the grains are thoroughly coated with butter. Pour the stock into the casserole, taking care, as the stock will sizzle when it comes into contact with the hot butter. Season with salt and pepper to taste and quickly cover the casserole to prevent too much stock evaporating.

3 Transfer to the oven and bake for 35-40 minutes, or until the rice grains are fluffed and separate, and the liquid has been absorbed. Meanwhile, sauté the pine nuts in the remaining butter until golden, and drain the raisins.

4 Transfer the rice to a serving dish, add the drained, soaked raisins and sautéed pine nuts and toss them altogether with a fork to mix them in lightly. Season with more salt and pepper, if necessary. Garnish with a little flat-leaved parsley, if wished and serve immediately.

Radish flower salad

● *Preparation: 30 minutes, plus chilling* ● *Serves 4*

ICE CUBES
8 RADISHES
2 LARGE CARROTS
4 CELERY STALKS
8 SPRING ONIONS
LETTUCE LEAVES

For the dressing:
3tbls OLIVE OIL
2tsp LEMON JUICE
1tsp SOY SAUCE
1tsp SUGAR
PEPPER

1 Prepare a large bowl of water with ice cubes in it. With a small, sharp knife trim the radishes, then make four or five cuts lengthways down the radishes to make petals. Pare the skin of the centre tip so that it is white, then drop the radishes into iced water where they will open up to resemble flowers.

2 Slice the carrots thinly lengthways and cut into thin 4cm/1½in strips. Add to the bowl of iced water.

3 Cut the celery stalks into thin strips lengthways, then into 4cm/1½in lengths. Add to the bowl of iced water.

4 Trim the roots of the spring onions and cut off the green parts to make the onions about 6.5cm/2½in long, including the white bulbs. Make three or four cuts 2.5cm/1in long at the stalk end, taking care not to separate the onion strips completely. Add to the bowl of iced water. Leave the bowl of vegetables to soak in the refrigerator for at least 2 hours, during which time they will all curl up most attractively.

5 Just before serving, put all the ingredients for the dressing in a small bowl and beat together until they form an emulsion. To serve, drain the chilled vegetables thoroughly on a clean tea-towel. Toss them in the prepared dressing and arrange in a bowl lined with lettuce leaves, making sure the radishes point upwards. Serve immediately.

Variations

You could vary the way you cut the radishes. Long ones look attractive when cut at intervals along the length to open out concertina-fashion.

Lemon clouds

● ***Preparation: 10 minutes, plus chilling*** ● ***Serves 6***

FINELY GRATED ZEST of 1 LEMON
600ml/1pt SET YOGHURT
JUICE of 2 LEMONS, strained
1-2tbls CASTER SUGAR
3 EGG WHITES
SHREDS OF LEMON ZEST, to decorate
SMALL BISCUITS or RATAFIAS, to serve

1 Stir the grated lemon zest into the yoghurt in a large bowl. Stir in the lemon juice a little at a time. Add sugar to taste.

2 In a large, clean, dry bowl, whisk the egg whites until they form stiff peaks. Gently fold them into the yoghurt mixture using a large metal spoon.

3 Spoon the mixture into individual glass serving dishes and chill for 1-2 hours. Decorate with lemon shreds and serve with ratafias or other small biscuits.

Cook's tips

A tool called a zester will give you attractive, even strips of lemon zest to use as decoration for this dish. If you don't have one, use a potato peeler to peel off strips of zest, then slice them very thinly with a sharp knife.

Orangey plum crumble

● ***Preparation: 30 minutes***

● ***Cooking: 55 minutes*** ● ***Serves 4-6***

800g/1¾lb RED PLUMS, halved and stoned
150g/5oz SUGAR
½tsp GROUND CINNAMON
150ml/¼pt ORANGE JUICE or WATER
2 ORANGES, peeled, pith removed, segmented

For the crumble:
225g/8oz FLOUR
100g/4oz BUTTER, diced
100g/4oz SOFT BROWN SUGAR

1 Heat the oven to 180C/350F/gas 4. Place the plums, sugar and cinnamon in a heavy saucepan with the orange juice or water, then cook over low heat for 10-15 minutes or until tender.

2 Pour the fruit and syrup into a deep ovenproof dish and add the orange segments, stirring gently to mix them in with the plums.

3 To make the crumble, sift the flour into a large bowl, then add the butter and rub it into the flour lightly, using your fingertips. When the butter has been evenly dispersed and the mixture resembles fine breadcrumbs, add the sugar and mix in well.

4 Sprinkle the crumble mixture evenly over the fruit and bake for 30-40 minutes or until the crumble is a rich golden colour.

Variations

Instead of all flour, you can use half plain flour and half rolled oats; or half wholewheat flour and half rolled oats; or, for a delicious nut crumble topping, 175g/6oz wholewheat flour and 75g/3oz chopped nuts. You will need only 75g/3oz soft brown sugar and 75g/3oz butter for the nut crumble.

WELCOMING DINNER FOR FOUR

Italian pepper appetizer · Lamb bourguignon · Green bean purée · Sauté potatoes · Rhubarb fool

For a meal that is warming and satisfying but elegant at the same time, this menu selection is ideal. Begin on a colourful note with a starter of red, yellow and green peppers with a garlic and lemon dressing.

A little drop of alcohol has always been the traditional way to keep the chill out, and the red wine in the Lamb bourguignon does just that, while giving plenty of flavour to this welcoming, classic casserole. Serve it with Green bean purée, a smooth, stylish vegetable dish which contrasts beautifully with the crisp, golden sautéed potatoes. And if you've ever wondered how restaurants manage to get them just right every time, we now reveal the answer.

Nothing could be simpler, however, than Rhubarb fool. It is a beautiful dessert with which to finish the meal.

Setting the Scene

As this meal is a satisfying one, keep any pre-dinner nibbles very light. Given this, don't keep your guests waiting too long for the meal – about 20 minutes is long enough. You can prepare most of the dishes well before, so just relax and enjoy the evening.

Wine Ideas

The classic French bourguignon calls for an inviting red wine from Burgundy. Any from 1984 or 1985 will be particularly ripe-tasting with a hint of raspberries, but most of the wine from this region is straightforward and honest and it would be difficult to make a bad choice. After dinner you might like to serve a warming glass of Port or Madeira.

Countdown

The day before
Make the rhubarb purée for the fool, cool, then chill, covered.
Make the Italian pepper appetizer, cool, then cover and chill.

Four and a half hours before
Cook the Lamb bourguignon to the end of step 3.

Two hours before
Add the beurre manié and the mushrooms to the lamb and return to the oven to continue cooking.
Whip the cream for the fool; chill.
Cook the green beans. Drain, then purée and reserve.

One and a quarter hours before
Prepare the potatoes, soak them, then drain and dry thoroughly.

Thirty minutes before
Add the whipped cream to the rhubarb purée and flavour with the lemon juice. Spoon into glasses and decorate; then chill.
Finish the lamb; keep warm.
Sauté the potatoes and keep warm.
Meanwhile, reheat the green bean purée, add the cream, season and keep warm.

★ *Italian pepper appetizer*

● ***Preparation: 25 minutes***

● ***Cooking: 15 minutes, plus chilling*** ● ***Serves 4***

4 SWEET RED, GREEN or YELLOW PEPPERS
2tbls OLIVE OIL, plus extra for brushing
3 CANNED ANCHOVY FILLETS, drained
2 GARLIC CLOVES, finely chopped
2tbls FINELY CHOPPED PARSLEY
1tsp LEMON JUICE
SALT and PEPPER (optional)

1 Heat the grill to moderate. Brush the peppers all over with olive oil. Place them side by side in the grill pan, and grill steadily under moderate heat for about 10 minutes or until their skins blister and blacken all over, and the peppers become limp. Turn them regularly to ensure they cook evenly.

2 Plunge the grilled peppers into a large bowl of cold water. Leave for 2 minutes, then drain and peel. The skins will peel off easily if the peppers have been evenly grilled.

3 Slice the peppers in half. Cut out the core and rinse out the seeds under cold running water. Pat each piece of pepper dry with absorbent paper or a clean tea-towel. Cut each pepper half across into four.

4 Cut the anchovy fillets into 5mm/¼in lengths and combine them in a deep serving dish with the peppers and finely chopped garlic and parsley. Toss lightly until well mixed.

5 In a small saucepan, heat the oil and the lemon juice. When it is very hot, pour the dressing over the peppers and mix lightly to coat. Leave to become cold, then chill. The hot dressing will develop and blend together the flavours as it cools in a way that a simple cold dressing could never do.

6 Season lightly with salt and pepper, if wished. (This dish is so strongly flavoured that you are unlikely to need either salt or pepper, but taste and judge for yourself). Serve chilled.

Cook's tips

The slow steady grilling helps bring out the flavour of the peppers, so make sure the heat stays moderate.

Plan ahead

As this starter is served chilled, but is tossed originally in a hot dressing, it is ideal to prepare the day before and can be left to chill overnight.

Prawn and pineapple salad

• Preparation: 35 minutes **• Serves 4**

1 SMALL COS LETTUCE
1 PINEAPPLE
150ml/¼pt MAYONNAISE
1tsp SOY SAUCE
2tsp CLEAR HONEY
1tsp LEMON JUICE
1cm/½in PIECE OF FRESH ROOT GINGER, crushed
SALT and PEPPER
225g/8oz COOKED PEELED PRAWNS, defrosted if frozen
PRAWNS IN THEIR SHELLS, to garnish

1 Wash the lettuce in cold water and dry each leaf with absorbent paper. Roll in a clean tea-towel and place in the vegetable compartment of your refrigerator until needed.

2 Cut off the pineapple skin with a sharp knife and remove the 'eyes', then quarter the pineapple lengthways and remove the core from each wedge. Cut across each quarter into 5mm/¼in slices.

3 In a bowl, combine the mayonnaise, soy sauce, honey, lemon juice and crushed ginger. Stir everything together to blend well and season with salt and pepper to taste.

4 Stir the prawns and the pineapple slices into the mayonnaise mixture. Taste and adjust the seasoning if necessary.

5 Arrange a bed of lettuce in a salad bowl or on a serving dish, spoon the prawn and pineapple salad in the centre, garnish and serve immediately.

Cook's tips

Serve the Prawn and pineapple salad as soon as it is assembled, as the dressing separates if left to stand.

★ Lamb bourguignon

• Preparation: 40 minutes

• Cooking: 3½-4 hours **• Serves 4-6**

1.4kg/3lb NECK FILLET or BONED LEG of LAMB, trimmed of all fat
50g/2oz SEASONED FLOUR
3tbls OLIVE OIL
65g/2½oz BUTTER
225g/8oz BUTTON ONIONS
2 CARROTS, cut into sticks
2 LEEKS, sliced
1-2 GARLIC CLOVES, crushed
BOUQUET GARNI
300ml/½pt LAMB or BEEF STOCK
300ml/½pt RED BURGUNDY
SALT and PEPPER
BEURRE MANIÉ, made from 3tbls flour and 25g/1oz butter
175g/6oz BUTTON MUSHROOMS
CHOPPED PARSLEY, to garnish

1 Heat the oven to 150C/300F/gas 2. Cut the lamb into 2.5cm/1in squares and toss in seasoned flour, shaking off the excess.

2 In a large flameproof casserole, heat 2tbls olive oil and 25g/1oz butter. Sauté the lamb in batches, just enough to cover the bottom of the casserole each time, for about 2 minutes each side, or until well browned all over, adding more oil and butter as necessary. Transfer to a plate with a slotted spoon.

3 Add the button onions to the fat remaining in the casserole and fry, stirring often, until lightly coloured on all sides. Return the lamb to the casserole. Add the carrots, leeks, garlic, bouquet garni, stock and red wine. Season with salt and pepper to taste and bring to the boil, then reduce the heat, cover and cook very gently for 2 hours.

4 Add the *beurre manié* in small pieces, stirring it in carefully. Add the mushrooms, cover and return to the oven for a further 1-1½ hours.

5 Remove the bouquet garni and correct the seasoning. Sprinkle the casserole with chopped parsley and serve at once.

Cook's tips

To make *beurre manié,* blend the softened butter with the flour, then add tiny pieces to the simmering liquid until thickened, stirring constantly.

Variations

For extra flavour, add a split calf's foot (prepared by your butcher) to the casserole with the bouquet garni and stock. Remove the calf's foot at the same time as removing the bouquet garni.

Pigeon in red wine

- ***Preparation: 40 minutes***
- ***Cooking: 1 hour 10 minutes*** ●***Serves 4***

4 x 175g/6oz PIGEONS, dressed weight
SALT and PEPPER
8 STRIPS of UNSMOKED STREAKY BACON
25g/1oz BUTTER
1 ONION, coarsely chopped
1 LARGE CARROT, chopped
1tbls FLOUR
300ml/½ pt CHICKEN STOCK
175ml/6fl oz RED WINE
1 BOUQUET GARNI (see Cook's tips, page 20)
1tsp TOMATO PUREE
100g/4oz MUSHROOMS, sliced

For the garnish:
SPRIGS of WATERCRESS
TRIANGULAR CROUTONS

1 Heat the oven to 220C/425F/gas 7. Wipe the birds carefully, both inside and out, with a damp cloth or absorbent paper. Pick off any stray feathers. Season generously inside and out with salt and pepper. Cover the birds completely with strips of streaky bacon, and secure with string.

2 Place the pigeons on racks in two roasting tins and roast for 10 minutes, basting frequently.

3 Discard the string, bacon and the pigeon skins. Cut the breasts of each pigeon away from the bone, reserving the legs and carcasses. Cut the breasts in two and place in a flameproof casserole. Cover and set aside. Chop up the carcasses and legs with a cleaver or heavy knife.

4 For the sauce, melt the butter in a saucepan. Add the chopped onion and carrots and cook for 10-15 minutes, until soft but not browned.

5 Stir the flour into the softened onion and carrot mixture and cook for 1-2 minutes more to make a pale roux. Gradually stir in the chicken stock and red wine. Add the bouquet garni and tomato purée. Continue cooking over low heat for 10 minutes.

6 Add the chopped carcasses and pigeon legs to the sauce. Season with salt and pepper to taste and simmer gently for 20 minutes.

7 Strain the sauce over the pigeon breasts. Add the sliced mushrooms to the casserole and simmer over low heat for 5-10 minutes or until the breasts are tender. Garnish and serve as soon as possible.

Freezer

Once cool, this casserole can be frozen for up to 2 months. Heat from frozen for 1 hour in an oven heated to 200C/400F/gas 6 then, if necessary, reduce the heat to 180C/350F/gas 4 and continue heating until thoroughly hot.

★ Green bean purée

- ***Preparation: 20 minutes***
- ***Cooking: 35 minutes*** ●***Serves 4***

450g/1lb WHOLE GREEN BEANS, fresh or frozen
SALT and PEPPER
4tbls DOUBLE CREAM
FRESHLY GRATED NUTMEG

1 Bring a pan of water to the boil. When it begins to bubble, add a generous pinch of salt and the beans. Boil briskly for 20-30 minutes – less for frozen beans – or until the beans are very tender. Drain off most of the cooking liquid.

2 Purée in small batches in a food processor or blender. Then, using a wooden spoon, press the purée through a fine sieve and return to the pan. Reheat over medium heat, beating vigorously with a wooden spoon to evaporate excess moisture. Add the cream and mix well.

3 Season the creamed bean purée with salt and pepper and a pinch of freshly grated nutmeg to taste. Spoon the bean purée into a heated serving dish, sprinkle with a little more grated nutmeg and serve immediately.

Variations

You can bind the purée with a little butter instead of cream.

This dish is excellent served cold, mixed with a little well-flavoured mayonnaise.

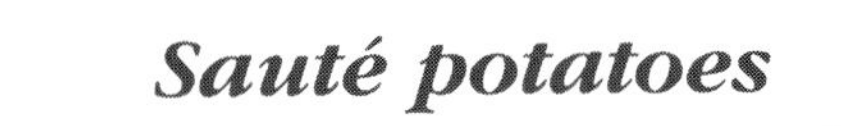

Sauté potatoes

● *Preparation: 20 minutes, plus soaking*

● *Cooking: 20 minutes* ● *Serves 4*

450-700g/1-½lb EVEN-SIZED POTATOES
50-75g/2-3oz BUTTER
1tbls OLIVE OIL
SALT and PEPPER
2tbls FINELY CHOPPED PARSLEY (optional)

1 Slice the potatoes thinly and soak them in cold water for a few minutes. This removes some of the starch and helps prevent them sticking later when they are fried. Drain and dry them thoroughly on absorbent paper or a clean tea-towel.

2 Use butter for frying for the flavour it gives, plus a small amount of oil to prevent burning. Melt the butter and oil in two heavy frying pans. When really hot, add the potatoes in a single layer, without overcrowding the pans. Sauté over moderate heat, until the potatoes are crisp and golden, turning frequently with a spatula. Season with salt and pepper to taste towards the end of the cooking time, adding a little more butter if necessary.

3 Turn the potatoes out onto a heated serving dish and serve immediately, sprinkled with finely chopped parsley, if wished.

Cook's tips

This popular dish is often very badly cooked. Undercooked, hard potatoes or overcooked, mushy potatoes are usually caused by overcrowding the potatoes in the pan. The potatoes must cook in a single layer, or the rising steam will moisten them instead of giving them that crisp golden finish.

Sauté potatoes are a wonderful way of using up uneaten baked potatoes; leave until completely cold then slice thinly, leaving the skins on, and cook in very hot fat as before.

Celery with toasted garlic breadcrumbs

● *Preparation: 10 minutes*

● *Cooking: 20 minutes* ● *Serves 4*

450g/1lb CELERY STALKS
425ml/¾pt BEEF STOCK
50g/2oz BUTTER
1 GARLIC CLOVE, crushed
6tbls WHITE BREADCRUMBS, toasted (see Cook's tips)
SALT and PEPPER
CELERY LEAVES, to garnish (optional)

1 Cut the celery stalks into 7cm/2¾in lengths, then cut each length into narrow batons.

2 In a medium-sized saucepan, bring the stock to the boil. Add the celery batons, bring back to the boil, reduce the heat and simmer gently for 4 minutes. Drain well.

3 Heat the butter in a large frying pan. Stir in the crushed garlic and the toasted breadcrumbs.

4 Add the drained celery batons and toss over moderate heat for 3 minutes, or until the batons are coated in garlic breadcrumbs.

5 Season with salt and pepper to taste and transfer to a heated serving dish. Garnish with celery leaves, if wished, and serve immediately.

Cook's tips

To make toasted breadcrumbs, grate one-day-old bread through the coarse holes of a grater, then rub down the lumps with your fingers. Heat the oven to 180C/350F/gas 4 and bake the crumbs on a baking tray for about 10 minutes or until coloured, shaking the tray occasionally.

★ Rhubarb fool

● ***Preparation: 15 minutes***

● ***Cooking: 10 minutes, plus chilling*** ● ***Serves 4***

350g/12oz RHUBARB, cut into 2.5cm/1in pieces
100g/4oz SUGAR
2tbls LEMON JUICE
200ml/7fl oz DOUBLE CREAM, whipped
ROSE or MINT LEAVES, to decorate (optional)

1 In a heavy saucepan, combine the rhubarb, sugar and 1tbls lemon juice. Bring to the boil, stirring constantly with a wooden spoon.

2 Lower the heat and simmer gently for 5-8 minutes, stirring all the time, until the rhubarb is soft but not mushy.

3 Purée in a food processor or blender until smooth or press through a fine sieve into a bowl, using the back of the wooden spoon. Allow to cool, then chill the cooled purée in the refrigerator until ready to use.

4 Shortly before serving, fold the whipped cream into the purée with a large metal spoon, reserving 4tbls to decorate. Flavour to taste with the remaining lemon juice. Spoon into individual glass dishes and decorate each dish with whipped cream and rose or mint leaves, if using, or serve the rhubarb fool in a large bowl and decorate as before.

Variations

If fresh rhubarb is unavailable, you can use frozen instead. Use the same amount as for fresh, but defrost and drain before using.

Apple upside-down pudding

● ***Preparation: 30 minutes, plus chilling***

● ***Cooking: 45 minutes, plus cooling*** ● ***Serves 4***

25g/1oz BUTTER
150g/5oz SOFT DARK BROWN SUGAR
4 DESSERT APPLES
7 GLACÉ CHERRIES
6 WALNUT HALVES
DOUBLE CREAM, to serve

For the batter:
50g/2oz BUTTER
5tbls CASTER SUGAR
3tbls GOLDEN SYRUP
1tbls BLACK TREACLE
1 LARGE EGG, lightly beaten
100g/4oz FLOUR
¼tsp SALT
1tsp BAKING POWDER
½tsp BICARBONATE OF SODA
1tsp GROUND GINGER
1tsp GROUND CINNAMON
1tbls MILK (optional)

1 Heat the oven to 180C/350F/gas 4. In a small saucepan melt the butter and add the soft dark brown sugar, stirring until the sugar has dissolved. Pour this mixture into a 20cm/8in cake tin and chill.

2 Peel and core the apples; cut each apple in half crossways. Arrange seven apple halves, cut-side down, in the syrup-coated tin. Place a glacé cherry in the bottom of each core cavity and the walnut halves between the apples.

3 To make the batter, cream the butter and caster sugar until light and fluffy. Stir in the golden syrup, black treacle and beaten egg and beat until smooth. Sift the flour, salt, baking powder, bicarbonate of soda and ground ginger and cinnamon into the batter and fold in with a large metal spoon. Stir in 1tbls milk, if necessary, to make the batter a soft dropping consistency.

4 Pour the batter over the apples in the tin and, with a palette knife, smooth the batter evenly around the apples. Bake in the oven for 35-40 minutes, or until the cake is well risen and springs back when pressed lightly with a finger. Allow the pudding to cool in the tin.

5 Turn the pudding out, upside down, onto a serving platter and serve warm or at room temperature, accompanied by double cream.

INFORMAL DINNER FOR FOUR

Mushroom soup · Baked chicken · Braised cabbage with tomatoes · Baked stuffed potatoes · Lemon-poached peaches

COOK THIS MENU when you want to invite close friends round for an evening meal without making a big thing of it. All the recipes are easy to do – and easy on the pocket too.

Start off with Mushroom soup, equally delicious hot or chilled. Follow with Baked chicken, derived from the French *poulet en persillade* and baked in a crispy coating of breadcrumbs, cheese, onion, garlic and parsley. Accompany this with cabbage with tomatoes and half a baked potato shell piled high with potato mashed with soured cream. None of these dishes depends on split-second timing: once cooked they can be kept hot in a low oven if necessary.

To finish off, serve Lemon-poached peaches, a chilled dessert of peaches cooked in cinnamon-flavoured syrup.

Table Talk

Why not serve this dinner as an informal buffet? Let guests help themselves to what they like and wander around as they please – even outdoors if it's a fine evening. For ease in serving, have the soup cold, and the main course very hot – put the dishes on a hotplate if you have one.

What to Drink

Continue the informal theme by having big jugs of cider available for guests to help themselves. Cider contains only about 5.8% alcohol by volume, roughly half that of wine, and is much cheaper. So you can afford to be generous, and non-driving guests can drink deeply without worrying about the consequences. Make sure to pick a dry cider, which will make a perfect partner for the baked chicken. Most commercially produced ciders are slightly sparkling; if you want something with lots of fizz to start the evening off with a bang, open a bottle of vintage cider, packaged in gold-foil topped bottles just like champagne.

Countdown

The day before
Make the Lemon-poached peaches and chill, lightly covered.

In the morning
Make the Mushroom soup, cool, cover and chill.

Two hours before
Bake the potatoes and prepare the soured cream mixture. When they are cooked, reduce the oven temperature to 200C/400F/gas 6.
Cut the chicken into serving pieces and season.
Prepare the breadcrumb mixture.

One hour before
Start cooking the chicken pieces.

Fifteen minutes before
Sprinkle the breadcrumbs over the chicken and continue to cook.
Start reheating the soup over low heat, if serving hot.
Add the garnish just before serving.
Fill the potato shells and finish cooking them.

Before serving the main course
Take the Lemon-poached peaches out of the refrigerator and decorate with mint sprigs.

★ *Mushroom soup*

- ***Preparation: 15 minutes***
- ***Cooking: 25 minutes***
- ***Serves 4***

225g/8oz MUSHROOMS
50g/2oz BUTTER
2tbls FLOUR
425ml/¾pt CHICKEN OR VEGETABLE STOCK
150ml/¼pt MILK
2tbls FINELY CHOPPED PARSLEY
juice of ½ LEMON
150ml/¼pt SINGLE CREAM
SALT AND PEPPER
SLICED MUSHROOMS and FRESH CHERVIL, to garnish

1 Chop the mushrooms finely, then purée them in a blender or food processor.

2 Melt the butter in a saucepan. Add the flour and cook over low heat for 3-4 minutes, stirring constantly. Gradually stir in the chicken or vegetable stock. Bring to the boil, stirring constantly until smooth.

3 Add the milk, puréed mushrooms, parsley and lemon juice. Cook for 5 minutes, then stir in most of the cream and season with salt and pepper to taste. Heat through if serving the soup hot; allow to cool, then chill, if serving it cold. Garnish with a swirl of cream, sliced mushrooms and chervil.

Variations

You can use button mushrooms or, for slightly more flavour, try flat mushrooms. For a soup with more of an oriental taste, use shiitake mushrooms; these also look attractive sliced and used as a garnish as shown in the photograph above.

Broccoli starter

- ***Preparation: 10 minutes***
- ***Cooking: 5 minutes, plus cooling*** • ***Serves 4***

450g/1lb BROCCOLI, separated into florets

For the dip:

175g/6oz FULL-FAT SOFT CHEESE
3tbls MAYONNAISE
JUICE and GRATED ZEST OF ½ SMALL LEMON
3 SPRING ONIONS, chopped
1-2 GREEN CHILLIES, seeded and chopped
BASIL SPRIGS, to garnish

1 Steam the broccoli florets for 4-5 minutes or until just tender, but still crisp. Leave to cool.

2 Place all the dip ingredients in a blender or food processor and blend until smooth. Chill lightly and garnish with the basil sprigs before serving. Arrange the broccoli florets around the bowl and use them to scoop up the dip.

★ Baked chicken

- ***Preparation: 20 minutes***
- ***Cooking: 1 hour 10 minutes*** • ***Serves 4-6***

1.4kg/3lb ROASTING CHICKEN
SALT AND PEPPER
50g/2oz BUTTER
40g/1½oz COARSE BREADCRUMBS
4tbls FINELY CHOPPED PARSLEY
2tbls GRATED PARMESAN CHEESE
1 SMALL ONION, finely chopped
1 GARLIC CLOVE, crushed
FLAT-LEAVED PARSLEY and LEMON WEDGES, to garnish

1 Heat the oven to 200C/400F/gas 6. Cut the chicken into eight pieces, then season generously with salt and pepper.

2 Heat the butter in a flameproof baking dish large enough to hold all the chicken pieces in one layer. Put in the chicken pieces and toss them in the butter until well coated all over. Then arrange them in the dish and bake for 45 minutes. Drain off the cooking juices.

3 Combine the breadcrumbs and finely chopped parsley with the Parmesan, onion and garlic and season; sprinkle the mixture over the chicken. Return to the oven and bake for 15-20 minutes or until the chicken pieces are cooked through and the topping is golden brown.

4 Serve the chicken in its baking dish, if wished, garnished with parsley sprigs and lemon wedges.

Cook's tips

If it is more convenient, use eight small chicken portions instead of cutting up a whole bird yourself. However, this will make the dish more expensive.

Macaroni pizza bake

• ***Preparation: 30 minutes***

• ***Cooking: 40 minutes*** • ***Serves 4***

225g/8oz MACARONI
2 LARGE EGGS, beaten
4tbls DOUBLE CREAM
CAYENNE PEPPER
BUTTER, for greasing
50g/2oz CANNED ANCHOVY FILLETS, drained
1-2tsp DRIED OREGANO
100g/4oz MOZZARELLA CHEESE, very finely chopped
3-4tbls GRATED PARMESAN CHEESE
12-14 BLACK OLIVES, stoned

For the tomato sauce:
1tbls OLIVE OIL
1 SMALL ONION, finely chopped
1 GARLIC CLOVE, finely chopped
400g/14oz CANNED TOMATOES, chopped
¼tsp DRIED BASIL
1tsp TOMATO PUREE
SALT and PEPPER

1 First make the sauce: heat the oil in a saucepan and fry the onion and garlic gently until transparent. Add the tomatoes with their juice, the basil and tomato purée; season lightly with salt and pepper. Simmer for 30 minutes, then purée in a blender or food processor. Taste and adjust the seasoning.

2 Meanwhile, heat the oven to 200C/400F/gas 6. Bring a large pan of lightly salted boiling water to the boil and drop in the macaroni. Stir once or twice. When the water returns to the boil, boil briskly for 10-12 minutes or until the macaroni is cooked but still firm. Drain at once.

3 Combine the drained macaroni with the eggs and cream. Season to taste with salt, pepper and cayenne pepper; mix well. Butter a large shallow baking dish. Pour in the macaroni mixture, put in the oven and bake for 10 minutes. Meanwhile, cut the anchovy fillets in half lengthways.

4 Pour the tomato sauce over the macaroni base; sprinkle with oregano, Mozzarella and Parmesan cheese. Arrange the anchovy fillets on top in a lattice pattern and put an olive in the centre of each square. Return to the oven for 10 minutes or until the top is lightly browned. Serve hot.

★ *Braised cabbage with tomatoes*

• ***Preparation: 15 minutes***

• ***Cooking: 45 minutes*** • ***Serves 4***

1tbls OLIVE OIL
1 LARGE ONION, finely chopped
1 BOUQUET GARNI (parsley, bay leaf and thyme)
1 GARLIC CLOVE, finely chopped
4 LARGE, RIPE TOMATOES, skinned, seeded and diced
SALT and PEPPER
15g/½oz BUTTER
175g/6oz STREAKY BACON, cut into strips
700-900g/1½-2lb WHITE CABBAGE, cored and shredded

1 Heat the oil in a saucepan. Add the onion and cook over medium heat for about 10 minutes, until soft and golden brown, stirring occasionally.

2 Add the bouquet garni, garlic and tomatoes. Season with salt and pepper to taste. Simmer over low heat for 15 minutes or until the tomatoes are reduced to a purée, stirring occasionally. Keep warm.

3 Meanwhile, heat the butter in a flameproof casserole. Add the bacon strips and cook, tossing frequently, for 5 minutes or until golden.

4 Stir in the cabbage and season with salt and pepper to taste. Cover and cook for 10 minutes or until the cabbage is almost tender, stirring occasionally.

5 Pour the tomato purée over the cabbage and stir it in gently. Cook for a further 5 minutes, stirring occasionally, until the cabbage is cooked but still crisp and the flavours have blended together.

6 Remove the bouquet garni, correct the seasoning and transfer to a heated serving dish. Serve hot.

★ Baked stuffed potatoes

- **Preparation: 25 minutes**
- **Cooking: 1 hour 35 minutes** • **Serves 4**

3 × 225g/8oz POTATOES
150ml/¼pt SOURED CREAM
2tbls FINELY SNIPPED CHIVES
½tsp GROUND CUMIN
1 LARGE EGG, lightly beaten
25g/1oz BUTTER
SALT and PEPPER
PAPRIKA

1 Heat the oven to 220C/425F/gas 7. Scrub the potatoes until absolutely clean. Pat dry with absorbent paper and prick all over with a fork. Bake for 1-1¼ hours or until cooked through.

2 Mix the soured cream, chives, cumin and egg together in a bowl. Remove the potatoes from the oven and reduce the temperature to 200C/400F/gas 6.

3 Cut the potatoes in half horizontally and scoop out the centres with a sharp-edged spoon, taking care not to break the skins and leaving a shell about 5mm/¼in thick. Sieve or mash the potato in a large bowl. Beat in the butter and the soured cream mixture. Season with salt and pepper to taste.

4 Arrange four of the best potato shells on a baking sheet. Spoon the potato mixture into them, mounding it up slightly, and sprinkle with paprika. Bake the potato shells for 15-20 minutes or until golden brown. Serve hot.

Variations

Try topping each potato half with a bacon roll. Cut two bacon rashers in half and roll each one up tightly, then arrange them on the filled potatoes before baking them in step 4.

Green beans with pimiento

- **Preparation: 10 minutes**
- **Cooking: 20 minutes** • **Serves 4**

450g/1lb GREEN BEANS
SALT and PEPPER
1 ONION, finely chopped
50g/2oz BUTTER
2tbls OLIVE OIL
2 CANNED PIMIENTOS, drained and thinly sliced
LEMON JUICE
STRIPS OF FLAT-LEAVED PARSLEY and LEMON SLICES, to garnish

1 Cut the beans into 5cm/2in lengths and cook in plenty of boiling salted water for 3-8 minutes, until tender but still crisp. Drain and refresh in cold water.

2 Fry the onion in the butter and oil over low heat for about 5 minutes until transparent, stirring ocasionally. Add the cooked beans and toss for a few minutes more, just until they are warmed through.

3 Add the pimiento to the beans, sprinkle with lemon juice and season with salt and pepper to taste. Toss once more to heat the pimiento.

4 To serve, transfer the beans to a heated serving dish. Sprinkle with parsley, garnish with lemon slices and serve as soon as possible.

Plan ahead

The beans can be cooked ahead of time to the end of step 1 if this is more convenient.

★ *Lemon-poached peaches*

● ***Preparation: 10 minutes***

● ***Cooking: 20 minutes*** ● ***Serves 4***

8 THIN SLICES of LEMON, unpeeled
4 RIPE PEACHES
JUICE OF ½ LEMON
6tbls SUGAR
½tsp VANILLA ESSENCE
GROUND CINNAMON
4 MINT SPRIGS

1 Lay four of the lemon slices in the bottom of a saucepan. Put the peaches on top, just as they are. Add 425ml/¾pt water, the lemon juice, 4tbls of the sugar, the vanilla essence and a pinch of cinnamon. Bring to the boil, lower the heat, then cover the pan and simmer gently for 4-6 minutes, depending on the ripeness of the peaches, until tender.

2 Remove the peaches from the syrup and gently pull away the skins. Remove the lemon slices from the pan and discard.

3 Return the pan of syrup to the heat and boil for about 10 minutes or until it has reduced to about 4tbls.

4 Put the remaining sugar in another pan, add 2tbls water and boil for about 4 minutes or just until it turns a pale golden colour. Then add the remaining lemon slices. Toss them in the caramel and carry on boiling for about 2 minutes or until they take on a rich golden colour. Lift out the slices and put them onto shallow individual serving dishes.

5 Put a poached peach on top of each lemon slice, pour the cinnamon-flavoured syrup over the top and chill. Serve the peaches decorated with mint sprigs.

Clafoutis

● ***Preparation: 30 minutes, plus soaking***

● ***Cooking: 1 hour, plus cooling*** ● ***Serves 4***

600g/1¼lb FRESH BLACK CHERRIES, or 400g/14oz canned stoned black cherries in syrup
50ml/2fl oz KIRSCH
BUTTER, for greasing
65g/2½oz FLOUR
SALT
50g/2oz CASTER SUGAR
3 EGGS
225ml/8fl oz MILK
VANILLA ESSENCE
1tbls ICING SUGAR

1 Stone fresh cherries or drain canned ones. Heat the oven to 200C/400F/gas 6.

2 Soak the cherries in the kirsch for 1 hour. Drain, reserving the kirsch. Put the cherries into a lightly buttered 1.1L/2pt ovenproof dish.

3 Sift the flour and a pinch of salt into a mixing bowl; stir in the sugar. Make a well in the centre and break in the eggs. Add about 75ml/3fl oz of the milk. Beat the eggs and milk with a wire whisk, gradually incorporating flour from the sides of the bowl.

4 Add two drops of vanilla essence to the rest of the milk and beat the mixture into the batter in the bowl. Then beat in the reserved kirsch. Continue beating until the batter is very smooth. Pour the batter over the cherries and bake the clafoutis for 50 minutes-1 hour.

5 Cool the clafoutis in the tin for 15 minutes. Sift the icing sugar over the top and serve while still warm.

Variations

Try making the clafoutis without the kirsch; if you do this, increase the milk to 300ml/½pt.

STORE-CUPBOARD SUPPER FOR FOUR

Garlic bread ·

Eggs in onion sauce · Artichoke and pimento salad ·

Sliced oranges

WHEN FRIENDS DROP in unexpectedly for supper, you need to be able to come up with dishes which are out of the ordinary, but based on ingredients which you already have. This menu is planned for such an occasion.

With a French stick ready in the freezer, you have the main ingredient for delicious buttery Garlic bread. Serve this on its own as a starter, or to accompany the main course, Eggs in onion sauce. These are simply hard-boiled eggs lifted into gourmet class by the sauce. Accompany this with an unusual salad based on canned vegetables (artichoke hearts and pimentos). To finish, serve a simple orange salad, prettily arranged.

Table Talk

The ability to produce a delicious meal quickly and without advance notice requires no magic, just a little forethought and a well-stocked store cupboard, fridge and freezer.

If you have a large freezer and keep it filled with meat, fish, vegetables and fruit you have no real problem, and, with a microwave as well, you can quickly defrost ready-frozen complete meals and desserts.

Use the fridge to make sure you always have basics such as eggs, hard cheese, bacon and milk. (Unopened long-life milk and cream keep indefinitely.)

Use the store cupboard for basic cans and dry goods like tomatoes, pasta and rice, plus slightly more unusual or luxurious items like ham, salmon, crab, artichoke hearts and palm hearts. Canned pulses (red kidney beans, chick peas, etc) are invaluable as they need no soaking. Onions appear in almost all savoury recipes, so keep a standby carton of dried ones in case the vegetable rack supply runs out, or keep a stock of ready-chopped onion in the freezer.

For dessert, keep a can or two of exotic fruit such as mangoes or lychees to mix with whatever fresh fruit you have on hand to make a fruit salad. Serve it with ice cream or long-life cream.

Countdown

One and a half hours before
Prepare the Sliced oranges to the end of step 2 and chill.
Boil the eggs for the Eggs in onion sauce.

One hour before
Prepare the Artichoke and pimiento salad ingredients and make the dressing.
Prepare the Eggs in onion sauce to the end of step 3 and keep hot.
Heat the oven for the Garlic bread.

30 minutes before
Prepare and bake the Garlic bread.

15 minutes before
Finish the Artichoke and pimiento salad.

Before serving the main course
Garnish the Eggs in onion sauce.

Before serving the dessert
Decorate the Sliced oranges with cream

★

Garlic bread

● ***Preparation: 15 minutes***

● ***Cooking: 15 minutes*** ● ***Serves 4-6***

1 FRENCH STICK (BAGUETTE)
For the garlic butter:
175g/6oz BUTTER, softened
3 GARLIC CLOVES, crushed
3tbls FINELY CHOPPED PARSLEY
PEPPER

1 Heat the oven to 190C/375F/gas 5. Put the butter in a bowl with the garlic, parsley and pepper to taste. Beat with a wooden spoon until the ingredients are well mixed.

2 Cut the French stick into 1cm/½in diagonal slices, without cutting through the crust on the bottom, so that the loaf is still in one piece. Generously spread both sides of the cut slices with the garlic butter.

3 Wrap the loaf tightly in a large sheet of foil and put it on a baking sheet. Bake for 10-12 minutes or until the bread is crisp and the butter has melted.

4 Unwrap the bread and finish cutting the slices. Either leave it in the foil or pile the slices into a basket. Serve very hot.

French liver pâté

• Preparation: 20 minutes, plus chilling **• Serves 4**

225g/8oz LIVER SAUSAGE, skinned
2tbls MAYONNAISE
2tbls DOUBLE CREAM
SALT and PEPPER
LEMON JUICE
HARD-BOILED SIEVED EGG YOLKS and PARSLEY to garnish (optional)
TOAST, RYE or PUMPERNICKEL BREAD, to serve

1 Combine the liver sausage, mayonnaise and cream in a blender or food processor. Season with salt, pepper and lemon juice to taste and process until smooth.

2 Put the pâté into four individual ramekin dishes or one larger terrine. Cover and chill until needed; it will keep for several days.

3 Just before serving, garnish the ramekins or terrine with sieved egg yolks and/or finely chopped parsley. Accompany with toast or bread.

Variations

For a special occasion, add a little brandy instead of the lemon juice. Try serving the pâté with thin slices of ripe pear instead of toast or bread.

★ Eggs in onion sauce

• Preparation: 15 minutes

• Cooking: boiling eggs, then 25 minutes **• Serves 4**

600ml/1pt MILK
½ CHICKEN STOCK CUBE, crumbled
25g/1oz BUTTER
225g/8oz ONIONS, sliced
2tbls CORNFLOUR
SALT and PEPPER
pinch of CAYENNE PEPPER
pinch of GRATED NUTMEG
6 LARGE HARD-BOILED EGGS, quartered
4 PARSLEY SPRIGS and GRATED NUTMEG, to garnish

1 Heat the milk in a saucepan and dissolve the chicken stock cube in it. Melt the butter in a flameproof casserole, add the onions and fry gently for 10 minutes, stirring occasionally, until soft but not browned.

2 Sprinkle the cornflour over the onions and mix well. Gradually stir in the flavoured milk and bring to the boil, stirring constantly, then reduce the heat and simmer for 10 minutes, stirring occasionally. Season generously with salt, pepper, cayenne and nutmeg.

3 Stir in the hard-boiled eggs and heat through. Pour the egg mixture into four heated ramekin dishes.

4 Garnish each ramekin with a grating of nutmeg and a parsley sprig and serve hot.

Spaghetti with clam sauce

• *Preparation: 15 minutes*

• *Cooking: 20 minutes* **• *Serves 4***

600g/1¼lb CANNED CLAMS, drained
225g/8oz SPAGHETTI
SALT and PEPPER
4tbls OLIVE OIL
2 GARLIC CLOVES, finely chopped
1-2 DRIED RED CHILLIES, seeded and finely chopped
25g/1oz BUTTER
3tbls FINELY CHOPPED PARSLEY

1 Spread the clams on absorbent paper to get rid of any remaining moisture. Cook the spaghetti in plenty of lightly salted boiling water until just tender, about 2 minutes for fresh, 10 minutes for dried.

2 Meanwhile, put the olive oil, garlic and chillies in a saucepan and heat gently until the garlic just begins to change colour, stirring occasionally. Add the clams and cook over medium heat for 2 minutes or until heated through, shaking the pan occasionally. Taste and adjust the seasoning. Keep hot.

3 Drain the spaghetti, rinse under hot running water and drain again. Return to the rinsed-out pan, add the butter and season generously with salt and pepper. Toss until the butter has melted.

4 Transfer the spaghetti to a heated serving bowl. Pour the clam mixture over the top and sprinkle with parsley. Serve at once.

Cook's tips

If you are using fresh pasta, cook the sauce first and keep it hot while cooking the spaghetti.

Asparagus flan

• *Preparation: making pastry case, then 30 minutes*

• *Cooking: 35 minutes* **• *Serves 4-6***

25cm/10in PASTRY CASE, baked blind (see Fruity treacle tart, p.18)
1 LARGE EGG, separated
50g/2oz BUTTER
1 ONION, finely chopped
4tbls FINELY CHOPPED HAM
100g/4oz BUTTON MUSHROOMS, finely chopped
SALT and PEPPER
2½tbls FLOUR
225ml/8fl oz MILK
GRATED NUTMEG
2tbls DOUBLE CREAM
400g/14oz CANNED ASPARAGUS TIPS, drained
2tbls GRATED PARMESAN CHEESE

1 Leave the pastry case in its tin. Brush it inside with lightly beaten egg white to seal the surface.

2 Melt half the butter in a saucepan, add the onion and cook over medium heat for about 5 minutes or until soft and golden, stirring occasionally. Add the ham and mushrooms and cook for a further 4-5 minutes or until the mushrooms are a pale golden colour, stirring. Season with salt and pepper to taste. Leave to cool, then drain.

3 Melt the remaining butter in a saucepan. Add the flour and cook for 2-3 minutes, stirring constantly. Add the milk, whisking constantly to prevent lumps from forming. Season with salt, pepper and nutmeg to taste. Cook over low heat for 5 minutes or until thick, stirring occasionally.

4 Meanwhile, heat the oven to 230C/450F/gas 8. Mix the egg yolk and cream together in a small bowl. Add to the thickened sauce, stirring constantly.

5 Spread the onion, ham and mushroom mixture over the base of the prepared pastry case. Arrange the asparagus tips on top like the spokes of a wheel, stalk ends to the centre, trimming them to fit, if necessary. Pour in the sauce and sprinkle with the Parmesan cheese. Bake for 10-12 minutes or until the sauce has set and the top is golden brown. Serve hot, warm or cold.

★ Artichoke and pimiento salad

• *Preparation: 15 minutes* **• *Serves 4***

400g/14oz CANNED ARTICHOKE HEARTS, drained
185g/6½oz CANNED PIMIENTOS, drained
1 ROUND LETTUCE

For the dressing:
3tbls OLIVE OIL
2tsp LEMON JUICE
½tsp CASTER SUGAR
1tsp CHOPPED FRESH HERBS (optional)
SALT and PEPPER

1 Rinse the artichoke hearts under cold running water, drain and pat dry. Cut them into halves. Wipe the pimientos and slice thinly.

2 Mix the oil, lemon juice, caster sugar and herbs (if using) together. Season with salt and pepper to taste and beat or shake until emulsified.

3 Line a serving dish with lettuce leaves. Arrange the artichoke halves and pimientos on top. Pour the dressing over and serve at once.

Tomato and onion salad

• *Preparation: 20 minutes* **• *Serves 4-6***

6 RIPE, FIRM TOMATOES
1 SMALL SPANISH ONION
PARSLEY SPRIG, to garnish

For the dressing:
1tsp CASTER SUGAR
1tbls WINE VINEGAR
3tbls OLIVE OIL
SALT and PEPPER

1 Using a freshly sharpened knife, cut the tomatoes into very thin slices. Discard the end slices of each tomato. Slice the onion as thinly as possible and separate into rings.

2 Combine the sugar, vinegar and oil in a small bowl or screw-topped jar. Season with salt and pepper to taste and beat or shake until the mixture emulsifies.

3 Arrange alternating slices of tomato and onion overlapping on a small, round serving dish. Pour the dressing over and garnish with a sprig of parsley. Serve at once.

Sliced oranges

• Preparation: 15 minutes, plus chilling **• Serves 4**

4 LARGE ORANGES
150ml/¼pt FRESH ORANGE JUICE
2tbls CASTER SUGAR
300ml/½pt DOUBLE CREAM

1 Grate the zest of one orange and add to the orange juice. Peel all the oranges and cut off all the pith with a sharp knife. Cut the flesh into thin slices and remove the pips.

2 Arrange the orange slices in overlapping rows in a shallow serving dish. Sprinkle with orange juice and 1tbls caster sugar. Cover and chill until serving time.

3 Whip the cream and fold in the remaining caster sugar. Spoon the sugared cream over the orange slices, keeping it away from the edges to prevent the orange juice from flowing into the cream. Serve at once.

Apple snowballs

• Preparation: 50 minutes

• Cooking: 35 minutes **• Serves 4-6**

4-6 LARGE, FIRM EATING APPLES
1tsp LEMON JUICE
50g/2oz BUTTER, softened
3 EGG YOLKS
100g/4oz CASTER SUGAR
65g/2½oz GROUND ALMONDS
1tbls DARK RUM
4-6tsp REDCURRANT JELLY

For the meringue mixture:
3 EGG WHITES
pinch of SALT
75g/3oz ICING SUGAR, sifted

1 Peel the apples and carefully remove the cores without piercing the bases. Immediately put the apples in a large bowl of water to which you have added the lemon juice to prevent discoloration. Heat the oven to 190C/375F/gas 5.

2 Put half the butter in a bowl and cream it with a fork. Add the egg yolks, half the sugar, the almonds and rum. Beat vigorously until well mixed together. Drain the apples and dry them thoroughly. Divide the almond filling between the apples, pressing it tightly into each cavity.

3 Generously grease a large, shallow, ovenproof dish with the remaining butter. Sprinkle with the remaining sugar. Put the apples in the dish, spaced well apart, and bake for 10 minutes. Then raise the oven temperature to 220C/425F/gas 7 and bake the apples for a further 15-20 minutes or until they are golden and soft but not disintegrating.

4 About 5 minutes before the end of the cooking time, make the meringue. Whisk the egg whites and salt in a large, clean, dry bowl until they just begin to hold the shape of the whisk. Then whisk in the icing sugar, a spoonful at a time. Put the bowl over a pan half filled with simmering water and whisk the egg white mixture until it is thick and firm.

5 Remove the apples from the oven and, using a round-bladed knife, cover each one with meringue, leaving the central cavity free. Lower the oven temperature to 150C/300F/gas 2 and bake for 10-15 minutes until the meringue is set and golden.

6 Allow the apples to cool slightly, then put 1tsp redcurrant jelly into the centre of each one. Serve on individual plates.

Cook's tips

A simple way to fill the apple cavities with the almond mixture is to use a piping bag fitted with a large plain nozzle.

FAMILY DINNER FOR FOUR

Stuffed beetroot · German meatballs · Noodles with caraway seeds · Braised leeks with bacon · Ginger, fruit and nut ice cream

HERE'S A MENU for easy entertaining: the dishes are not only easy to cook, but easy on the housekeeping money. It's ideal for a family gathering, or for close friends.

For starters serve each person that much-neglected but delicious vegetable, beetroot, stuffed with a tasty mixture of egg, ham, mayonnaise and mushrooms. The main course recipe, German meatballs, features a sauce created from beef consommé, mushrooms and soured cream which transforms the humble meatball into a delicacy. Serve this with a suitably Germanic accompaniment, Noodles with caraway, and juicy Braised leeks with bacon. Finish with simply made but unusual Ginger, fruit and nut ice cream.

Table Talk

Make the meal a little more special by serving a fourth course: a cheese board, either before or after the dessert. The cheeses don't have to be ruinously expensive to be good; but buy them from a specialist cheese shop if you can, rather than a supermarket, if possible on the morning of the meal. Keep them in a cool place, not in the refrigerator. A choice of four is quite adequate, say a mature Cheddar, creamy ripe Brie, Danish Mycella blue and Norwegian Jarlsberg (very like Emmental but much cheaper, and just as good when fresh). Serve the cheeses with some crisp unflavoured crackers and unsalted butter to allow their taste to be savoured fully.

What to Drink

The best accompaniment to an informal meal with a German flavour is – naturally – German beer. For authenticity, try to find one brewed in Germany, not under licence in the UK. Names to look out for include Holsten, Dortmunder, Herforder Pils or Munchener lager. But make sure whatever you drink is well chilled.

Countdown

The day before
Make the Ginger, fruit and nut ice cream and freeze overnight.

In the morning
Prepare the Stuffed beetroot to the end of step 3 and chill.
Prepare the German meatballs to the end of step 1 and chill.

Forty five minutes before
Cook the Braised leeks with bacon and keep hot in the oven.

Thirty minutes before
Take the Stuffed beetroot out of the refrigerator, arrange and garnish.
Brown the German meatballs and leave to simmer.
Cook the Noodles with caraway seeds and keep hot in the oven.

Before serving the starter
Transfer the ice cream from freezer to fridge.
Finish the German meatballs and keep hot.

★ Stuffed beetroot

• *Preparation: cooking beetroots and egg, then 30 minutes*

• *Cooking: 10 minutes, plus cooling* **• *Serves 4***

15g/½oz BUTTER
100g/4oz BUTTON MUSHROOMS, finely chopped
4 BEETROOTS, cooked and peeled
1 LARGE HARD-BOILED EGG, finely chopped
100g/4oz LEAN COOKED HAM, diced
100g/4oz COOKED CHICKEN, diced
8tbls MAYONNAISE
½tsp DIJON MUSTARD
SALT and PEPPER
LETTUCE LEAVES, to serve
FLAT-LEAVED PARSLEY, to garnish

1 Melt the butter in a saucepan, add the mushrooms and fry over medium heat for 10 minutes or until tender, stirring occasionally. Leave to cool.

2 Slice the tops off the beetroots. With a sharp-edged teaspoon, hollow out the centre of each beetroot, being careful not to break through. (Use the centre bits in a salad.) If necessary slice a little off the bottom of the beetroot shells to help them stand upright.

3 Put the egg, ham, chicken, mayonnaise, mustard and mushrooms in a bowl and mix together. Season with salt and pepper to taste. Spoon the mixture into the prepared beetroots.

4 Arrange the lettuce leaves on a serving platter, put the beetroots in the centre and garnish with parsley.

Cook's tips

Make sure the beetroots you use for this recipe are not cooked or preserved in vinegar – the flavour would be too strong.

Variations

Use other left-over meats, such as roast pork or garlic sausage, to stuff the beetroots instead of the ham or chicken.

Tomato soup with rice

● *Preparation: 10 minutes*

● *Cooking: 20 minutes* ● *Serves 4*

600ml/1pt BEEF STOCK
2 x 400g/14oz CANNED CHOPPED TOMATOES
SALT and PEPPER
SUGAR
1-2tsp TOMATO PURÉE (optional)
50g/2oz COOKED RICE
DILL or PARSLEY SPRIG, to garnish

1 Put the beef stock in a saucepan. Add the tomatoes to the stock and simmer gently for 10 minutes.

2 Allow to cool slightly, then purée the mixture in a blender or food processor. If you want to get rid of the seeds pass the purée through a sieve into the rinsed-out pan. (Alternatively put the mixture through a vegetable mill to purée it and remove seeds.)

3 Bring the soup to the boil, then season with salt and pepper to taste and a generous pinch of sugar. If it seems bland add a little tomato purée.

4 Just before serving the soup stir in the rice and garnish with a sprig of dill or parsley.

Cook's tips

Use fresh tomatoes to make soup in late summer when they are both cheap and flavoursome. Cut them in half, scoop out the seeds and chop the flesh roughly. The skins can be discarded when the soup is puréed.

★ German meatballs

● *Preparation: 30 minutes*

● *Cooking: 35 minutes* ● *Serves 4*

450g/1lb LEAN MINCED BEEF
4tbls FRESH BREADCRUMBS
½tsp DRIED MARJORAM
1tbls FINELY CHOPPED PARSLEY
SALT and PEPPER
4tbls MILK
1 LARGE EGG, lightly beaten
25g/1oz BUTTER
1tbls OIL
1 SMALL ONION, finely chopped
100g/4oz MUSHROOMS, quartered
300ml/½pt BEEF CONSOMME
150ml/¼pt SOURED CREAM
FRESH HERBS, to garnish

1 Put the meat in a bowl and mix in the breadcrumbs and herbs. Season generously with salt and pepper, then stir in the milk and egg. With wet hands, shape the mixture into 24 balls.

2 Heat the butter and oil in a frying pan large enough to take all the meatballs in one layer (use two pans, if necessary). Brown the meatballs over medium heat for 4 minutes, shaking the pan so that they colour evenly. Transfer them to a plate with a slotted spoon and keep warm.

3 Put the onion and mushrooms in the pan and fry for 5 minutes, stirring occasionally, just until beginning to soften. Stir in the consommé and return the meatballs to the pan. Simmer, uncovered, for 25 minutes or until the meatballs are cooked and the sauce has reduced by half, turning the meatballs frequently.

4 Transfer the meatballs to a serving dish using a slotted spoon. Stir the soured cream into the sauce; do not let it boil. Pour the sauce over the meatballs and serve hot, garnished with fresh herbs.

Serving ideas

German meatballs are equally good accompanied by rice or by a South German speciality called *Spätzle* (batter dumplings).

Pork chops with almonds

• Preparation: 10 minutes

• Cooking: 15 minutes **• Serves 4**

4 x 225g/8oz PORK CHOPS, about 1cm/½in thick
SALT and PEPPER
4tsp CURRY PASTE
50g/2oz BUTTER
2tbls OIL
75g/3oz FLAKED ALMONDS
1 LIME, sliced, to garnish

1 Trim the excess fat from the pork chops but leave a thin layer to protect the meat. Season with pepper, leave to come to room temperature and season with salt just before cooking.

2 Spread ½tsp of curry paste on each side of each chop. Heat the butter and oil in a frying pan large enough to take the chops in one layer. When the foaming subsides, cook the chops over medium heat for 5-6 minutes. Turn them over with a spatula to avoid releasing the juices and cook for a further 5-6 minutes or until tender and cooked through. Transfer to a heated serving platter with a slotted spoon and keep hot.

3 Put the flaked almonds in the pan and fry over high heat for 1-2 minutes or until golden brown, stirring occasionally. Remove them with a slotted spoon and sprinkle over the chops. Serve hot, garnished with lime slices.

Cook's tips

Curry paste has a milder taste than many commercial curry powders. Alternatively, you can mix a good-quality curry powder with a little water to make a smooth paste.

★ Noodles with caraway seeds

• Preparation: 5 minutes

• Cooking: 20 minutes **• Serves 4**

225g/8oz DRIED EGG NOODLES
SALT and PEPPER
40g/1½oz BUTTER
2tbls CARAWAY SEEDS
6tbls FRESH BREADCRUMBS
DILL SPRIGS, to garnish (optional)

1 Bring a large saucepan of salted water to the boil and put in the noodles. Return to the boil, stir, then simmer gently for 10-15 minutes or until cooked through but still firm.

2 Meanwhile, melt the butter in a frying pan, add the caraway seeds and breadcrumbs and fry for 4-5 minutes, stirring constantly, until the breadcrumbs are golden.

3 Drain the noodles thoroughly and put them in a heated serving dish. Sprinkle over the breadcrumb and caraway seed mixture, season with pepper to taste and toss gently. Serve hot, garnished with sprigs of dill, if wished.

★Braised leeks with bacon

● ***Preparation: 20 minutes***

● ***Cooking: 25 minutes*** ● ***Serves 4***

8 LARGE or 12 SMALL LEEKS
40g/1½oz BUTTER
425ml/¾pt CHICKEN STOCK
PEPPER
175g/6oz BACON
THYME SPRIGS, to garnish (optional)

1 Heat the oven to 190C/375F/gas 5. Thickly slice the leeks, then wash them thoroughly in cold running water to remove grit. Drain well.

2 Put the leeks in a flameproof and ovenproof dish. Dot with the butter, pour in the chicken stock and season with pepper to taste. Bring to the boil over medium heat, then put the dish in the oven to braise, uncovered, for 15-20 minutes or until tender.

3 Meanwhile, grill the bacon until crisp and crumble it into small pieces. Scatter the crumbled bacon over the leeks, garnish with sprigs of thyme, if wished, and serve hot.

Cucumber with fresh dill

● ***Preparation: 25 minutes***

● ***Cooking: 25 minutes*** ● ***Serves 4***

2 CUCUMBERS
50g/2oz BUTTER
SALT and PEPPER
3 SPRIGS FRESH DILL
25g/1oz COLD BUTTER, diced
EXTRA DILL, to garnish (optional)

1 Peel the cucumbers. Cut each one in half lengthways and remove the seeds with a teaspoon. Cut each half into 2.5cm/1in lengths and then slice these lengthways to make batons about 5mm/¼in wide.

2 Put the butter in a large saucepan with 8tbls water. Bring to the boil and stir to mix. Add the cucumber batons; season with salt and pepper to taste and add the dill sprigs. Cover and simmer gently for 20 minutes, shaking the pan occasionally to stop the batons from sticking to the bottom.

3 Using a slotted spoon, transfer the cucumber batons to a heated serving dish, arranging them in neat rows. Keep hot. Discard the dill sprigs. Over medium heat, whisk the diced butter, a piece at a time, into the liquids remaining in the pan. Taste and adjust the seasoning and pour the sauce over the cucumber batons. Serve hot, garnished with more dill, if liked.

★ *Ginger, fruit and nut ice cream*

● ***Preparation: 30 minutes, plus cooling and freezing***

● ***Cooking: 5 minutes*** ● ***Serves 6***

2 EGGS
1tbls CORNFLOUR
100g/4oz CASTER SUGAR
150ml/¼pt MILK
150ml/¼pt SINGLE CREAM
3tbls GINGER SYRUP
50g/2oz STEM GINGER, chopped
50g/2oz RAISINS
50g/2oz SLIVERED ALMONDS
300ml/½pt DOUBLE CREAM
STEM GINGER SLICES, to decorate

1 Whisk the eggs, cornflour and sugar together until the mixture is thick and has a mousse-like consistency.

2 Heat the milk and single cream together gently until they are almost boiling, then pour onto the egg mixture, whisking constantly. Return to the pan and cook over low heat until thickened, stirring constantly. Remove from the heat, stir in the ginger syrup, chopped ginger, raisins and almonds and leave to cool.

3 Whip the double cream until it forms soft peaks, then fold into the cooled custard mixture. Turn into a shallow freezer container, cover and freeze for 4-6 hours or until firm.

4 Transfer the ice cream from the freezer to the refrigerator about 30 minutes before serving to allow it to soften slightly. Serve in scoops, decorated with slices of stem ginger.

Cherry pie

● ***Preparation: 35 minutes***

● ***Cooking: 55 minutes*** ● ***Serves 4***

450g/1lb FRESH CHERRIES or 275g/10oz FROZEN CHERRIES, defrosted and drained
6tbls CASTER SUGAR
1tbls FLOUR
20g/¾oz BUTTER, plus extra for greasing
1tbls KIRSCH
450g/1lb SHORTCRUST PASTRY (see Cook's tips, p.18, and make double the quantity)
1 LARGE EGG YOLK, lightly beaten
DOUBLE CREAM, to serve

1 Wash the fresh cherries, then remove the stones and any stalks. Put the fruit in a small, heavy saucepan with 4tbls sugar and 125ml/4fl oz water. Cook over low heat for 10-15 minutes (15 minutes for frozen cherries) or until the fruit is very soft. Drain in a sieve set over a large measuring jug. Make the juice up to 150ml/¼pt with water.

2 Put the remaining sugar and the flour in a small saucepan, add a little of the cherry juice and mix to a smooth paste, then add the remaining juice. Cook over a low heat for 2-3 minutes to thicken the mixture, stirring constantly. Add the butter and kirsch, stir well, then leave to cool. Heat the oven to 200C/400F/gas 6.

3 Roll out two-thirds of the pastry and use it to line a buttered 19cm/7½in flan tin. Reserve the trimmings. Put the drained cherries in the pastry case and pour the cooled sauce over them.

4 Roll out the remaining pastry to cover the pie. Trim the edges, then seal them with a little egg yolk. Crimp the edges together, then glaze the top with egg yolk. Cut the trimmings into leaves and small circles (to represent cherries), arrange on the pie lid and glaze with the remaining egg yolk.

5 Bake for 10 minutes, then reduce the temperature to 180C/350F/gas 4 and bake for a further 20-25 minutes until lightly browned. Leave to cool before serving with a jug of cream.

CONVENIENT DINNER FOR FOUR

Watercress and potato soup · Almond veal parcels · Green beans with soy sauce · Chocolate Swiss roll

ENTERTAINING NEW FRIENDS for the first time can be a daunting experience so it's important to feel confident and relaxed about the occasion – then you can enjoy yourself.

Plan a menu so that as much as possible can be done in advance. This way you will be free to concentrate on your guests and make them feel welcome.

The smooth, creamy yet peppery Watercress and potato soup can be prepared earlier in the day, as can the main dish: escalopes of veal enveloping a Madeira-flavoured filling of mushrooms and tongue, with a crisp, nutty coating contrasting with the tender veal inside.

Chocolate Swiss roll sounds unremarkable, but kirsch-soaked glacé cherries make it really special – and this, too, can be prepared ahead of time. Have a nice dinner!

Table Talk

A well-balanced meal makes a dinner party more enjoyable so make sure that light courses are included with more substantial dishes. This menu starts with soup which can be filling, so serve in small bowls then offer another helping to guests with good appetites. As the Chocolate Swiss roll is deliciously rich, the main course is deliberately light – veal with green beans. Offer a tossed green salad and a selection of breads as accompaniments, if you wish.

Wine Ideas

To complement the delicate veal, choose a white wine from Germany: a crisp light Moselle from the Saar and Ruwer region or a popular medium wine, Niersteiner Gutes Domtal from the Rheinhessen region. If you prefer a dry white wine with more body and more alcohol, choose an Italian wine like Gavi or Orvieto to serve with the main course and save the lighter German wines for the sweet course. Chill any of these wines before serving.

Countdown

The day before
Marinate the cherries for the Chocolate Swiss roll.

In the morning
Prepare the orange julienne strips and bake the Swiss roll. Roll up and leave to cool.
Make the Watercress and potato soup to the end of step 3.
Make the veal parcels to the end of step 3, cover lightly and chill.

Forty minutes before
Prepare the beans and assemble the ingredients for the Green beans with soy sauce.
Egg-and-breadcrumb the veal parcels and chill.
Fill the Chocolate Swiss roll and decorate. Keep cool.

Ten minutes before
Heat the soup, add the cream, then garnish and serve.

Before serving the main course
Cook the veal parcels.
Cook the Green beans with soy sauce.

★*Watercress and potato soup*

- ***Preparation: 20 minutes***
- ***Cooking: 30 minutes*** • ***Serves 4***

225g/8oz POTATOES, peeled and thinly sliced
1 LARGE LEEK, sliced
1 BUNCH WATERCRESS
600ml/1pt CHICKEN STOCK
1 HAM BONE (optional)
SALT and PEPPER
200ml/7fl oz DOUBLE CREAM
WATERCRESS SPRIGS, to garnish

1 Put the potatoes and leek in a saucepan. Wash the watercress, discard any yellow or damaged leaves and cut off the bottom third of the stalks. Chop the leaves and remaining stalks and add to the potatoes and leek.

2 Add the chicken stock and ham bone, if using. Bring to the boil, season lightly with salt and pepper to taste, cover and simmer gently for 25 minutes or until the vegetables are tender. Leave to cool slightly.

3 Put half the soup in a blender or food processor and blend until smooth, then pass it through a fine sieve into a clean saucepan. Repeat with the remaining soup.

4 Reheat if necessary, then stir in the double cream. Heat through gently and check the seasoning.

5 To serve, pour into a heated soup tureen or individual bowls and garnish with the watercress sprigs. Serve immediately.

Anchovy and potato salad

• Preparation: 35 minutes

• Cooking: 20 minutes, plus cooling **• Serves 4**

6 MEDIUM-SIZED NEW POTATOES
SALT and PEPPER
8tbls DRY WHITE WINE
2tbls OLIVE OIL
2tbls WINE VINEGAR
2 SHALLOTS, finely chopped
1tsp FINELY SNIPPED CHIVES
2 GARLIC CLOVES, crushed
1 GREEN PEPPER, seeded and sliced
3 TOMATOES, skinned, seeded and quartered
75g/3oz BLACK OLIVES, stoned
12 ANCHOVY FILLETS, cut into fine strips lengthways
1tbls FINELY CHOPPED PARSLEY

1 Boil the potatoes in salted water for 15-20 minutes or until tender but still firm. Cool, peel and cut into slices. Place in a mixing bowl.

2 Bring the wine to the boil in a small saucepan and pour over the potato slices. Season generously with salt and pepper. Allow to cool.

3 In a large bowl, combine the oil, vinegar, shallots, chives and garlic. Beat with a fork until the mixture emulsifies. Season with salt and pepper to taste. Add the sliced green pepper, tomatoes, olives and potato slices. Check the seasoning and toss the salad carefully, taking care not to break the potato slices.

4 Arrange the potato salad on a serving platter. Lay the anchovy fillets diagonally across the salad and sprinkle with finely chopped parsley in fine lines to form a lattice with the anchovy strips. Serve the salad at room temperature.

Cook's tips

This refreshing summer salad is reminiscent of Salade niçoise. If new potatoes are not available, use old ones, but follow this method to keep them firm; boil potatoes in their jackets, then leave them to cool completely in their water before peeling carefully.

★ Almond veal parcels

• Preparation: 40 minutes, plus chilling

• Cooking: 20 minutes **• Serves 4**

40g/1½oz BUTTER
3tbls OLIVE OIL
100g/4oz BUTTON MUSHROOMS, thinly sliced
SALT and PEPPER
1½tbls MADEIRA
4 × 100-150g/4-5oz VEAL ESCALOPES
100g/4oz COOKED TONGUE
2 LARGE EGGS, beaten
50g/2oz FRESH WHITE BREADCRUMBS
40g/1½oz FLAKED ALMONDS, roughly chopped
FLOUR, for coating
MAYONNAISE, to serve

1 In a frying pan, heat one-third each of the butter and oil. Cook the mushrooms for 5 minutes or until golden, turning them with a spatula. Season with salt and pepper to taste, sprinkle the Madeira over them and leave to cool.

2 Beat the veal escalopes between sheets of stretch wrap with a meat bat or rolling pin until they are as thin as possible. Season the meat generously with salt and pepper.

3 Cut the tongue into thin strips. Pile a quarter of the strips in the centre of each escalope. Spoon the mushrooms over the top. Fold first the short ends, then the long edges, of each escalope over the filling, to make an envelope-shaped parcel, securing with cocktail sticks if necessary.

4 Pour the eggs into a shallow dish. Combine the breadcrumbs and chopped almonds in another shallow dish. Coat the veal parcels with flour, shaking off any excess. Dip into the beaten egg, then coat with the almond and breadcrumb mixture, patting the mixture on firmly. Chill for at least 15 minutes to set the coating.

5 To cook the veal, heat the remaining butter and olive oil in a frying pan large enough to take the escalopes in one layer. Lay them in the hot fat side by side. Cook over low heat for 5 minutes. Turn over and cook for a further 5 minutes, or until golden brown.

6 Arrange the escalopes on a heated serving platter or place on individual plates. Remove the cocktail sticks if used. Serve as soon as possible with the mayonnaise.

Pork chops with orange stuffing

● ***Preparation: 35 minutes***

● ***Cooking: 20 minutes*** ● ***Serves 4***

4 PORK LOIN CHOPS, trimmed
SALT and PEPPER
50g/2oz BUTTER, softened
1 SPANISH ONION, finely chopped
2 CELERY STALKS, finely chopped
GRATED ZEST of 1 ORANGE
2tbls ORANGE JUICE
4tbls FRESH BREADCRUMBS
OIL, for greasing
ORANGE SLICES and PARSLEY SPRIGS, to garnish

1 Slice the pork chops horizontally through the width on the opposite side to the bone to make a pocket, leaving a 2.5cm/1in border next to the bone. Season the chops with salt and pepper to taste.

2 In a small saucepan heat 25g/1oz of the butter and cook the onion and celery for 5 minutes or until soft, stirring constantly. Add the orange zest, orange juice and breadcrumbs and season with salt and pepper to taste. Leave to cool.

3 Heat the grill to high. Stuff each pork chop with a quarter of the stuffing and sew up the cut side with strong thread.

4 When ready to grill, brush the grid of the grill pan with a little oil. Place the pork chops on the grid and grill 7.5cm/3in in from the heat for 5-6 minutes on each side, basting often with the remaining butter. Remove the thread from the pork chops and arrange on a heated serving platter. Garnish with orange slices and sprigs of parsley. Serve immediately.

★*Green beans with soy sauce*

● ***Preparation: 10 minutes***

● ***Cooking: 10 minutes*** ● ***Serves 4***

450g/1lb FRENCH BEANS
3tbls PEANUT OIL
1tsp SALT
2tsp SOY SAUCE
2tbls DRY SHERRY

1 Wash and trim the beans. Cut them into 5cm/2in lengths. Heat the peanut oil in a wok or frying pan. Add the beans and cook over a medium heat for 1 minute, stirring constantly with a wooden spoon.

2 Add the salt and 150ml/¼pt water. Cover the pan and cook the beans for 3 minutes.

3 Remove the lid and simmer gently, stirring from time to time, for 5 minutes or until all the water has evaporated, then stir in the soy sauce and sherry. Transfer to a serving dish and serve as soon as possible.

Juniper cabbage

• Preparation: 20 minutes

• Cooking: 15 minutes **• Serves 4**

- 3tbls OLIVE OIL
- 100g/4oz STREAKY BACON IN ONE PIECE, diced
- 1 SPANISH ONION, sliced
- 2tsp JUNIPER BERRIES, crushed
- 450g/1lb WHITE CABBAGE, shredded
- SALT and PEPPER

1 Heat the olive oil in a flameproof casserole. Add the bacon and onion and cook for 5 minutes or until the onion is soft but not brown.

2 Add the crushed juniper berries and cook for 1-2 minutes. Add the shredded cabbage and toss in the oil. Season with salt and pepper to taste. Cook, stirring occasionally, for 10 minutes, until the cabbage is lightly cooked but still crunchy. If you like cabbage softer, cover the pan while it is cooking; the steamy vapour will cook it faster.

Cook's tips

Juniper berries are best known as flavouring for gin; they give it both its oiliness and 'scented' flavour. They are also used in the kitchen to season pâtés, game and pork. Partnering them with cabbage in this dish makes an unusual and delicious combination.

Carrots with raisins

• Preparation: 20 minutes

• Cooking: 25 minutes **• Serves 4-6**

- 2tbls RAISINS
- BOILING WATER
- 450-700g/1-1½lb CARROTS
- 50g/2oz BUTTER
- 4tbls CHICKEN STOCK
- ½tsp SUGAR
- SALT and PEPPER
- FINELY CHOPPED PARSLEY or MINT, to garnish

1 Soak the raisins in boiling water to cover. Meanwhile, slice the carrots, then cut them into matchstick strips.

2 Place the carrots in a saucepan of cold water. Bring to the boil, then drain immediately.

3 Melt the butter in a heavy pan over low heat and add the stock, carrots, drained raisins, sugar, salt and pepper to taste. Simmer, covered, for 15-20 minutes until tender, shaking the pan occasionally to make sure the carrots are not sticking.

4 Just before serving, turn into a heated serving dish and garnish with a sprinkling of chopped parsley or mint.

★ Chocolate Swiss roll

• Preparation: overnight marinating, then 30 minutes

• Cooking: 25 minutes, plus cooling **• Serves 4**

3 LARGE EGGS
75g/3oz CASTER SUGAR, plus extra for sprinkling
1tsp VANILLA ESSENCE
50g/2oz FLOUR
pinch of SALT
25g/1oz COCOA

For the filling:
100g/4oz GLACÉ CHERRIES
3tbls KIRSCH
150ml/¼pt DOUBLE CREAM, whipped

For the decoration:
1 LARGE ORANGE
2tbls ICING SUGAR

1 In a small bowl, marinate the glacé cherries for the filling in the kirsch overnight.

2 The next day, pare the zest from the orange with a potato peeler and cut into 2.5cm/1in lengths, then into very fine julienne strips. Blanch for 5 minutes in simmering water. Drain, refresh under cold running water and drain again.

3 Heat the oven to 200C/400F/gas 6. Line a 33cm x 23cm/13in x 9in Swiss roll tin with non-stick baking paper or greased greaseproof paper.

4 Choose a bowl that fits over a saucepan of simmering water, and put in the eggs, sugar and vanilla essence. Whisk with a hand-held electric whisk until the mixture is very thick and pale (this takes about 10 minutes). Remove the bowl from the saucepan and whisk for another 5 minutes or until cold.

5 Sift the flour, salt and cocoa onto a plate. Then sift again over the egg mixture and fold in with a large metal spoon. Pour into the tin and level the surface. Bake for 12-15 minutes or until the sponge shrinks slightly from the sides of the tin and the surface springs back when touched.

6 Lay a large piece of greaseproof paper on a flat surface and sprinkle with 1tbls caster sugar. Carefully turn the sponge out onto the paper and peel off the lining paper. Trim the edges with a sharp knife. Lay another piece of greaseproof paper on top. Carefully roll up the Swiss roll from one short edge with the paper inside. Leave to cool on a wire rack.

7 Unroll the Swiss roll carefully, discarding the paper. Spread with the whipped cream. Drain the marinated cherries and spread them over the cream. Re-roll the Swiss roll and sift over the icing sugar. Sprinkle with the orange julienne and serve.

Brandied apple tart

• Preparation: making pastry case, then 40 minutes

• Cooking: 40 minutes, plus cooling **• Serves 4-6**

20cm/8in PASTRY CASE, baked blind (see Fruity treacle tart, page 18)
2tbls APRICOT JAM
WHIPPED CREAM, to serve (optional)

For the filling:
15g/½oz BUTTER
450g/1lb CRISP DESSERT APPLES
1tbls CASTER SUGAR
1 LARGE EGG YOLK
1tbls BRANDY

For the topping:
2tsp BRANDY
1tsp LEMON JUICE
2 CRISP DESSERT APPLES
2tsp MELTED BUTTER
1tbls SUGAR

1 Leave the pastry case in its tin. Put a large baking sheet in the oven, then heat to 230C/450F/gas 8.

2 Make the filling: melt the butter in a heavy saucepan. Remove from the heat. Chop the apples coarsely, without coring, into the butter. Cover tightly and cook the apples over a moderate heat for 15 minutes or until soft, shaking the pan occasionally and making sure the apples do not burn.

3 Rub the apples through a sieve into a bowl, using the back of a spoon. Discard the skins and cores. Beat in the sugar, followed by the egg yolk and brandy. Leave to cool.

4 Meanwhile, in a small saucepan, heat the jam with ½tbls water, stirring until melted. Work the melted jam through a fine sieve over the base of the pastry case, then spread it evenly with a brush. This will prevent the filling soaking into the pastry. Spread the cooled apple purée evenly over the base of the pastry case.

5 Prepare the topping: in a bowl, combine the brandy and lemon juice. Quarter and core the apples, slicing them thinly into the bowl. Toss to coat. Arrange the apple slices neatly on top of the purée in overlapping, concentric circles, starting from the outside edge.

6 Brush the apple slices with melted butter and sprinkle with sugar. Bake in the oven on the baking sheet for 20 minutes or until the apple slices are tender and tinged with brown. Leave to cool in the tin until lukewarm, then remove from the tin onto a serving platter and serve with whipped cream, if wished.

COUNTRY DINNER FOR SIX

Provençal and onion strips ·

Boiled chicken and rice · Steamed carrots and green beans ·

Baked sultana pudding

ENTERTAINING COUNTRY-STYLE MEANS serving top-quality food, plainly but perfectly cooked and unfussily presented. The starter, Provençal and onion strips, hails from the French countryside, where it would be made with home-grown onions and olives.

Boiled chicken and rice is deliciously old-fashioned, with its smooth, gently seasoned sauce. Make it with a boiling fowl if you wish, allowing a longer cooking time. Serve this mildly flavoured dish with steamed baby carrots and green beans; both the carrots and the beans should ideally be picked from your vegetable garden, but if not, at least fresh, not frozen. To finish serve a traditional English sweet, Baked sultana pudding, plain but delicious served with warm cream.

Table Talk

Serve suitably peasant-style bread to go with your country meal. Round loaves have a nice rustic look about them, and can be cut into wedges instead of slices. Choose wholemeal or granary rather than white bread; or you might be able to find a round of soda bread or scofa, which is ready-scored to break into four sections. If time allows you could make your own quick wholemeal or soda bread, or a scone round. As this doesn't involve yeast it is even quicker, and delicious served straight from the oven.

Wine Ideas

To go with the chicken serve a light, young red wine or a medium-dry white. With six people at the table two bottles will not be too much, so you could please all tastes by having one red and one white. Nothing grand is called for: a French *vin de pays* or country wine would be just right.

Alternatively you could buy a couple of the Californian wines which are packaged in glass decanters rather than bottles. Simply shaped like those used in French family restaurants, these will look just right on the table.

Countdown

Two and a quarter hours before
Start cooking the chicken for the Boiled chicken and rice.
Prepare the carrots and green beans; keep in a cool place.
Make the Provençal and onion strips and keep warm.
Complete step 1 of the Baked sultana pudding and assemble the remaining ingredients.

Forty five minutes before
Cook the rice and make the cream sauce for the chicken. Keep warm.

Twenty five minutes before
Finish preparing the pudding and lower the oven temperature to 190C/375F/gas 5.

Ten minutes before
Steam the carrots and green beans; keep warm.

Before serving the starter
Bake the pudding; keep warm.

Before serving the main course
Finish the Steamed carrots and green beans.

Before serving the dessert
Warm the cream gently. Cut the pudding into squares, sprinkle with sugar and serve with the cream.

★ *Provençal and onion strips*

● ***Preparation: 30 minutes, plus chilling***

● ***Cooking: 1 hour*** ● ***Serves 6***

8tbls OLIVE OIL
2 SPANISH ONIONS, thinly sliced
450g/1lb FROZEN PUFF PASTRY, defrosted and cut in half lengthways
SALT and PEPPER
50g/2oz CANNED ANCHOVY FILLETS
2 TOMATOES
36 SMALL BLACK OLIVES, stoned
MELTED BUTTER, for sealing

1 For the topping, heat the oil in a large heavy saucepan and cook the onions over low heat, stirring occasionally, until pale golden and translucent, 15-20 minutes. Divide the onions into two batches.

2 Meanwhile, roll out both halves of the pastry into rectangles 30cm/12in long, slightly wider than the tomatoes and 3mm/⅛in thick. Lay them on a dampened baking sheet and chill for 30 minutes.

3 Drain the onions on absorbent paper, then season well with salt and pepper and leave to cool. Heat the oven to 200C/400F/gas 6.

4 For the Provençal strip, drain the anchovy fillets, reserving the oil. Cut each fillet lengthways into thin strips and slice the tomatoes thinly. Spread one strip of pastry with half the onions, not quite to the edge, and put the tomatoes on top in a row. Arrange a lattice of anchovy strips on top, then put an olive in the centre of each lattice. Sprinkle with a little of the anchovy oil. Brush the edges of the strip with melted butter, fold over to just touch the tomatoes and press down firmly to seal.

5 For the onion strip, spread the second strip of pastry with the remaining onion, not quite to the edge. Brush the edges with butter and fold the pastry as for the Provençal strip.

6 Bake both strips for 20-25 minutes until the pastry has risen and is golden. Cut each into eight pieces, arrange on a heated platter and serve.

Serving ideas

These tasty puff pastry strips are ideal for passing around with drinks before guests are seated at the dining table.

Mushroom and barley soup

• Preparation: overnight soaking, then 20 minutes

• Cooking: 50 minutes **• Serves 6**

15g/½oz BUTTER
1 LARGE ONION, finely chopped
100g/4oz BUTTON MUSHROOMS, chopped
100g/4oz PEARL BARLEY, soaked overnight
1.1L/2pt BEEF STOCK
1 CARROT, diced
SALT and PEPPER
225g/8oz POTATOES, diced
150ml/¼pt SINGLE CREAM
150ml/¼pt MILK

1 Melt the butter in a large saucepan, add the onion and mushrooms and fry for 7-10 minutes, stirring occasionally, until soft and golden.

2 Drain the pearl barley and add to the pan along with the stock, carrot and salt and pepper to taste. Bring to the boil, cover and simmer gently for 30 minutes, stirring occasionally.

3 Add the potatoes and simmer for another 10 minutes or until the potatoes are cooked but not disintegrating and the other vegetables are tender.

4 Stir in the cream and milk. Heat through, correct the seasoning and pour into a heated tureen or individual bowls. Serve hot.

★ Boiled chicken and rice

• Preparation: 25 minutes

• Cooking: 2 hours **• Serves 6**

1.4kg/3lb OVEN-READY CHICKEN
1 ONION stuck with 2 CLOVES
2 LARGE CARROTS, quartered
1 BOUQUET GARNI
2 CELERY STALKS, coarsely chopped
175ml/6fl oz DRY WHITE WINE
1.1L/2pt CHICKEN STOCK
SALT and PEPPER
BLACK PEPPERCORNS
15g/½oz BUTTER
1 ONION, finely chopped
225g/8oz LONG-GRAIN RICE

For the cream sauce:
25g/1oz BUTTER
2tbls FLOUR
450ml/¾pt DOUBLE CREAM
FRESHLY GRATED NUTMEG

1 Put the chicken in a flameproof casserole with the onion stuck with cloves, carrots, bouquet garni and celery. Pour in the wine and stock, season with salt to taste and add a few peppercorns. Simmer gently for 1-1½ hours or until the chicken is tender. Remove the chicken and keep it warm; strain the stock and reserve.

2 Melt the butter in a saucepan. Add the chopped onion and cook over low heat for 4-5 minutes, stirring occasionally, until translucent. Stir in the rice, 300ml/½pt of the stock and 600ml/1pt hot water. Season with salt and pepper to taste, bring to the boil, then stir once. Reduce the heat to low, cover and simmer for 15-25 minutes or until the rice is tender but not mushy.

3 Meanwhile, make the cream sauce. Melt the butter in a heavy saucepan. When it just begins to bubble, stir in the flour and cook over low heat for 2-3 minutes, stirring constantly to make a pale roux. Gradually add 150ml/¼pt of the stock and the cream, stirring vigorously with a wire whisk. Bring to the boil, stirring, then reduce the heat and simmer for 5-10 minutes or until the sauce is thick and smooth, stirring occasionally. Season with salt and pepper to taste and a pinch of nutmeg.

4 To serve, put the chicken in the centre of a large, heated serving platter with the rice. Pour a little of the sauce over the chicken and serve the rest separately.

Hunters' lamb casserole

● ***Preparation: 30 minutes***

● ***Cooking: 2½ hours*** ● ***Serves 6***

2kg/4½lb SHOULDER OF LAMB
4-6tbls OLIVE OIL
2 GARLIC CLOVES, crushed
2tsp DRIED ROSEMARY
1tsp DRIED SAGE
2tsp FLOUR
6tbls WINE VINEGAR
25g/1oz BUTTER
200g/7oz BUTTON MUSHROOMS
4-6 ANCHOVY FILLETS, drained and finely chopped
SALT and PEPPER

For the garnish:
2tbls CHOPPED PARSLEY
GRATED ZEST of ½ LEMON

1 Trim all fat from the lamb and cut the meat into 4cm/1½in cubes. Pat the cubes dry with absorbent paper. Heat 4tbls oil in a heavy flameproof casserole. Add the meat and brown on all sides, adding more oil as necessary. Add the garlic, rosemary and sage, then sprinkle in the flour. Fry the meat gently until golden, turning the cubes frequently.

2 Pour in the vinegar and 125ml/4fl oz hot water. Cover and simmer over very low heat for 1½-2 hours or until tender, stirring frequently and adding a little hot water if the sauce reduces too quickly.

3 Meanwhile, melt the butter in a frying pan and sauté the mushrooms until golden. About 15 minutes before the end of the cooking time, put the anchovy fillets in a small saucepan with 4tbls liquid from the lamb. Simmer very gently, stirring, until the fillets have disintegrated into a purée. Add them to the casserole along with the drained mushrooms. Turn the meat until evenly coated with sauce and simmer for 10 minutes more to develop the flavour. Correct the seasoning, bearing in mind the salty anchovy. Sprinkle with chopped parsley and lemon zest and serve hot.

Cook's tips

The original Italian version of this lamb casserole, *abbachio alla cacciatore,* would also contain dried mushrooms. If you can get them, soak 12 in boiling water for 15 minutes, drain and add to the casserole along with the button mushrooms.

Country pork and vegetable casserole

● ***Preparation: 25 minutes***

● ***Cooking: 55 minutes*** ● ***Serves 4-6***

350g/12oz CARROTS
225g/8oz TURNIPS
2 LEEKS
¼ CABBAGE
65g/2½oz BUTTER
1.2L/2¼pt CHICKEN STOCK
SALT and PEPPER
CAYENNE PEPPER
350g/12oz STREAKY SALT PORK
75g/3oz RICE
4tbls GRATED GRUYERE CHEESE

1 Cut the carrots and turnips into dice, the leeks into rings. Remove the core from the cabbage and shred the leaves finely.

2 Heat 40g/1½oz of the butter in a large saucepan. Add the vegetables and fry, stirring often, until they are soft and golden brown, about 15 minutes. Add the stock, season with pepper, salt if needed and a pinch of cayenne. Bring to the boil, then skim, cover and simmer gently for 10 minutes. Remove from the heat while preparing the salt pork.

3 Bring 600ml/1pt water to the boil in a saucepan, add the pork and simmer for 10 minutes. Drain and cut into small dice. Heat the remaining butter in a frying pan and fry the pork until golden brown, stirring often. Add to the casserole along with the rice and simmer gently for 20 minutes or until the rice is tender and has absorbed the stock. Sprinkle with the cheese and serve at once.

Cook's tips

Salt pork is not widely available; if you can't get any use diced bacon pieces instead. There is no need to parboil them.

★ Steamed carrots and green beans

● **Preparation: 15 minutes**

● **Cooking: 20 minutes** ● **Serves 6**

450g/1lb BABY CARROTS, scrubbed
350g/12oz GREEN BEANS, topped, tailed and halved
2tsp LEMON JUICE
25g/1oz BUTTER
SALT and PEPPER

1 Put the carrots in a steamer or a metal colander set over a saucepan of simmering water. Cover tightly and steam for 5 minutes.

2 Push the carrots to one side and add the green beans. Cover again and steam for a further 15 minutes or until both vegetables are just tender.

3 Put the carrots in a warm bowl. Pour in the lemon juice, add half the butter, and toss until the carrots are well coated. Season with salt and pepper to taste.

4 Put the green beans in another warm bowl, toss with the remaining butter and season to taste. Arrange the vegetables on a heated serving platter and serve hot.

Tossed green salad with Roquefort

● **Preparation: 20 minutes, plus chilling** ● **Serves 4-6**

1 CRISP LETTUCE
½ BUNCH WATERCRESS
½ HEAD CURLY ENDIVE

For the dressing:
6-8tbls OLIVE OIL
2tbls WINE VINEGAR
2tbls SINGLE CREAM
25g/1oz ROQUEFORT CHEESE, crumbled
BLACK PEPPER
HOT PEPPER SAUCE
1 HARD-BOILED EGG, finely chopped

1 Prepare the lettuce, watercress and endive, wrap in a clean tea-towel and chill in the salad drawer of the refrigerator until needed.

2 Make the dressing: combine the oil, vinegar, cream and Roquefort cheese in a small bowl. Whisk briskly with a fork until smooth. Season with pepper to taste, add a pinch of hot pepper sauce and stir in the chopped egg.

3 Just before serving, arrange the lettuce, watercress and endive in a salad bowl and pour over the dressing. Toss thoroughly to coat all the leaves with the dressing and serve at once.

★ Baked sultana pudding

• Preparation: 20 minutes

• Cooking: 35 minutes **• Serves 6**

75g/3oz COLD BUTTER, diced, plus extra for greasing
225g/8oz FLOUR
pinch of SALT
1tsp BAKING POWDER
75g/3oz SULTANAS
3tbls CASTER SUGAR, plus extra for sprinkling
1-2tbls CANDIED PEEL, finely chopped
GRATED ZEST of ½ ORANGE
2 LARGE EGGS, well beaten
1tsp VANILLA ESSENCE
175ml/6fl oz MILK
300ml/½pt DOUBLE CREAM, to serve

1 Heat the oven to 190C/375F/gas 5. Lightly butter an 18cm/7in square cake tin. Sift the flour, salt and baking powder into a bowl. Rub in the diced butter with your fingertips until the mixture resembles breadcrumbs.

2 Add the sultanas, sugar, candied peel and orange zest to the mixture and stir well. Make a well in the centre, then pour in the eggs and vanilla essence and gradually mix in the milk, using a wooden spoon. Beat until well blended and smooth.

3 Spoon the mixture into the prepared cake tin and level off the top with a palette knife. Bake for 30-35 minutes or until the pudding is well risen and firm to the touch.

4 Just before serving, warm the cream gently, taking care not to let it boil. Cut the warm pudding into squares, sprinkle with sugar and hand the cream separately.

Chocolate cake with fudge icing

• Preparation: 40 minutes

• Cooking: 55 minutes, plus cooling **• Serves 10-12**

100g/4oz BUTTER, plus extra
50g/2oz COCOA
2tsp INSTANT COFFEE
275g/10oz CASTER SUGAR
2 LARGE EGGS, beaten
175g/6oz FLOUR
1tsp BICARBONATE OF SODA
½tsp BAKING POWDER

For the fudge icing:
450g/1lb CASTER SUGAR
1tbls GOLDEN SYRUP
50g/2oz BUTTER
50g/2oz COCOA

1 Grease and base line two 20cm/8in sandwich tins. Heat the oven to 180C/350F/gas 4. Put the cocoa into a small saucepan and mix it with 200ml/7fl oz cold water. Bring to the simmer, simmer for 5 minutes then stir until well mixed and free from lumps. Add the coffee and leave to cool slightly.

2 Meanwhile, cream the butter with a wooden spoon or electric mixer. Gradually add the sugar and cream until light and fluffy. Add the beaten eggs, a little at a time, beating well after each addition. Stir in the cooled cocoa mixture. Sift the flour, bicarbonate of soda and baking powder over the cake mixture and fold in lightly but thoroughly with a large metal spoon.

3 Divide the mixture equally between the two greased and lined sandwich tins, levelling the tops lightly with a knife. Bake for 30-35 minutes or until the cakes shrink back slightly from the sides of the tins and spring back into shape when lightly pressed with a finger. Remove from the oven and leave to cool in the tins for 5 minutes, then turn the cakes out onto a wire rack, peel away the lining paper and leave to cool.

4 Meanwhile, make the fudge icing. Combine all the ingredients in a large, heavy saucepan with 300ml/½pt cold water. Stir over low heat until the sugar has dissolved and the ingredients are well blended. Bring to the boil and boil to 115C/230F on a sugar thermometer (soft ball stage), stirring very occasionally. Remove the pan from the heat and leave the icing to cool until lukewarm, but do not allow it to get cold and hard. Then beat it with a wooden spoon until the icing holds its shape.

5 Assemble the cake. With a palette knife, spread one-third of the icing on the bottom cake round. Sandwich the rounds together. Spread the remaining icing evenly over the top and sides of the cake. Allow the icing to set before serving.

DINNER PARTY FOR FOUR

Mozzarella cigars ·

Normandy wild duck · Duchesse potatoes · French beans with hazelnuts ·

Apricot brandy sorbet

THIS IS A MENU of elegant simplicity. The starter, Mozzarella cigars, is a variation on the croustade – the soft white cheese is rolled up in white bread, fried in butter and drained.

These tasty morsels precede a substantial main course, Normandy wild duck, which allows each guest half a duck, casseroled Normandy style with apples, calvados and double cream. This is accompanied by two vegetable dishes cooked in French style: Duchesse potatoes – creamy mashed potato piped into rosettes and browned in the oven; and French beans with hazelnuts, in which the beans are served in a nutty, buttery, garlicky dressing.

The dessert, Apricot brandy sorbet, provides a refreshing finish with its sharp lemon flavour.

Table Talk

When your guests have cleansed their palates with the sorbet, serve a selection of cheeses from Normandy to finish this memorable meal in fitting style. Camembert is a must – look for boxes marked *fabriqué en Normandie.* Two other famous Normandy cheeses are Livarot and Pont L'Evêque, both fairly strong soft cheeses with brine-washed rinds. For something more delicate serve Petit-Suisse or Demi-sel, imported versions of the little soft fresh cream cheeses made all over Normandy.

Wine Ideas

To do full justice to the wild duck serve a really first-class wine. Its rich but subtle flavour calls for a full-bodied red, preferably a fine claret from Bordeaux. Saint-Emilion is the biggest top-quality Bordeaux district: look for Cheval Blanc, Ausone, Canon, Magdelaine or Figeac.

Countdown

The day before
Prepare the Apricot brandy sorbet and keep in the freezer.

Three hours before
Season the wild ducks and bring to room temperature.
Skin, chop and reserve the hazelnuts for French beans with hazelnuts.
Peel the potatoes and prepare to the end of step 2.

Two hours before
Prepare and blanch the beans for French beans with hazelnuts.
Prepare the Mozzarella cigars to the end of step 3.
Wrap in foil and store in a cool place.

One hour 15 minutes before
Prepare the Normandy wild duck and put in the oven.

One hour before
Finish the Duchesse potatoes ready for baking.

Thirty minutes before
Put the Apricot brandy sorbet in the body of the refrigerator to soften.
Add the cream and lemon juice to the duck and return to the oven to finish cooking.

Twenty minutes before
Cook the French beans with hazelnuts and keep hot.
Sauté the Mozzarella cigars.

Before serving the first course
Remove the duck from the oven, increase the heat and put in the Duchesse potatoes.

Between the first and main courses
Finish the Normandy wild duck.

★ Mozzarella cigars

● ***Preparation: 20 minutes***

● ***Cooking: 5 minutes*** ● ***Serves 4***

8 PIECES SLICED WHITE BREAD
4-5tsp DIJON MUSTARD
225g/8oz MOZZARELLA CHEESE
PEPPER
75g/3oz BUTTER
2tbls OIL

For the garnish:
4 TOMATO WEDGES
2 BLACK OLIVES, halved
WATERCRESS SPRIGS

1. Cut the crusts off the bread and flatten each slice with a rolling pin until very thin. Spread each slice with Dijon mustard to taste.
2. Slice the Mozzarella cheese as thinly as possible and cover each slice of bread with pieces of cheese. Season generously with pepper.
3. Roll up each Mozzarella-covered slice of bread very tightly and secure with a wooden cocktail stick, taking a long 'stitch' through the loose edge along the length of the roll.
4. Heat the butter and oil in a frying pan large enough to take the Mozzarella cigars in a single layer. Put them in side by side and sauté for 2 minutes or until they are evenly browned and the cheese has melted inside. Turn once and shake the pan frequently.
5. Remove from the pan and lay on absorbent paper to absorb the excess fat. Carefully remove the cocktail sticks.
6. Arrange the Mozzarella cigars on a heated serving dish. Garnish with tomato wedges, olives and watercress sprigs. Serve at once.

Cook's tips

This is a variation on the Italian favourite *Mozzarella in carozza.*

Stuffed mushrooms

● ***Preparation: 15 minutes***

● ***Cooking: 20 minutes*** ● ***Serves 4***

8 LARGE FLAT MUSHROOMS
50g/2oz BUTTER
SALT and PEPPER
8 LAMBS' KIDNEYS
4 SMALL LEEKS, white part only
1tbls RED WINE
1tbls FINELY CHOPPED PARSLEY
PARSLEY SPRIG, to garnish

1 Heat the oven to 190C/375F/gas 5. Trim off the mushroom stalks level with the caps. Melt 25g/1oz of the butter in a small saucepan and grease a large baking tray with a little of it.

2 Brush the mushrooms all over with the remaining melted butter and lay them, cap side down, on the prepared baking tray. Season with salt and pepper to taste and bake for 10 minutes. Keep warm.

3 Remove the skin from the kidneys, cut in half horizontally and cut out the core. Chop the kidneys roughly. Slice the leeks into thin rings, then put them in a colander, wash under cold running water and drain well.

4 Heat the remaining 25g/1oz butter in a large frying pan and cook the leeks for 4 minutes, stirring occasionally. Remove with a slotted spoon and keep warm. Add the chopped kidneys to the pan and fry for 3 minutes or until cooked but still slightly pink inside, turning frequently.

5 Return the leeks to the pan and add the wine. Season the sauce with salt and pepper to taste and simmer for 3 minutes. Put two mushroom caps on each of four individual serving plates and spoon the leek and kidney sauce over the top. Sprinkle with parsley, garnish with a parsley sprig and serve hot.

★ Normandy wild duck

● ***Preparation: bringing to room temperature, then 15 minutes***

● ***Cooking: 1¼ hours*** ● ***Serves 4***

2 × 700g/1½lb WILD DUCKS (dressed weight)
SALT and PEPPER
50g/2oz BUTTER
2tbls OLIVE OIL
2 LARGE TART DESSERT APPLES
6tbls CALVADOS (APPLE BRANDY)
300ml/½pt DOUBLE CREAM
2tbls LEMON JUICE

1 Wipe the ducks well with absorbent paper and rub the body cavities with pepper. Leave to come to room temperature.

2 Heat the oven to 190C/375F/gas 5. Season the ducks with salt. Heat 25g/1oz of the butter with the olive oil in a large frying pan. When the foaming subsides put in the ducks, side by side, and brown on all sides. Remove from the pan and keep warm.

3 Core the apples with an apple corer and slice into thick rings. Melt the remaining 25g/1oz butter in an ovenproof casserole large enough to take the ducks comfortably side by side. Fry the apple rings in the casserole for 2-3 minutes on each side or until lightly browned, turning with a spatula.

4 Arrange the ducks on top of the apple slices. Pour over the calvados and put in the oven for 30 minutes, basting frequently, uncovered.

5 Add the cream and lemon juice; return to the oven covered for 20-30 minutes or until the ducks are tender and the sauce is creamy and thick.

6 Transfer the ducks to a board and cut each one in half. Arrange them on a heated serving platter. Taste the sauce and correct the seasoning if necessary; spoon over the ducks and serve at once.

Lamb with prunes

● ***Preparation:* soaking raisins, then 25 minutes**

● ***Cooking:* 55 minutes** ● ***Serves 4***

900g/2lb LEG or SHOULDER OF LAMB, boned
2tbls FLOUR
3tbls OLIVE OIL
1 LARGE ONION, sliced into rings
1 GARLIC CLOVE, finely chopped
¼tsp TURMERIC
¼tsp SAFFRON POWDER
¼tsp GROUND CINNAMON
large pinch GROUND GINGER
large pinch CAYENNE PEPPER
SALT and PEPPER
350ml/12fl oz CHICKEN STOCK
1tbls CLEAR HONEY
225g/8oz NO-SOAK DRIED PRUNES
75g/3oz RAISINS, soaked for 2 hours and drained
PARSLEY SPRIG and LEMON SLICE, to garnish
RICE, to serve

1 Trim all the fat off the lamb and cut the meat into 4cm/1½in cubes. Toss the cubes in the flour. Heat the oil in a large flameproof casserole, add the lamb and fry over medium heat until brown on all sides, stirring occasionally. Remove with a slotted spoon and set aside.

2 Add the onion to the casserole and fry until golden brown, stirring continuously. Add the garlic and spices; season with salt and pepper to taste. Fry for 5 minutes, stirring, before gradually adding the stock. Bring to the boil.

3 Return the meat to the casserole. Lower the heat to minimum, cover the casserole and simmer the stew very gently for 30 minutes.

4 Stir in the honey, prunes and raisins, cover and cook for a further 10 minutes or until the lamb is tender.

5 Serve hot with plain boiled rice: spoon the rice around the edges of a large heated serving platter, pour the stew in the centre and garnish with parsley and lemon.

Variations

This is a classic Arab dish, and would traditionally be served with couscous. For a family supper omit the saffron, which is expensive but does give the authentic flavour, and use ½tsp turmeric.

★ *Duchesse potatoes*

● ***Preparation:* 20 minutes**

● ***Cooking:* 40 minutes** ● ***Serves 4***

450g/1lb POTATOES
SALT and PEPPER
15-25g/½-1oz BUTTER
1 LARGE EGG
1 LARGE EGG YOLK
GRATED NUTMEG
OIL, for greasing
For the glaze:
1 LARGE EGG, beaten with 1tbls MILK

1 Heat the oven to 200C/400F/gas 6. Slice the peeled potatoes thickly and cook in lightly salted simmering water for 10 minutes or until soft but not mushy. Drain well. Return the potatoes to the pan and remove all moisture by shaking the pan over the heat until they are quite dry.

2 Pass the potatoes through a sieve or vegetable mill. Add the butter while they are still warm and beat with a wooden spoon until the mixture is very smooth.

3 Put the egg and egg yolk in a small bowl and mix together; then beat gradually into the potato mixture. Season with salt, pepper and nutmeg to taste. Beat the mixture until fluffy.

4 Lightly oil a baking tray. Spoon the potato mixture into a piping bag fitted with a 1cm/½in star nozzle and pipe in rosettes onto the baking tray. Brush lightly with the egg and milk glaze. Bake for 20-25 minutes until golden.

Freezer

These potatoes freeze extremely well. Pipe the mixture onto baking trays. Put in the freezer, open freeze, uncovered, until hard. Pack in plastic boxes or bags and seal. When required lay on a lightly oiled baking sheet, brush with egg and cook.

★ French beans with hazelnuts

● *Preparation: 10 minutes*

● *Cooking: 20 minutes* ● *Serves 4*

450g/1lb FRENCH BEANS
SALT and PEPPER
50g/2oz BUTTER
4tbls CHICKEN STOCK
1tsp LEMON JUICE
50g/2oz HAZELNUTS, skinned and coarsely chopped
1 GARLIC CLOVE, very finely chopped

1 Top and tail the beans, stringing them if necessary, then cut them in half. Bring a saucepan of salted water to the boil, add the prepared beans. Return the water to the boil and blanch for 1 minute. Drain well.

2 Heat 25g/1oz of the butter in a large frying pan with the chicken stock and lemon juice. Add the blanched beans and season with salt and pepper to taste. Simmer gently for 12 minutes or until just tender, tossing frequently with a spatula.

3 Meanwhile heat the remaining 25g/1oz butter in a small frying pan and add the hazelnuts. Fry for 3 minutes over moderate heat, tossing frequently with a spatula. Stir in the garlic.

4 Stir the hazelnut and garlic mixture into the cooked beans. Taste and adjust the seasoning and transfer to a heated serving dish. Serve as soon as possible.

Peas with mint butter

● *Preparation: 10 minutes*

● *Cooking: 6 minutes* ● *Serves 4*

450g/1lb FROZEN PEAS
50g/2oz BUTTER
4tbls FINELY CHOPPED FRESH MINT
SALT and PEPPER
1 CANNED PIMIENTO
MINT SPRIG, to garnish

1 Bring a saucepan of salted water to the boil and put in the peas. Return to the boil over high heat, then reduce the heat to low and simmer the peas for 2-3 minutes. Drain and keep warm.

2 Melt the butter in another saucepan. Add the mint and cook for 1-2 minutes, stirring constantly. Add the peas and season with salt and pepper to taste. Toss well to coat the peas with the minted butter. Transfer to a heated serving dish.

3 Open out the pimiento and cut it into long thin strips from top to bottom. Arrange the strips criss-cross fashion over the peas to make a fine lattice garnish. Tuck the sprig of mint into one side of the dish and serve.

Cook's tips

Fresh mint is essential for this dish. If you use fresh peas in the pod buy 1kg/2¼lb.

★ Apricot brandy sorbet

● ***Preparation: 5 minutes, plus cooling, beating and freezing***

● ***Cooking: 10 minutes*** ● ***Serves 4***

175g/6oz SUGAR
GRATED ZEST and JUICE OF 1 LEMON
5tbls APRICOT BRANDY
2 EGG WHITES
SHINY GREEN LEAVES, to decorate

1 If you are using the freezing compartment of the refrigerator turn it down to its coldest setting one hour before starting to make the sorbet.

2 Bring the sugar and 375ml/12fl oz water slowly to the boil in a saucepan, stirring until dissolved. Then boil for 5 minutes without stirring. Remove from the heat, add the lemon zest and leave the syrup to stand until lukewarm.

3 Add the lemon juice and apricot brandy to the syrup, stir once and leave until cold. Then strain it through a fine sieve into a shallow freezer-proof container. Cover and put in the freezing compartment. leave until the sorbet mixture freezes 2.5cm/1in thick around the sides of the container, which will take about 2½ hours.

4 Whisk the sorbet with a fork or wire whisk to break up the ice crystals, cover and return to the freezer for 1 hour.

5 Remove from the freezer and transfer to a bowl if the container is very shallow. Whisk until smooth. Whisk the egg white until soft peaks form, then fold into the sorbet. Cover and return to the freezer until the sorbet is firm; about 2-5 hours depending on the size of the container.

6 About 30 minutes before serving transfer the sorbet to the main part of the refrigerator to soften it slightly. To serve scoop the sorbet out into eight scoops. Pile the scoops into a glass dish or individual coupes. Decorate with shiny green leaves and serve at once.

Grand Marnier soufflé

● ***Preparation: 15 minutes, plus chilling***

● ***Cooking: 45 minutes*** ● ***Serves 4***

4 LARGE EGGS, separated
100g/4oz CASTER SUGAR
6tbls GRAND MARNIER
GRATED ZEST of 1 ORANGE
1 SACHET POWDERED GELATINE
150g/¼pt DOUBLE CREAM, lightly whipped

For the decoration:
150ml/¼pt DOUBLE CREAM, whipped
1 ORANGE, cut into segments

1 Prepare a strip of doubled greaseproof paper or foil, long enough to wrap round a 600ml/2pt soufflé dish and wide enough to stand 5cm/2in above the rim. Tie it round the dish with string.

2 Combine the egg yolk, sugar, Grand Marnier and orange zest in the top of a double boiler or in a bowl set over a pan of simmering water. Whisk over simmering water until the mixture is thick and mousse-like (and the whisk leaves a trail behind it).

3 Put 2tbls cold water in a small bowl, sprinkle on the geltatine and leave for 5 minutes until softened.

4 Remove the thickened egg mixture from the simmering water and continue whisking until cool.

5 Put the bowl of gelatine in a saucepan of hot water until dissolved, then stir it into the egg mixture. Continue stirring until on the point of setting. using a large metal spoon, fold in the whipped cream.

6 Whisk the egg whites in a clean dry bowl until stiff but not dry. Fold them lightly into the Grand Marnier mixture pouring it in a thin stream. Pour into the prepared soufflé dish and put in the refrigerator for 3-4 hours to set. Remove the paper collar very carefully, using a knife to ease it away from the soufflé.

7 Shortly before serving fit a piping bag with a 1cm/½in star nozzle. Spoon the whipped cream into the bag and pipe a continuous line of cream around the edge of the soufflé. Arrange the orange segments decoratively on top of the cream.

EASY DINNER FOR FOUR

Marinated pepper and prawn salad · Roast chicken with mushroom sauce · Jerusalem artichoke purée · Perfect Brussels sprouts · Pears with raspberry sauce

HERE'S AN INEXPENSIVE and easy-to-cook menu for times when you are just entertaining close friends or relatives. It's a good mid-week menu, as most of the cooking can be done in advance.

Start with Marinated pepper and prawn salad, a colourful mixture of pink prawns with red and green peppers. The main dish is a Jewish speciality, often served at Passover: Roast chicken with mushroom sauce. The whole dish can be prepared in advance, then chilled and reheated just before the meal.

Accompany this with two hearty vegetable dishes served separately: Jerusalem artichoke purée, and Perfect Brussels sprouts.

To finish, serve each guest an individual dessert, poached Pears with raspberry sauce. These can be made in advance, chilled and finished with raspberry sauce.

Wine Ideas

Virtually any wine can be served with roast chicken, from a dry or medium white to a full-bodied red. A bottle of each kind would be nice, as many people have a definite preference for one or the other. As a change from the usual French or German wines, why not try one of the excellent vintages now coming in from Australia? Many of their reds are made from the Cabernet Sauvignon grape, which produces wines every bit as good as those made from it in Europe. On the white side, a Milawa Chardonnay from Brown Brothers, one of the original Australian wine-making families, would serve the chicken well. If you feel like chilling a second bottle, it makes a wonderful aperitif, or could be drunk with the Marinated pepper and prawn salad starter.

Countdown

Two days before
Make the Roast chicken with mushroom sauce, cool and chill.
Poach the pears and make the raspberry sauce; chill separately.

The night before
Scrub the artichokes and prepare the Brussels sprouts. Store in the salad drawer of the refrigerator.

Two hours before
Prepare the peppers for the Marinated pepper and prawn salad and marinate in the vinaigrette dressing.
Defrost the prawns.
Carve the chicken.

45 minutes before
Preheat the oven and reheat the Roast chicken with mushroom sauce.
Cook the Jerusalem artichokes, finish and keep hot.

Before serving the starter
Cook the Perfect Brussels sprouts and keep hot.
Dry the prawns, mix with the marinated peppers and toss to mix; sprinkle with parsley.

Before serving the dessert
Put the pears on individual serving plates and spoon a little raspberry sauce over each one; decorate with crystallized violets.

★ *Marinated pepper and prawn salad*

● ***Preparation: 50 minutes, plus marinating***

● ***Cooking: 10 minutes*** ● ***Serves 4***

1 LARGE GREEN PEPPER
1 LARGE RED PEPPER
OLIVE OIL
225g/8oz FROZEN PRAWNS, defrosted
1tbls CHOPPED PARSLEY, to garnish

For the vinaigrette dressing:
6tbls OLIVE OIL
2tbls RED WINE VINEGAR
1 GARLIC CLOVE, finely chopped
1tbls FINELY CHOPPED PARSLEY
SALT and PEPPER

1 Heat the grill to high. Halve, core and seed the peppers. Brush the grid of the grill pan with a little olive oil and lay the pepper halves side by side on the grid, skin side up. Brush with olive oil and cook, 12.5cm/5in away from the heat, for 7-10 minutes, or until the skins are well-browned and blistered. Leave until cool enough to handle.

2 Peel the skins from the pepper halves. Using a sharp knife, slice each half into fine strips. Put the strips in a shallow serving dish.

3 Prepare the vinaigrette: put the oil in bowl or screw-topped jar along with the vinegar, garlic and parsley. Season with salt and pepper to taste; beat or shake until the mixture emulsifies. Pour the dressing over the pepper strips and leave to marinate in a cool place for 30 minutes.

4 To serve, drain the defrosted prawns on absorbent paper and add to the pepper slices. Toss to mix, garnish with a sprinkling of parsley and serve as soon as possible.

Cook's tips

This salad is also good made with a mixture of peppers in other colours – yellow, purple and black – which are now quite commonly available.

Belgian chicken liver pâté

• Preparation: 20 minutes, plus chilling

• Cooking: 25 minutes **• Serves 4**

450g/1lb CHICKEN LIVERS
SALT and PEPPER
225g/8oz BUTTER, softened
4tbls FINELY GRATED ONION
2tsp MUSTARD POWDER
½tsp GRATED NUTMEG
¼tsp GROUND CLOVES
HOT TOAST, to serve
LETTUCE LEAVES, to garnish

1 Cover the livers with salted water. Bring to the boil, then cover and simmer for 20 minutes. Drain and pat dry with absorbent paper, then pass twice through the finest blade of a mincer, or liquidize to a paste in a blender or food processor.

2 Return the paste to the saucepan and beat with a wooden spoon over medium heat for 1 minute to evaporate the excess moisture.

3 Work the butter with a wooden spoon until it is soft and creamy. Flavour it with the onion, mustard, nutmeg and cloves. Season with salt and pepper to taste. Mix with the liver paste.

4 Pack the pâté firmly into a small earthenware pot or terrine and chill until needed. Serve with fresh fingers of hot toast: trim off all crusts and cut the toast into thin strips. Garnish each serving with a small lettuce leaf.

Cook's tips

This deliciously rich but simple chicken liver pâté is a convenient one because it will keep for up to a week in the refrigerator.

If you want the pâté to be absolutely smooth-textured, pass it through a fine sieve after adding the flavourings.

★ Roast chicken with mushroom sauce

• Preparation: 20 minutes

• Cooking: 1¼ hours **• Serves 4**

1.8kg/4lb OVEN-READY CHICKEN
SALT and PEPPER
OIL, for greasing
3 ICE CUBES
150ml/¼pt DRY WHITE WINE
225g/8oz BUTTON MUSHROOMS, sliced
2 LARGE RIPE TOMATOES, skinned, seeded and chopped

1 Heat the oven to 220C/425F/gas 7. Wipe the chicken inside and out with absorbent paper and pat dry. Season inside the cavity of the chicken with salt and pepper.

2 Truss the chicken and season the outside with salt and pepper. Lightly grease a small roasting tin and put the chicken in it, breast side up. Roast it for about 1¼ hours, turning it over after about 45 minutes. When you turn it, pour off any fat and juices that run from the chicken into a small bowl and reserve them for making the sauce.

3 Test that the chicken is cooked by inserting a skewer into the thickest part of the inside leg; the juices should run perfectly clear. Lower the heat to 150C/300F/gas 2. Remove the trussing skewer and strings from the chicken and put the chicken on a heated serving platter. Keep it warm in the oven while you make the sauce.

4 Add any fat and juices in the tin to those already reserved. Drop in the ice cubes and stir for a few moments until the fat hardens and rises to the surface. Lift off the fat and discard the ice cubes. Reserve juices and fat.

5 Add the wine to the roasting tin and bring to the boil over high heat, stirring to remove the sediment from the base of the tin. Reserve.

6 Put 1tbls of the reserved chicken fat into a frying pan over medium heat. Fry the mushrooms until golden, then add the tomatoes, chicken juices and the wine. Season with salt and pepper, then boil the sauce until it becomes syrupy. Pour over the chicken and serve at once.

Plan ahead

Cut the chicken into serving pieces, cover with sauce and put in an ovenproof serving dish. Cover with foil, cool rapidly and chill. Reheat in an oven preheated to 170C/325F/gas 3 for at least 30 minutes.

Foil-baked fish steaks

● ***Preparation:*** ***20 minutes***

● ***Cooking:*** ***35 minutes*** ● ***Serves 4***

4 x 175g/6oz FISH STEAKS
3tbls OLIVE OIL
90g/3½oz BUTTER
1 LARGE GREEN PEPPER, seeded and finely chopped
1 STALK CELERY, chopped
1 LARGE ONION, finely chopped
200ml/7fl oz TOMATO KETCHUP
1-2 GARLIC CLOVES, finely chopped
1-2 BAY LEAVES, crumbled
SALT and PEPPER

1 Heat the oven to 190C/375F/gas 5. Heat the oil and 40g/1½oz of the butter in a frying pan and fry the green pepper, celery and onion until soft but not coloured, stirring occasionally.

2 Add the tomato ketchup, garlic and bay leaves; season with salt and pepper to taste. Simmer gently for 10 minutes, stirring occasionally.

3 Wipe the fish steaks with absorbent paper and season them lightly with salt and pepper. Cut 4 pieces of double-thickness foil each large enough to envelope a fish steak completely and make a parcel or papillote.

4 Heat the remaining 50g/2oz butter in a large frying pan and fry the fish steak briefly until golden on both sides, turning once.

5 Spread one-eighth of the tomato and pepper sauce in the centre of each piece of foil. Put a fish steak on top and spread with the remaining sauce. Wrap the foil around the steaks and pinch the edges together securely and neatly.

6 Lay the parcels on a baking tray, join upwards, and bake for 10-15 minutes, so that the fish steaks are cooked but not disintegrating. Serve in the foil papillotes.

Cook's tips

Any firm white fish steaks can be used: cod, halibut, mock halibut, conger or sword fish.

Avocado green salad

● ***Preparation:*** ***20 minutes, plus marinating***

● ***Serves 4***

1 LETTUCE
100g/4oz YOUNG SPINACH LEAVES
1 LARGE AVOCADO
400g/4oz CANNED ARTICHOKE HEARTS, drained

For the dressing:
6tbls OLIVE OIL
2tbls LEMON JUICE
½ GARLIC CLOVE, finely chopped
SALT and PEPPER
¼tsp DRIED OREGANO
2tbls FINELY CHOPPED PARSLEY

1 Prepare the lettuce and spinach. Separate the lettuce into leaves. Remove any tough lengths of stalk and damaged leaves from the spinach. Dry both thoroughly and put in a salad bowl. (Or put in the salad drawer in the refrigerator if preparing well in advance.)

2 To make the dressing, put the oil in a small bowl or screw-topped jar along with the lemon juice and garlic. Season with salt and pepper to taste; beat or shake until the mixture emulsifies. Stir in the oregano and parsley. Taste for seasoning.

3 Halve and stone the avocado. Remove the skin by scoring down it and peeling off sections. Slice the flesh thinly.

4 Toss the artichoke hearts and avocado in the prepared dressing until well coated. Taste and adjust the seasoning and leave to marinate for about 30 minutes.

5 To serve, add the artichoke and avocado mixture to the lettuce and spinach leaves. Toss lightly to mix and serve at once.

★Jerusalem artichoke purée

● **Preparation: 20 minutes**

● **Cooking: 45 minutes** ● **Serves 4**

900g/2lb JERUSALEM ARTICHOKES
SALT and PEPPER
2tbls DOUBLE CREAM, whipped
25g/1oz BUTTER, diced
1 LARGE EGG YOLKS
2 CHILLI FLOWERS, to garnish

1 Scrub the artichokes clean. Bring a large saucepan of salted water to the boil. Add the artichokes, unpeeled, return to the boil, then lower the heat and simmer for 25-30 minutes, or until tender, according to size. Drain in a colander, hold in a cloth and peel.

2 Pass the cooked artichokes through a sieve or vegetable mill into a clean saucepan. Simmer the purée for 3-4 minutes over medium heat, stirring constantly. It will thicken considerably, and the delicate flavour of the artichokes will be intensified.

3 Beat in the whipped cream, then gradually add the diced butter, stirring after each addition until it is incorporated into the purée.

4 When all the butter has melted, remove the pan from the heat and beat in the egg yolks, one at a time. Season with salt and pepper to taste.

5 To serve, transfer the purée to a heated serving dish. Garnish with chilli flowers, if wished, and serve hot.

Cook's tips

To make chilli flowers cut the tips of fresh chillies, then cut down in strips towards the stalk end. Gently fold back the strips to make the 'petals'.

★ Perfect Brussels sprouts

● **Preparation: 15 minutes, plus soaking**

● **Cooking: 15 minutes** ● **Serves 4**

700g/1½lb BRUSSELS SPROUTS
SALT and PEPPER
2tbls MELTED BUTTER
LEMON JUICE

1 Cut a slice from the base of each Brussels sprout and remove the tough outer leaves entirely. Nick a small cross in the base of each sprout; as this is the densest part, it is the slowest to cook. The cross lets in the hot water and helps the sprouts to cook evenly.

2 Soak the sprouts in cold water with a little salt added for about 15 minutes. Drain them well.

3 Bring a large saucepan of salted water to the boil. Drop the sprouts into the boiling water and simmer, uncovered, for 5 minutes. Cover the saucepan and continue to cook for 2-10 minutes, depending on their age and size, until the sprouts are tender but still crisp.

4 Drain the sprouts well, then return to the pan and season generously with salt and pepper. Add the melted butter and lemon juice to taste; toss lightly to coat the sprouts in lemony butter. Pile the sprouts up on a shallow heated serving dish and serve at once.

Cook's tips

Really fresh, young, top-quality Brussels sprouts will not need to have anything removed beyond the odd yellow leaf. But still cut the cross in the base to aid cooking.

★ Pears with raspberry sauce

- ***Preparation: 30 minutes, plus chilling***
- ***Cooking: 55 minutes*** ***Serves 4***

4 FIRM PEARS
JUICE OF ½ LEMON
225g/8oz SUGAR
½ CINNAMON STICK
1 CLOVE
1 THIN STRIP ORANGE ZEST
1 THIN STRIP LEMON ZEST
1tsp VANILLA EXTRACT
150ml/¼pt DRY WHITE WINE
RED FOOD COLOURING (optional)
CRYSTALLIZED VIOLETS, to decorate

For the raspberry sauce:
275g/10oz FRESH or FROZEN RASPBERRIES
1tbls ICING SUGAR
LEMON JUICE

1 Peel the pears but do not core them. As they are peeled, drop them into a bowl of cold water acidulated with a little lemon juice to stop them turning brown.

2 Pour 300ml/½pt water into a saucepan just large enough to hold the pears upright side by side. Add the sugar, spices, strips of zest and the vanilla extract. Bring to the boil, stirring until the sugar has dissolved. Add the pears. Cover the pan and simmer for about 15 minutes, shaking the pan gently from time to time.

3 Pour in the wine and continue to cook over a low heat, uncovered, for 15-30 minutes, or until the pears are meltingly tender but not mushy.

4 Using a slotted spoon, carefully transfer the pears to a deep serving dish. Boil the cooking juices rapidly until they have reduced to the consistency of a light syrup. If desired, colour it pale pink with a few drops of red food colouring. Spoon the syrup over the pears to glaze them. Allow to cool, then chill until needed.

5 To make the raspberry sauce, defrost the frozen raspberries, if using. Rub the fruit through a fine sieve, or purée in a blender and sieve to remove seeds. Add the icing sugar and lemon juice to taste. Chill.

6 To serve, put each pear on an individual serving plate and spoon a little raspberry sauce over. Decorate with crystallized violets.

Orange bowl with sabayon

- ***Preparation: 55 minutes, plus chilling***
- ***Cooking: 5 minutes*** ***Serves 4***

2-3 ORANGES
4tbls SOFT BROWN SUGAR
4 LARGE EGGS, separated
6tbls RUM
⅛tsp GRATED NUTMEG
150ml/¼pt DOUBLE CREAM, stiffly whipped
50g/2oz DESSERT CHOCOLATE, chopped
CHOCOLATE CURLS, to decorate

1 Finely grate a little zest from one of the oranges and reserve for decorating. Peel and slice into rings enough oranges to line an 850ml/1½pt glass bowl. Line the bowl with orange slices and chill.

2 Put the brown sugar in a saucepan with 2tbls water and set over low heat until dissolved, stirring constantly. Then increase the heat to high and boil for 2 minutes to make a syrup. Set aside to cool, but do not allow the syrup to set.

3 Put the egg yolks in a small mixing bowl with the rum and grated nutmeg and beat until the yolks are thick and pale. Fill a saucepan one-third full of boiling water. Put the bowl containing the egg yolk mixture over the pan and put the pan over medium heat. Do not let the bowl touch the water, or the mixture will curdle. Continue beating until the mixture stiffens and rises slightly. Remove the saucepan from the heat and continue to beat until the mixture is cool.

4 Put the egg whites in a clean dry bowl and beat until they form stiff peaks. Pour the cooled syrup onto the egg whites and fold in with a large metal spoon.

5 Pour the cooled egg yolk mixture onto the whipped cream. Fold in the chopped chocolate with a metal spoon, then fold in the egg white and syrup mixture. Fill the orange-lined bowl with the rum-flavoured sabayon cream and chill. Just before serving, decorate with chocolate curls and reserved orange zest.

Cook's tips

To make chocolate curls (caraque) melt some dessert chocolate, then spread it on a work surface covered with greaseproof paper and allow to set. Using a knife, shave off a thin layer; it will curl as it is shaved. Use to decorate all kinds of cakes and desserts.

FAMILY DINNER FOR FOUR

Prawn and green bean salad · Chicken with cucumber · Rice pilaff with mushrooms and raisins · Green salad with chiffonade dressing · Blackberry sponge

THIS IS THE perfect menu for a relaxed dinner party or a country-style lunch. Start with crisp, light Prawn and green bean salad, simple to prepare and easy to serve. This is followed by a splendid French-style dish – chicken served with, unusually, cucumber poached in a delicate cream sauce.

Serve the main course with a delicious Rice pilaff with mushrooms and raisins, which will cook happily in the oven while you get on with the rest of the meal. Follow this with a tossed green salad with a piquant vinaigrette dressing.

Finish off the meal with a comforting blackberry and apple sponge.

Setting the Scene

Create a relaxed atmosphere by planning your table setting to reflect the homeliness of the meal. Use a crisp checked table cloth and napkins, with everyday cutlery, plain Paris goblets and cheerful coloured candles. The chicken would look good served in an earthenware dish.

Wine Ideas

To go with the chicken, choose a crisp, dry, medium-bodied white wine such as Maçon blanc. This would go well with both the starter and the main course. Another good choice would be a clean-tasting Sauvignon blanc. Alternatively you could serve a red and a white – a fresh, fruity Beaujolais Villages would be a suitable red.

Countdown

In the morning
Prepare the Prawn and green bean salad to the end of step 3 and chill.
Prepare the giblets and vegetables for the Chicken with cucumber and store in the refrigerator.
Prepare the raisins and vegetables for the rice pilaff.
Prepare the lettuce and the chiffonade dressing and chill separately.

One and a half hours before
Start cooking the Chicken with cucumber. After 15 minutes, make additions to the chicken. Blanch the cucumber.
Prepare and cook the Blackberry sponge.

Thirty minutes before
Start cooking the rice pilaff. Sauté the mushrooms and pine nuts and keep warm.

Ten minutes before
Remove the Blackberry sponge from the oven and keep warm.
Assemble the Prawn and green bean salad.
Cook the cucumber for the Chicken with cucumber in butter and cream; keep warm.

Before serving the main course
Complete the sauce for the chicken.
Add the mushrooms, raisins, pine nuts and butter to the pilaff.
Toss the green salad.

★ Prawn and green bean salad

- ***Preparation: 20 minutes, plus cooling***
- ***Cooking: 5 minutes***
- ***Serves 4***

350g/12oz YOUNG FRENCH BEANS, trimmed
SALT and PEPPER
9tbls OLIVE OIL
3tbls WINE VINEGAR
2tbls FINELY CHOPPED PARSLEY
1 GARLIC CLOVE, finely chopped
350g/12oz COOKED PRAWNS, in their shells
4tbls COARSELY CHOPPED SPRING ONIONS or SHALLOTS

1 Cut the beans into 2.5cm/1in lengths and cook in boiling salted water for 5 minutes or until barely tender.

2 Meanwhile, to make the French dressing, place the olive oil, vinegar and salt and pepper to taste in a screw-topped jar and shake to mix. Drain the beans and toss immediately in half the dressing. Add the parsley and garlic. Leave until cold, then chill.

3 Peel the prawns and toss them in the remaining French dressing with the spring onions.

4 When ready to serve, place the beans and the prawn mixture in a bowl and toss until well mixed. Correct the seasoning if necessary and transfer to a serving plate.

Cook's tips

It's best to use prawns in the shell for this recipe as they have a better flavour than peeled ones. Unless using frozen ones, always prepare and use prawns on the day of purchase as they deteriorate quickly. Cooked prawns should be bright pink and smell fresh. To peel them, carefully pull off the head and legs and then peel away the shell from the body and tail.

Oriental fish soup

● ***Preparation: 15 minutes***

● ***Cooking: 15 minutes*** ● ***Serves 4***

350g/12oz HADDOCK FILLET
1½tbls CORNFLOUR
1½tbls DRY SHERRY
3tbls SOY SAUCE
¾tsp SALT
1 SPANISH ONION, thinly sliced
850ml/1½pt FISH STOCK
2tbls LEMON JUICE
1½tbls FINELY CHOPPED PARSLEY
1tbls FINELY CHOPPED CORIANDER LEAVES

1 Using a sharp knife, skin the haddock and cut it into 2.5cm/1in squares. In a medium-sized bowl, blend the cornflour with 1tbls water to a smooth paste. Stir in the sherry and half the soy sauce. Add the fish pieces and stir to coat.

2 In a saucepan, combine the salt, onion and fish stock. Bring to the boil, then simmer for 10 minutes. Add the fish mixture to the simmering liquid. Stir in the remaining soy sauce and the lemon juice. Simmer, uncovered, for 5 minutes or until the fish flakes easily with a fork.

3 Pour into four warmed soup bowls and sprinkle with the chopped parsley and coriander leaves. Serve immediately.

★ *Chicken with cucumber*

● ***Preparation: 30 minutes***

● ***Cooking: 1¾ hours*** ● ***Serves 4***

1.8kg/4lb CHICKEN, with giblets
5 CARROTS, thinly sliced
1 SPANISH ONION, thinly sliced
25g/1oz BUTTER, plus extra for greasing
6-8tbls MELTED BUTTER
¼tsp DRIED THYME
1 BAY LEAF, crumbled
SALT and PEPPER
2 LARGE, FIRM TOMATOES, skinned, seeded and coarsely chopped
1 CUCUMBER, peeled
PAPRIKA
150ml/¼pt DOUBLE CREAM

1 Heat the oven to 190C/375F/gas 5. Chop the chicken giblets and place with the carrots and onion in the bottom of a well-buttered flameproof casserole. Cook over low heat for 5 minutes, stirring now and then.

2 Brush the chicken all over with melted butter and place it on top of the vegetables and giblets. Place in the oven. After 15 minutes, add the thyme and bay leaf, a sprinkling of salt and the chopped tomatoes.

3 Continue roasting for a further 1-1¼ hours, turning the chicken several times and basting well with melted butter.

4 Meanwhile, cut the cucumber in half lengthways and remove the seeds with a pointed teaspoon. Cut into 5cm/2in lengths and round off the edges to make attractive oval shapes. Blanch in boiling salted water for 1 minute, then drain. Season the cucumber with salt, pepper and paprika to taste. Place the butter and cream in a small pan with a tightly fitting lid. Add the cucumber, cover and simmer gently for 5 minutes or until tender. Remove from the heat.

5 When the chicken is cooked (the juices should run clear, not pink, when the thickest part of the leg is pierced with a skewer), transfer it, with the vegetables and giblets, to a dish, using a slotted spoon and draining well. Add 2tbls of the cooking liquid to the cucumber and bring to the boil. Simmer for 2 minutes. Check the seasoning and pour the sauce over the chicken. Arrange the cucumber pieces around the chicken and serve immediately.

Chinese beef with oyster and soy marinade

- ***Preparation: 15 minutes, plus marinating***
- ***Cooking: 10 minutes*** ***Serves 4***

700g/1½lb SIRLOIN STEAK, cut into 2.5cm/1in cubes
thin slices of STEM GINGER (optional)
2 SPRING ONIONS, thinly sliced
2-4 WHOLE SPRING ONIONS, to garnish

For the marinade:
3tbls OYSTER SAUCE
½tsp CHINESE CHILLI SAUCE or other HOT PEPPER SAUCE
2tbls SOY SAUCE
3tbls PEANUT OIL
3tbls DRY WHITE WINE

1 Place the meat in a large bowl. Combine the marinade ingredients and pour over the meat. Mix well and leave to marinate in the refrigerator for at least 4 hours or overnight.

2 When ready to cook, heat the grill to high. Drain the meat, reserving the marinade. Thread the meat on long skewers with thin slices of preserved ginger between every two or three cubes, if wished.

3 Brush the meat with the marinade and grill for 8-10 minutes, turning the skewers and basting with the marinade several times during cooking.

4 When cooked to your taste, transfer the brochettes to a serving dish and sprinkle with the thinly sliced spring onion. Serve immediately, garnished with the whole spring onions.

Serving ideas

Cooked rice, either plainly boiled or as a pilaff, would make a good accompaniment to this dish.

★ *Rice pilaff with mushrooms and raisins*

- ***Preparation: 10 minutes***
- ***Cooking: 40 minutes*** ***Serves 4***

50g/2oz RAISINS
BOILING WATER
65g/2½oz BUTTER
½ SPANISH ONION, finely chopped
225g/8oz LONG-GRAIN RICE
1 CHICKEN STOCK CUBE
SALT and PEPPER
100g/4oz BUTTON MUSHROOMS, sliced
25g/1oz PINE NUTS

1 Put the raisins in a small bowl and pour over boiling water to plump them. Heat the oven to 190C/375F/gas 5. Melt 25g/1oz butter in a heavy, flameproof casserole and cook the onion gently for 10 minutes or until soft, stirring occasionally. Add the rice and stir over moderate heat for 2-3 minutes until the grains are thoroughly coated with butter.

2 Dissolve the stock cube in 425ml/¾pt boiling water in a saucepan and bring back to the boil. Pour the boiling stock into the casserole. Season to taste with salt and pepper and quickly cover the casserole to prevent too much stock evaporating. Cook the pilaff in the oven for 20-25 minutes or until the rice grains are tender, fluffy and separate, and the liquid has been absorbed.

3 Meanwhile, gently sauté the mushroom slices in 25g/1oz of the butter for 5 minutes. Sauté the pine nuts in the remaining butter in a separate pan until golden, stirring constantly.

4 When the rice is cooked, transfer it to a serving dish. Add the drained mushrooms, raisins and pine nuts. Toss with a fork to mix them in lightly. Season to taste and serve immediately.

Variations

If you cannot buy pine nuts, try using flaked almonds or unpeeled whole almonds cut in two lengthwise.

★ Green salad with chiffonade dressing

• Preparation: 15 minutes **• Serves 4**

1 HEAD LETTUCE
For the chiffonade dressing:
6-8tbls OLIVE OIL
2tbls WINE VINEGAR
1tbls FINELY SNIPPED CHIVES or CHOPPED SPRING ONIONS
1tbls FINELY CHOPPED PARSLEY
1tbls FINELY CHOPPED GHERKIN or STONED GREEN OLIVES
1 HARD-BOILED EGG, finely chopped
SALT and PEPPER

1 Wash the lettuce leaves well. Drain and dry thoroughly in a cloth, absorbent paper or salad basket, so that there is no water left on the leaves to dilute the dressing. Wrap and store in the crisper drawer of the refrigerator until needed.

2 To prepare the dressing, put all the ingredients, with salt and pepper to taste, in a screw-top jar and shake well to mix.

3 Pour the dressing into a salad bowl and arrange the lettuce leaves on top. At table, toss the lettuce in the dressing, making sure that every leaf is covered. Check the seasoning and serve.

Peas with water chestnuts

• Preparation: 15 minutes

• Cooking: 15 minutes **• Serves 4**

450-600g/1-1¼lb FROZEN PEAS
BOILING WATER
5mm/¼in THICK SLICE BACON
1tbls OIL
225g/8oz CANNED WATER CHESTNUTS, drained and thinly sliced
50g/2oz BUTTER
4tbls CHICKEN STOCK
1tbls CASTER SUGAR
SALT and PEPPER
LETTUCE LEAVES

1 Put the peas in a saucepan and cover with boiling water. As soon as the water returns to the boil, drain the peas thoroughly, refresh under cold running water and drain again.

2 Cut the bacon slice into 5mm/¼in wide strips. Heat the oil in a frying pan and sauté the bacon until golden. Remove from the pan with a slotted spoon and reserve.

3 Place the water chestnuts in a saucepan with the peas and bacon and add the butter, chicken stock, sugar and salt and pepper to taste. Cook gently for about 10 minutes, shaking the pan occasionally, until all the liquid has been absorbed. Serve on a bed of lettuce leaves.

★ Blackberry sponge

- ***Preparation: 30 minutes***
- ***Cooking: 40 minutes*** ***Serves 4-6***

900g/2lb FIRM DESSERT APPLES
225g/8oz BLACKBERRIES
2tbls CASTER SUGAR, plus extra for dusting
SINGLE CREAM or CUSTARD, to serve

For the sponge:
75g/3oz BUTTER
6tbls CASTER SUGAR
2 LARGE EGGS, beaten
100g/4oz FLOUR
2tbls CORNFLOUR
pinch of SALT
1½tsp BAKING POWDER

1 Heat the oven to 190C/375F/gas 5. Peel, quarter and slice the apples into a 1.7L/3pt pie dish. Add the blackberries and sprinkle with caster sugar.

2 To make the sponge, cream the butter and sugar in a bowl until light and lemon-coloured, then add the beaten eggs gradually. Sift together the flour, cornflour, salt and baking powder. Fold into the butter mixture with a large metal spoon.

3 With a palette knife, spread the sponge over the apple and blackberry mixture, smoothing the top. Bake for 40 minutes or until a skewer inserted into the centre of the sponge comes out clean.

4 Sift the caster sugar over the top of the sponge and serve hot, with a jug of cream or custard.

Cook's tips

Fresh blackberries are available from July to October. Wash them before using by dipping briefly in cold water to remove any dust and drain well. If you can't get fresh blackberries, frozen ones will do.

Cherry praline bombe

- ***Preparation: 50 minutes, plus allow for overnight freezing***
- ***Cooking: 30 minutes*** ***Serves 4-6***

425ml/¾ pt good quality VANILLA ICE CREAM
WHIPPED CREAM and MARASCHINO CHERRIES, to decorate

For the almond praline:
OIL, for greasing
50g/2oz SUGAR
½tsp LEMON JUICE
50g/2oz ALMONDS, skinned and toasted

For the cherry mousse:
50g/2oz SUGAR
2 LARGE EGG YOLKS and 1 LARGE WHITE
2tbls DOUBLE CREAM, lightly whipped
2tbls quartered MARASCHINO CHERRIES and 2tsp SYRUP

1 About 30 minutes before you start, put a 600ml/1pt bombe mould to chill, and transfer the ice cream to the main part of the refrigerator to soften slightly. Lightly oil a baking sheet.

2 To make the praline, combine the sugar, 2tbls water and the lemon juice and almonds in a small heavy saucepan. Stir over a gentle heat until the sugar has dissolved. Raise the heat and boil, without stirring, to a rich golden caramel. Pour onto the baking sheet. Leave to cool and harden, then ease off with a spatula. Crush finely with a rolling pin.

3 Add the praline to the softened ice cream and work in until evenly mixed, without stirring too much. Line the mould with a 2cm/¾in thick, even layer of the ice cream. Cover and freeze for 1-1½ hours or until set.

4 Meanwhile, make the mousse. Put the sugar into a small heavy-based saucepan with 50ml/2fl oz water and stir over a gentle heat until the sugar is dissolved. Boil to 102C/217F without stirring and leave to cool.

5 In the top pan of a double boiler, beat the egg yolks until light and creamy. Gradually pour in the cooled syrup, whisking constantly with a wire whisk. Cook over simmering water, continuing to beat, until thick and doubled in bulk, about 10-15 minutes. Remove from the heat and immerse the pan in a bowl of iced water. Whisk until the mousse is thick and cold.

6 Turn the mousse into a bowl and gently fold in the lightly whipped cream, cherries and their syrup. In another bowl, whisk the egg white until stiff but not dry. Fold into the mousse and pour into the centre of the bombe. Cover and freeze overnight.

7 About 15 minutes before serving, unmould the bombe and place in the refrigerator to soften. To serve, spoon the cream into a star-nozzled piping bag and decorate the bombe with piped cream and whole cherries.

TASTY DINNER FOR SIX

Chicken liver terrine ·

Blanquette of turbot · Carrot ring with peas · Pilaff ·

Raspberry meringue baskets

THE CHICKEN LIVER terrine which starts this menu can be tackled with confidence even if you have never made one before. And to make life easy, this chicken liver dish actually improves in flavour if made a day or two in advance.

For the main course serve Blanquette of turbot, a meaty fish presented in a rich cream sauce and garnished with glazed button onions and crisp crescents of puff pastry.

Accompany the fish with an attractive ring of carrot purée filled with peas and a tasty pilaff of rice cooked in stock.

Finish the meal with Raspberry meringue baskets, individual desserts which can be prepared in advance and finished at the end.

Wine Ideas

The main course of fish demands a dry or medium dry white wine. Serve one with enough flavour to hold its own – and why not take the opportunity to sample one of the English vintages, which are invariably white? Lamberhurst Vineyards' Müller Thurgau is perhaps the best known, but there are others of equal interest. There are now over 300 English vineyards, some of whose distribution may be largely local, and none the worse for it. It is an interesting exercise to include English wines in a meal as many people have not tasted them.

It is not widely remembered that vineyards tended by monks once panned from Trafalgar Square through the Strand down to the River Thames.

Countdown

The day before

Make the Chicken liver terrine and store in the refrigerator.
Make the meringues, bake, cool and store. Make the raspberry sauce for the Raspberry meringue baskets and store in the refrigerator, covered.

Two hours before

Prepare the Carrot ring with peas ready for baking.
Cube the fish and prepare the onions and mushrooms for the Blanquette of turbot.

30 minutes before

Bake the Carrot ring with peas.
Prepare the Pilaff and keep warm.
Cook the onions and fish for the Blanquette of turbot.
Transfer the ice cream for the Raspberry meringue baskets to the main part of the refrigerator.

Fifteen minutes before

Turn the Chicken liver terrine out onto a serving dish and garnish.
Finish the Blanquette of turbot and keep warm.

Before serving the main course

Heat the peas and fill the carrot ring.
Reheat the pastry crescents for the Blanquette of turbot in the oven for 2 minutes.

Before serving the dessert

Fill and decorate the Raspberry meringue baskets.

★ Chicken liver terrine

● *Preparation: 40 minutes, plus chilling*

● *Cooking: 55 minutes* ● *Serves 6*

450g/1lb CHICKEN LIVERS
1 ONION, finely chopped
1 LARGE GARLIC CLOVE, crushed
1 BAY LEAF, crumbled
¼tsp DRIED MARJORAM
¼tsp DRIED THYME
SALT and PEPPER
25g/1oz BUTTER
4tbls BRANDY
75g/3oz UNSMOKED STREAKY BACON RASHERS
175g/6oz PIE VEAL, cubed
150ml/¼pt DOUBLE CREAM

For the garnish:
LETTUCE LEAVES
QUARTERED TOMATOES
STONED BLACK OLIVES

1 Trim the membranes or green parts from the livers and pat them dry. Put them in a bowl with the onion, garlic and herbs; season to taste.

2 Melt the butter in a heavy frying pan. Add the liver mixture and fry for 3-4 minutes over high heat until the livers are browned outside, but still pink in the middle, turning frequently. Slice, reserving the best two.

3 Remove the pan from the heat, quickly pour on the brandy, then stand well back and set it alight. Shake the pan until the flames die down, then turn the pan contents into a bowl and leave to cool.

4 Heat the oven to 190C/375F/gas 5. Lay the bacon rashers well apart between two sheets of stretch wrap and pound until almost paper-thin.

5 Line the base and sides of an 850ml/1½pt loaf tin or mould with the rashers, allowing the ends to hang down outside. They should be long enough to fold over the top when the tin is full.

6 Combine the cooled liver mixture with the veal and chop coarsely in a food processor, or put through the coarse blade of a mincer. Beat in the cream and correct the seasoning. Spoon half the mixture into the lined tin. Arrange the reserved sliced livers in a row down the centre and cover with the remaining mixture.

7 Fold the bacon over the top to cover the liver mixture completely. Seal the top of the tin with foil. Put in a deep baking dish and pour in hot water to come one-third of the way up its side; bake for 45-50 minutes. To test, plunge a fine skewer into the centre, leave it there for 10 seconds, then quickly put it to your lips; it should feel hot. Allow the terrine to cool, then chill overnight.

8 To serve, line a serving dish with lettuce leaves. Loosen the terrine by dipping the base of the tin in hot water for 1-2 seconds. Turn it out onto the lettuce and garnish with tomatoes and olives.

Deep-fried crab rolls

● ***Preparation: making crêpes, then 30 minutes***

● ***Cooking: 25 minutes*** ● ***Serves 6***

CREPE BATTER (see page 84, and make double the quantity)
BUTTER, for frying
For the filling:
200g/7oz CANNED CRABMEAT
ABOUT 150ml/¼pt MILK
1 BAY LEAF
½ CHICKEN STOCK CUBE
SMALL STRIP LEMON ZEST
1-2 PARSLEY SPRIGS
1 SMALL ONION, quartered
25g/1oz BUTTER
2tbls FLOUR
1tsp TOMATO PUREE
6tbls DOUBLE CREAM
2tsp BRANDY
2tsp LEMON JUICE
1tsp GRATED HORSERADISH
SALT and PEPPER
CAYENNE PEPPER
LEMON SLICES and PARSLEY SPRIGS, to garnish
For deep-frying:
2 LARGE EGGS, beaten
75g/3oz FINE WHITE BREADCRUMBS
OIL, for deep-frying

1 Prepare and fry 24 small crêpes, using a 15cm/6in diameter pan. Stack them on a plate under a folded cloth to keep them moist.

2 Make the crabmeat filling. Drain the juices from the crab into a measuring jug, make up to 150ml/¼pt with milk and pour into a saucepan. Add the bay leaf, ½ stock cube, lemon zest, parsley and onion; bring slowly to the boil. Remove, cover, infuse for 10 minutes, then strain.

3 Melt the butter in a saucepan. Blend in the flour and cook over a low heat for 3-4 minutes to make a pale roux, stirring constantly. Gradually add the infused milk, stirring vigorously. Bring to the boil and cook, stirring, for 2-3 minutes, then remove from the heat.

4 Beat in the tomato purée, cream and brandy. When smooth mix in the crabmeat, lemon juice and horseradish. Season with salt, pepper and a pinch of cayenne. Cool, then chill for 1 hour or until needed.

5 Heat the oil in a chip pan or deep-fat fryer, basket in place, to 190C/375F. At this temperature a day-old cube of bread browns in 50 seconds.

6 Divide the chilled crabmeat mixture into 24 equal portions and put a portion at one edge of a crêpe. Roll over once, then fold in the ends to enclose the filling and roll up. Coat each roll with egg, draining off excess. Roll in breadcrumbs and shake off any excess.

7 Lay four or five rolls in the frying basket and deep-fry for 2-3 minutes until crisp and golden. Drain on absorbent paper and keep hot. Repeat until all the rolls are cooked; garnish with lemon and parsley.

★ Blanquette of turbot

● ***Preparation: making stock, then 30 minutes***

● ***Cooking: 1 hour*** ● ***Serves 6***

24 BUTTON ONIONS, peeled
150g/5oz BUTTER
2tbls CASTER SUGAR
SALT and PEPPER
900g/2lb TURBOT FILLETS
300ml/½pt DRY WHITE WINE
25g/1oz FLOUR
225g/8oz BUTTON MUSHROOMS
2 LARGE EGG YOLKS
200ml/7fl oz DOUBLE CREAM
1-2tbls LEMON JUICE
3-4tbls FINELY CHOPPED PARSLEY
6 BAKED CRESCENTS OF PUFF PASTRY, reheated in the oven
FISH or VEGETABLE STOCK CUBES

1 Prepare the stock using the correct number of fish or vegetable stock cubes, as stated on the packet, for 1.7L/3pt of water. Keep hot.

2 Meanwhile put the button onions in a small pan and cover with water. Add 25g/1oz butter, the caster sugar, and salt and pepper to taste. Bring to the boil and simmer for about 10 minutes, until the liquid has boiled away and the onions are lightly caramelized, shaking the pan towards the end to colour them evenly. Keep hot.

3 Cut the turbot into 24 even-sized cubes. heat 50g/2 oz butter in a frying pan until coloured and fry the cubes until a pale golden colour on all sides, taking great care not to break them. Add 850ml/1½pt fish stock and the wine. Bring to the boil over medium heat, then simmer very gently for about 5 minutes until the turbot is cooked through but still firm.

4 Remove the turbot with a slotted spoon and keep hot. Simmer the cooking liquor until reduced to 600ml/1pt.

5 Melt 25g/1oz butter in a large saucepan, add the flour and cook for 2 minutes, stirring constantly. Gradually stir in the reduced cooking liquor, beating vigorously, then bring to the boil, stirring constantly. Simmer for 10 minutes, stirring occasionally.

6 Meanwhile toss the mushrooms in 25g/1oz butter over low heat until softened. Keep hot.

7 Beat the egg yolks with the cream and lemon juice to taste. Off the heat, add this mixture to the sauce, mix well and return to a very low heat. Stir until it thickens; do not allow to boil.

8 Fold in the turbot and mushrooms, taste and adjust the seasoning, and heat through gently. Turn into a large heated serving dish, sprinkle with parsley, garnish with button onions and pastry crescents before serving.

Beef and pork kebabs

● ***Preparation: 30 minutes, plus marinating***

● ***Cooking: 15 minutes*** ● ***Serves 6***

700g/1½lb BONELESS PORK
700g/1½lb FILLET OF BEEF
OIL, for brushing
SALT
1 LETTUCE, shredded to serve
LEMON SLICES and BLACK OLIVES, to garnish

For the marinade:
1 ONION, finely chopped
3tbls FINELY CHOPPED PARSLEY
¼-½tsp DRIED OREGANO
6tbls OLIVE OIL
BLACK PEPPER

1 Cut any fat and gristle from the pork and cut the meat into 24 × 2.5cm/1in cubes. Do the same with the beef.

2 Prepare the marinade. Put the onion, parsley, oregano and oil in a large bowl. Season generously with pepper. Add the meat cubes and stir until well mixed. Cover and marinate for at least 2 hours in a cool place.

3 Heat the grill to high. When ready to grill brush the grid with a little oil. Remove the meat cubes from the marinade with a slotted spoon, reserving the marinade. Pat the meat dry with absorbent paper and season to taste with salt.

4 Skewer two pieces of pork and two pieces of beef alternately on each of twelve 10cm/4in long bamboo skewers. Put on the grid and cook, 7.5cm/3in away from the heat, for about 5-6 minutes on each side or until browned, basting frequently with the marinade.

5 Arrange the shredded lettuce on a serving platter. Put the skewers on top, garnish with lemon slices and olives and serve at once.

Cook's tips

To slice a lemon thinly enough to get 12 slices, chill the lemon for about an hour beforehand. Cut with a large, freshly sharpened knife.

★ *Carrot ring with peas*

● ***Preparation: 20 minutes***

● ***Cooking: 1½ hours*** ● ***Serves 6***

1kg/2lb CARROTS
100g/4oz BUTTER
150ml/¼pt CHICKEN STOCK
½-1tbls SUGAR
SALT and PEPPER
6tbls GRATED GRUYERE CHEESE
2 LARGE EGGS, beaten
225g/8oz COOKED PEAS
WATERCRESS SPRIGS, to garnish

1 Slice the cleaned carrots thickly and put in a saucepan. Cover with cold water and bring to the boil; drain.

2 Melt 40g/1½oz butter in a saucepan over low heat. Add the stock and carrots, plus sugar, salt and pepper to taste. Cover and simmer for 30-35 minutes, stirring occasionally. Uncover and simmer for a further 20-25 minutes until the carrots are tender and the liquid has been absorbed.

3 Heat the oven to 180C/350F/gas 4. Purée the carrots in a blender or food processor, or pass through a vegetable mill. Beat in 25g/1oz butter, the Gruyère cheese and finally the beaten eggs. Taste and adjust the seasoning.

4 Generously butter a 600ml/1pt ring mould. Press the carrot purée into it, levelling off the top with a palette knife. Bake for 25-30 minutes or until firm to the touch.

5 Meanwhile melt the remaining 25g/1oz butter in a frying pan. Add the cooked peas and cook for a further 1-2 minutes to heat through. Season with salt and pepper to taste.

6 Turn the carrot ring out unto a heated serving platter and fill the centre with peas. Garnish with watercress sprigs and serve hot.

Pilaff

● Preparation: 5 minutes

● Cooking: 30 minutes **● Serves 6**

75g/3oz BUTTER
1 ONION, chopped
450g/1lb LONG-GRAIN RICE
500ml/18fl oz WELL-FLAVOURED HOT STOCK
LARGE PINCH THYME
SALT and PEPPER
FRESH THYME SPRIG, to garnish

1 Heat the oven to 180C/350F/gas 4. Melt the butter in a flameproof casserole and fry the onion until it turns a light golden colour. Add the rice and continue to cook, stirring constantly, until the rice becomes translucent and just begins to colour.

2 Pour in the hot stock and season with thyme, salt and pepper to taste. Cover the casserole and put it in the oven for 15-20 minutes or until the liquid has been absorbed and the rice is tender.

3 Test to ensure rice does not become overcooked then turn the rice pilaff onto a heated serving platter, garnish with a thyme sprig and serve hot.

Cook's tips

Use a bay leaf instead of thyme for a slightly different flavour. For a spicy pilaff, add ½tsp crushed cumin seeds and a blade of mace. For golden-coloured pilaff, add a pinch of saffron or ½tsp turmeric.

Mixed bean salad with tomatoes

● Preparation: 20 minutes

● Cooking: 4 minutes **● Serves 6**

175g/6oz GREEN BEANS
SALT and PEPPER
200g/7oz CANNED HARICOT BEANS, drained
225g/8oz SMALL TOMATOES, quartered
10 BLACK OLIVES, stoned
4 CANNED ANCHOVY FILLETS, drained and finely chopped

For the vinaigrette:
6tbls OLIVE OIL
2tbls RED WINE VINEGAR
1 SMALL GARLIC CLOVE, finely chopped
2tbls FINELY CHOPPED PARSLEY
SALT and PEPPER

1 Top and tail the green beans. Bring a saucepan of salted water to the boil and blanch the beans for 3-4 minutes or until lightly cooked but still crisp. Drain, rinse under cold running water and drain again.

2 Put the beans in a serving dish and add with the haricot beans, tomatoes, olives and anchovy fillets. Toss lightly but thoroughly until well mixed.

3 Make the vinaigrette. Put the oil in a small bowl with the vinegar, garlic and parsley. Season with salt and pepper to taste. Beat with a fork until the mixture emulsifies. Pour over the salad, toss lightly to coat the ingredients and serve at once.

★Raspberry meringue baskets

● *Preparation: 30 minutes, plus cooling and chilling*

● *Cooking: 3-4 hours* ● *Serves 6*

300ml/½pt VANILLA ICE CREAM
For the meringue baskets:
MELTED BUTTER and SIFTED FLOUR, for the baking tray
5 EGG WHITES
SALT
275g/10oz CASTER SUGAR

For the raspberry sauce:
350g/12oz RASPBERRIES
4tbls ICING SUGAR, sifted
3tbls GRAND MARNIER
1tbls LEMON JUICE
EXTRA RASPBERRIES, to decorate

1 First make the meringue baskets. Heat the oven to 100C/200F/gas low. Brush a baking tray with melted butter and dust with sifted flour. Using an inverted cup as a guide, mark six 7.5cm/3in diameter circles in the flour, spaced well apart. Alternatively mark a baking sheet lined with non-stick paper.

2 Put the egg whites in a clean dry mixing bowl with a pinch of salt and whisk with an electric whisk until stiff and dry. Whisk in half the sugar, 1tbls at a time. Change to a balloon whisk and continue whisking by hand for 1 minute or until the mixture is very smooth and glossy. Using a metal spoon, fold in the remaining sugar.

3 Fit a piping page with a 1cm/½in plain nozzle. Spoon the meringue mixture into the bag and pipe six meringue baskets as follows. Pipe the bases to fit the circles marked on the baking tray, starting in the centre and working outwards in a spiral. Form the sides by piping around the edge of the base three times, one layer on top of the next.

4 Bake on the lowest shelf of the oven for 4½ hours, or until the meringue baskets are crisp on the outside but still soft in the centre. Cool on a wire rack completely before storing.

5 Meanwhile make the raspberry sauce. Push the raspberries into a bowl through a fine sieve, using the back of a wooden spoon, and discard the pips. Stir the sifted sugar into the raspberry purée, with the Grand Marnier and lemon juice to taste. Chill for 2 hours or until required.

6 About 30 minutes before serving transfer the ice cream to the main part of the refrigerator to soften slightly.

7 To assemble, scoop vanilla ice cream into the centre of each meringue basket. Spoon a little of the raspberry sauce over and decorate with whole raspberries. Serve the remaining sauce separately.

Apple jalousie

● *Preparation: 50 minutes*

● *Cooking: 30 minutes* ● *Serves 6*

400g/14oz FROZEN PUFF PASTRY, defrosted
225g/8oz MINCEMEAT
1 LARGE COOKING APPLE
1 LARGE EGG, beaten
FLOUR
1tbls ICING SUGAR, sifted
DOUBLE CREAM, to serve

1 Heat the oven to 230C/450F/gas 8. Put a baking tray on a centre shelf to heat through. (This ensures that when the jalousie is placed on it the bottom cooks as well as the top.)

2 Cut the pastry in half. Roll out into two strips about 30cm/12in long by 15cm/6in wide. Put one on another baking tray and spread with the mincemeat, leaving a good 2.5cm/1in of pastry visible around the edge.

3 Peel, core and thinly slice the apple and arrange the slices on top of the mincemeat in overlapping rows. Trim any uneven edges of the pastry to give a neat rectangle and brush the exposed pastry with beaten egg.

4 Fold the second piece of pastry in half lengthways and, using a sharp knife, cut slits into the fold about 5mm/¼in apart and to within 2.5cm/1in of the edges, making sure they go right through to the second side. Open out the pastry and put it carefully on top of the filling.

5 Knock up and flute the pastry edges to seal them and give a decorative finish. Brush with the rest of the beaten egg. Put on the heated baking tray and bake for 10 minutes. Reduce the heat to 190C/375F/gas 5 and cook for a further 5 minutes.

6 Remove the jalousie from the oven and sprinkle with the icing sugar. Return to the oven for a further 5-10 minutes or until the glaze is golden and the pastry crisp. Serve hot with lightly whipped cream.

Cook's tips

The name of this apple dessert comes from the French for shutter – *jalousie* – the oblong shape and slits in the pastry top resemble a miniature shutter.

DINNER FOR EIGHT

Spinach-stuffed mushrooms · Easy cassoulet · Polenta · Leek and curly endive salad · Oranges in Marsala

LAYING ON DINNER for eight is quite an undertaking, so make life easy by serving a large hearty casserole for the main course which is cooked the day before.

To begin, serve Spinach-stuffed mushrooms, button mushroom caps filled with a mouth-watering mixture of spinach, shallots and herbs baked in white wine. Easy cassoulet, the main course, is an adaption of the more elaborate French version, containing haricot beans, bacon and lamb slowly simmered together until tender with a crispy golden topping.

To accompany this simple peasant dish, serve no more than Leek and curly endive salad, and suitably rustic slices of Polenta topped with grated cheese.

As the main course is filling – serve Oranges in Marsala as a light fruity finale.

Wine Ideas

Cassoulet is a robust, hearty dish from south-west France, so serve it with a hearty red wine from the same area, something unpretentious that you can afford to dispense in good quantity to your eight guests. Cahors, the wine traditionally described as 'black' because of its very deep colour, from the vineyards around the Lot river, would be ideal. Or perhaps another deep-coloured wine, Corbières, from Southern France; not quite so full-bodied but still very rich. If you prefer a wine from another part of the world, choose an Italian Barbera, Australian Shiraz or Californian Cabernet Sauvignon.

The Marsala used to make the dessert is a fine sweet dessert wine; serve the rest of the bottle as a finishing touch, either with the dessert or afterwards with coffee.

Countdown

The day before
Cook the Easy cassoulet and chill overnight.

In the morning
Make the Oranges in Marsala and chill until needed.
Cook the leeks for the Leek and curly endive salad.
Prepare the endive and store in the salad drawer of the refrigerator. Make the vinaigrette.

Three hours before
Steam the polenta.

One hour before
Take the cassoulet out of the refrigerator.
Prepare the Spinach-stuffed mushrooms; put in the oven 20 minutes before sitting down to eat.

30 minutes before
Finish off and reheat the cassoulet.

15 minutes before
Assemble the Leek and curly endive salad.
Slice and dish up the Polenta.

Spinach-stuffed mushrooms

● ***Preparation: 15 minutes***

● ***Cooking: 35 minutes*** ● ***Serves 8***

450g/1lb FROZEN CHOPPED SPINACH
85-100g/3½-4oz BUTTER
32 BUTTON MUSHROOMS (about 450g/1lb)
8 SHALLOTS, finely chopped
½tsp DRIED THYME
SALT and PEPPER
1 LARGE EGG, beaten
2tbls FINELY CHOPPED PARSLEY
8tbls DRY WHITE WINE

1. Melt 25g/1oz butter in a large saucepan and add the frozen spinach. Cook over medium heat, breaking up the blocks with a wooden spoon.
2. Heat the oven to 190C/375F/gas 5. Remove the mushroom stalks and wipe the caps clean with a damp cloth. Finely chop the stalks.
3. Heat 50g/2oz butter in a saucepan and fry the shallots for 5 minutes or until soft, stirring frequently. Add the mushroom stalks and fry for a further 3 minutes. Drain the spinach and add to the pan along with the thyme. Season with salt and pepper to taste, remove from the heat and cool.
4. Butter a gratin dish large enough to take the mushrooms caps in one layer; use two dishes if necessary. Arrange the mushrooms, cap side down, in the dish and season with salt and pepper to taste.
5. Stir the beaten egg into the spinach mixture and spoon it into the mushroom caps.
6. Combine the breadcrumbs and parsley; sprinkle over the mushroom caps. Pour the wine down the side of the dish and bring to a simmer over low heat. Transfer to the oven for 15-20 minutes until the mushrooms caps are tender and the breadcrumbs golden. Serve hot.

Cucumber ring with prawns

● *Preparation: Making stock, then 30 minutes, plus setting* ● *Serves 8-10*

3 CUCUMBERS
1 ONION
JUICE of 2 LEMONS
SALT and WHITE PEPPER
425ml/¾ pt WARM CHICKEN STOCK
2tbls GELATINE
2tbls FINELY CHOPPED PARSLEY
2tbls FINELY CHOPPED TARRAGON
WHOLE PRAWNS and THIN CUCUMBER SLICES, to garnish

For the prawn mayonnaise:
6tbls MAYONNAISE
2tsp CHILLI SAUCE (HOT PEPPER SAUCE)
1tsp WORCESTERSHIRE SAUCE
350g/12oz COOKED PEELED PRAWNS
2 TOMATOES, skinned, seeded and diced
1tsp each FINELY CHOPPED TARRAGON, CHERVIL and CHIVES

1 Peel the cucumbers and grate them finely into a bowl. Grate the onion into a bowl and mix together. Stir in the lemon juice and season with salt and white pepper to taste. Pour in the warm chicken stock.

2 Sprinkle the gelatine over 125ml/4fl oz cold water and leave for 5 minutes to soften. Put the bowl in a saucepan of simmering water and leave until the gelatine has dissolved. Allow to cool slightly.

3 Pour the dissolved gelatine into the cucumber mixture and stir to blend. Stir in the parsley and tarragon; taste and adjust the seasoning. Pour the mixture into a wetted 1.4L/2 ½pt ring mould and chill until firm.

4 Meanwhile prepare the prawn mayonnaise. Put the mayonnaise, chilli sauce and Worcestershire sauce in a bowl. Stir in the prawns, tomatoes and herbs. Correct the sêasoning if necessary and continue stirring lightly until the prawns and tomatoes are well coated with mayonnaise.

5 Dip the mould into hot water for a few seconds and invert it onto a dampened serving platter slightly larger in diameter than the mould. Remove the mould and centre the ring on the plate. Spoon the prawn mayonnaise into the centre of the ring and garnish with whole prawns and cucumber slices.

Hungarian beef goulash

● *Preparation: 30 minutes*

● *Cooking: 1¾ hours* ● *Serves 8*

1.4kg/3lb TOP RUMP
50g/2oz BUTTER
2tbls OLIVE OIL
2 LARGE ONIONS, finely chopped
2 GARLIC CLOVES, finely chopped
6tbls FLOUR
SALT and PEPPER
2tbls PAPRIKA
1tsp GROUND CARAWAY SEEDS
1 BAY LEAF
¼tsp DRIED MARJORAM
PINCH CAYENNE PEPPER
450g/1lb BUTTON MUSHROOMS, sliced
2 RED PEPPERS, seeded and diced
850g/1lb 14oz CANNED TOMATOES
300ml/½pt SOURED CREAM
FINELY CHOPPED PARSLEY, to garnish

1 Heat the oven to 140C/275F/gas 1. Cut the beef into 5cm/2in cubes. Heat 25g/1oz of the butter with the oil in a large flameproof casserole. Add the onions and garlic and cook over low heat for 10 minutes or until the onions are transparent, stirring occasionally. Using a slotted spoon, transfer the onions and garlic to a heated serving plate and keep warm.

2 Sprinkle the flour onto a plate and season with salt and pepper. Toss each cube of meat in the flour, shaking off any excess. Heat the remaining 25g/1oz butter in the casserole and brown one-quarter of the meat for 2-3 minutes on each side. Transfer to a heated plate, using a slotted spoon, and keep warm while browning the remainder in three batches.

3 Return the onions, garlic and meat to the casserole. Sprinkle with the paprika and caraway seeds. Add the bay leaf, marjoram and thyme and season with salt, pepper and cayenne. Bring to a simmer over medium heat and cook for 10 minutes, stirring constantly.

4 Add the mushrooms, red peppers and tomatoes; bring to a simmer. Cover and transfer to the oven to cook for 1-1¼ hours or until the meat is tender. Taste and adjust the seasoning. Pour a little soured cream in the centre and garnish with parsley. Serve the remaining cream separately.

Easy cassoulet

• Preparation: overnight soaking, then 45 minutes, plus chilling

• Cooking: 3½ hours **• Serves 8**

800g/1¾lb DRIED WHITE HARICOT BEANS, soaked overnight
450g/1lb BACON in one piece
3 LARGE ONIONS
1 THYME SPRIG
1 CHICKEN STOCK CUBE, crumbled
1 BAY LEAF
3 GARLIC CLOVES
150g/5oz LARD or VEGETABLE SHORTENING
SALT and PEPPER
900g/2lb BONELESS BREAST OF LAMB
8 LARGE RIPE TOMATOES, skinned and seeded
6tbls TOMATO PURÉE
1.1L/2pt CHICKEN STOCK
75g/3oz FRESH WHITE BREADCRUMBS
BAY LEAVES, to garnish

1 Drain the beans and put them in a large saucepan. Cover with cold water and add the bacon, two onions, thyme, chicken stock cube, bay leaf, 1 garlic clove and 50g/2oz of the lard or vegetable shortening, season.

2 Bring the mixture to the boil and simmer for 30 minutes or longer, until the beans are soft. Drain the beans, reserving the liquor and bacon. Discard the flavourings.

3 Meanwhile cut the breast of lamb into serving pieces. Season with salt and pepper. Melt 50g/2oz of the remaining lard or vegetable shortening in a large frying pan and fry the pieces of lamb until golden.

4 Remove the lamb from the pan with a slotted spoon and transfer to a large flameproof casserole. Reserve. Slice the remaining onion and add to the pan along with one garlic clove. Fry for 5 minutes until soft.

5 Heat the oven to 150C/300F/gas 2. To assemble the cassoulet cut the bacon into chunks and put on top of the lamb. Cover with half the cooked beans. Crush the remaining garlic clove and add to the casserole with the tomatoes. Top with the remaining beans.

6 Put the tomato purée in a bowl and dilute with 300ml/½pt of the reserved bean liquor; add to the casserole, together with the remaining lard and the chicken stock. Sprinkle the surface with 25g/1oz breadcrumbs and cook in the oven for 2 ½ hours. Skim off excess fat.

7 After 1 hour cover the casserole with a lid or piece of foil to prevent the crust becoming too thick. At the end of the cooking time allow to cool, then chill overnight. Heat the oven to 170C/325F/gas 3. Gently stir the crust in with a fork. Sprinkle with the breadcrumbs and cook until heated through. Garnish with bay leaves and serve hot.

Polenta

• Preparation: 20 minutes

• Cooking: 3 hours **• Serves 8**

1½tsp SALT
350g/12oz FINE CORNMEAL
8tbls MELTED BUTTER
SALT and PEPPER
50g/2oz GRUYERE CHEESE, grated
FLAT-LEAVED PARSLEY and TOMATO SLICES, to garnish

1 Bring 1.2L/2¼pt salted water to the boil in a large heavy saucepan. Slowly, so that the water does not come off the boil, pour in the cornmeal, stirring vigorously with a wooden spoon to prevent lumps forming. Continue to cook, stirring vigorously, until the mixture is quite thick and smooth; about 1 minute.

2 Line a metal sieve or a colander with a large double thickness of muslin. Scrape the polenta mixture into it, fold the ends of the muslin neatly over the top and tie with string. Fit the sieve or colander over a pan of simmering water, cover and steam for 3 hours, topping up the water when necessary, until the polenta becomes a firm loaf.

3 Turn the polenta out onto a flat dish. Remove the muslin and cut into 1cm/½in thick slices. Pour 1tbls melted butter over each slice. Season with salt and pepper to taste and sprinkle with 1tbls Gruyère cheese. Garnish with parsley and tomato and serve at once.

Cook's tips

Fine cornmeal from North Italy is often sold under then name *polenta*, the famous dish made from it. Polenta slices are also delicious fried in butter until crisp and golden. Or try them baked in cream, sprinkled with Gruyère cheese.

Boiled meat with dumplings

● **Preparation: 30 minutes**

● **Cooking: 2 hours** ● **Serves 8**

800g/1¾lb UNSMOKED BACON HOCK
1.1kg/2½lb CHICKEN
6 POTATOES, quartered
2 LARGE ONIONS, quartered
6 CARROTS, cut into chunks
SALT and PEPPER
1 SMALL CABBAGE, cut into 8 wedges
2tbls FINELY CHOPPED PARSLEY, to garnish

For the cornmeal dumplings
65g/2½oz CORNMEAL
65g/2½oz SELF-RAISING FLOUR
¼tsp SALT
15g/½oz BUTTER
½ BEATEN EGG
4-5tbls MILK

1 Put the bacon and chicken into a heavy 4.5L/8pt saucepan, cover with water and bring to the boil. Cover the pan, reduce the heat and simmer for at least 1 hour.

2 Add the potatoes and simmer for a further 10 minutes. Add the onions and carrots and season to taste with pepper. Simmer for 15 minutes.

3 Meanwhile prepare the dumplings. Sift the cornmeal, flour and salt into a bowl. Rub in the butter until the mixture resembles fine breadcrumbs. Stir in the beaten egg and milk to make a soft dough.

4 Add the cabbage wedges to the saucepan and push them down into the simmering stock.

5 Drop rounded teaspoons of dough into the simmering stock. Cover and cook gently for 10-15 minutes or until the dumplings are fluffy and firm and all the vegetables are tender.

6 Remove the bacon to a board. With a large sharp knife, remove and discard the skin and fat, cut the meat into chunks. Put the chicken on the board, remove and discard the skin and cut the bird into eight portions. Divide the meat between eight large heated soup bowls.

7 Divide the vegetables, dumplings and broth between the bowls and sprinkle with parsley. Serve at once.

★ Leek and curly endive salad

● **Preparation: making stock, then 20 minutes**

● **Cooking: 30 minutes, plus cooling** ● **Serves 8**

850ml/1½pt CHICKEN STOCK
8 YOUNG LEEKS
1 HEAD CURLY ENDIVE

For the vinaigrette:
6tbls OLIVE OIL
2tbls RED WINE VINEGAR
1tsp DIJON MUSTARD
1 GARLIC CLOVE, finely chopped
2tbls FINELY CHOPPED PARSLEY
SALT and PEPPER

1 Put the chicken stock into a large saucepan and bring to the boil. Meanwhile prepare the leeks. Cut off and discard the roots and the tough parts of the green tops. Remove the outer leaves if they are very coarse. Rinse the trimmed leeks thoroughly under cold running water to remove any dirt and grit.

2 Add the prepared leeks to the boiling stock, bring back to the boil, then reduce the heat, cover and cook for 20-25 minutes or until tender but not too soft. Drain well and leave to get cold.

3 Meanwhile separate the curly endive leaves, discarding any discoloured or tough outer leaves. Cut off and discard the stems. Wash the leaves well, drain and pat dry with absorbent paper.

4 Prepare the vinaigrette. Put the oil in a bowl and combine with the vinegar, mustard, garlic and parsley. Season with salt and pepper to taste; beat with a fork until the mixture emulsifies.

5 Set out four individual serving dishes long enough to take the leeks. Arrange a bed of curly endive leaves on each one. Put two leeks side by side in the middle of each and spoon over some of the vinaigrette to coat. Serve at once, with the remaining vinaigrette in a sauceboat.

★ *Oranges in Marsala*

• *Preparation: 30 minutes, plus chilling*
• *Cooking: 20 minutes* **• *Serves 8***

8 JUICY THIN-SKINNED ORANGES
225g/8oz SUGAR
150ml/¼pt MARSALA
JUICE OF 1 LEMON

1 Using a potato peeler, pare the zest thinly from half the oranges. Cut it into neat strips, as thin as possible and of equal length.

2 Remove the remaining peel from all the oranges, making sure that you take off the outside membrane and every scrap of the bitter white pith.

3 Put the sugar in a heavy bottomed saucepan and pour in the Marsala, lemon juice and 150ml/¼pt water. Bring to the boil over low heat, stirring occasionally. Stir the strips of lemon zest into the syrup and simmer, stirring constantly, until the syrup is reduced by about one third. Remove the pan from the heat and allow the syrup to cool.

4 Using a sharp serrated knife, slice each orange horizontally on a shallow plate to catch the juice. Remove the pips with the point of the knife, then reassemble each orange by sticking a long cocktail stick vertically through the slices to hold them together.

5 Arrange the oranges in a glass bowl. Stir the orange juice caught on the plate into the syrup and spoon the syrup over the oranges. Decorate each one with a little pile of caramelized zest. Chill until ready to serve.

Cook's tips

This delicious dessert is known as *aranci alla Marsala* in its native Sicily, and uses two of Sicily's best-known exports: juicy oranges and the dessert wine, Marsala.

If you find that the syrup hardens before you are ready to pour it over the oranges, reheat it with a little extra orange juice.

Raspberry cheese

• *Preparation: 10 minutes, plus chilling* **• *Serves 8***

650g/1¼lb FULL-FAT SOFT CHEESE
100g/4oz CASTER SUGAR
250ml/9fl oz DOUBLE CREAM
JUICE OF 1 LEMON
550g/1¼lb RASPBERRIES

1 Put the cheese into a bowl and beat with a wooden spoon for 2 minutes until soft. Add the caster sugar and beat again until well blended.

2 Add the cream, together with the lemon juice, and mix well. Reserve 100g/4oz of the best raspberries for decorating and fold the remainder into the cheese and cream mixture. Cover and chill overnight.

3 To serve divide the raspberry cheese between eight champagne glasses or glass dessert dishes. Decorate with the reserved raspberries.

Serving suggestions

Serve this deliciously simple dessert with delicate crisp biscuits such as *langues de chats*.

NEW YEAR'S EVE DINNER FOR EIGHT

Chicken avocado aspic · Beef in red wine · Potatoes parisienne · Roquefort cheese and walnut savoury

Roquefort and walnut savoury (page 167)

FOR ENTERTAINING ON New Year's Eve, here's a menu with dishes which can be prepared well in advance, leaving very little to interfere with the celebrations.

The starter, spectacular Chicken avocado aspic, can be made the day before. The main course, Beef in red wine, is marinated in the wine for 12-24 hours, so this too can be started the day before. Once in the oven, it will come to no harm if cooked a little longer than stated.

Accompany the beef with Potatoes parisienne, potato balls tossed in hot butter and parsley, which are quickly cooked – the time-consuming preparation can be done ahead of time.

Finish the meal with Roquefort and walnut savoury rather than a sweet, as some may want to carry on drinking to see the Old Year out and ring the New Year in.

Setting the Scene

Christmas decorations traditionally stay in place until Twelfth Night (6th January) but if you're having a New Year's Eve celebration dinner give them a facelift for the occasion. A gold and silver colour scheme is easy to create: if you have got holly and ivy branches around, or Christmas wreaths, take them down and spray them with gold and silver paints. Similarly adapt the Christmas tree and room decorations, removing everything red and substituting gold and silver. Decorate the table with golden chrysanthemums and matching candles. Small gifts for the guests can be wrapped in gold or silver foil, and gold or silver crackers will complete the festive occasion.

Wine Ideas

New Year's Eve is probably not the right occasion to spend money on fine wines; quantity to last through the evening is more important! A good supply of a Bulgarian Cabernet or Merlot (or Country Wine, made from a blend of both grapes), inexpensive but fruity and full-bodied, will give you a good wine to use in the cooking of the beef main course, and to serve with it. If it's a cold evening, mull a bottle or two to welcome guests as they arrive. Then, to welcome the New Year in, bring out something bubbly; you don't need to spend much as there are some very drinkable and affordable alternatives to champagne to suit all tastes.

Countdown

The day before
Prepare the Chicken avocado aspic and chill.
Prepare and marinate the Beef in red wine.

In the morning
Prepare the Roquefort and walnut mixture and the salad leaves for the savoury and chill separately.

Three and a half hours ahead
Prepare the potato balls for Potatoes parisienne and store in cold water.
Cook the Beef in red wine for the suggested cooking time.

Thirty minutes before
Cook the Potatoes parisienne and keep warm.
Unmould the Chicken avocado aspic, decorate and chill.

Before serving the starter
Assemble the Roquefort and walnut savoury.
Slice the Beef in red wine and make gravy. Keep warm.

★ *Chicken avocado aspic*

● ***Preparation: 1½ hours*** ● ***Serves 8***

3tsps ASPIC POWDER
1.1L/2pt CANNED CHICKEN CONSOMMÉ
18 STUFFED OLIVES, sliced
½ CUCUMBER, cut into 5mm/¼in dice
3 BONED CHICKEN BREASTS, cooked and shredded
CUCUMBER and LEMON SLICES, to garnish (optional)

For the avocado mousse:
2 RIPE AVOCADOS
JUICE OF 1 LEMON
150ml/¼pt CHICKEN STOCK
SALT and PEPPER
HOT PEPPER SAUCE
25g/1oz POWDERED GELATINE
4-6tbls MAYONNAISE
150ml/¼pt DOUBLE CREAM

1 Make up the aspic with boiling water, add consommé. Chill a 2L/3½pt round mould. Put 300ml/½pt aspic in a bowl. Put over a bowl of ice cubes and stir until about to set. Spoon into the chilled mould, a little at a time, tilting the mould over ice until it is lined with aspic.

2 Arrange the olive slices on the aspic one at a time, in an overlapping circle 2.5cm/1in from the edge of the mould. Chill to set, then cover the olives with a little liquid aspic and chill again until set.

3 Meanwhile make the avocado mousse. Halve and peel the avocados and remove the stones. Put the flesh in a blender or food processor with the lemon juice and stock; season with salt and pepper and a few drops of hot pepper sauce. Process to a purée, then press through a fine nylon sieve.

4 Put 4tbls cold water into a small bowl and sprinkle on the gelatine. Leave for 5 minutes until softened, then stand in simmering water until the gelatine has dissolved. Leave to cool slightly.

5 Add the tepid gelatine to the avocado purée along with the mayonnaise and mix well. Whip the cream to soft peaks, then fold it gently into the mixture with a large metal spoon. Taste and adjust the seasoning. Spoon one-third of the mousse over the set aspic, spreading it evenly, and chill to set.

6 Arrange the diced cucumber over the mousse, making sure it goes right up to the sides of the mould. Put a little more liquid aspic into a bowl, set it over ice and stir until about to set. Spoon on an even layer, set.

7 Arrange the chicken over the set aspic. Stir the remaining liquid aspic until about to set, then spoon over the chicken. Chill to set. Spoon the remaining mousse over the set aspic and chill again until firmly set.

8 To unmould, dip the mould into hot water for a few seconds, then invert onto a dampened flat serving dish. Make sure the aspic is centred, then remove the mould. Garnish with cucumber and lemon slices and serve.

Real Russian salad

- *Preparation: 15 minutes*
- *Cooking: 20 minutes, plus cooling*
- *Serves 8*

225g/8oz POTATOES
175g/6oz CARROTS
100g/4oz SWEDE or TURNIP
SALT and PEPPER
50g/2oz FROZEN PEAS
50g/2oz CELERY, diced
50g/2oz PICKLED DILL CUCUMBER, diced
175g/6oz COOKED HAM, thickly sliced
6tbls SPRING ONION TOPS, sliced
150ml/¼pt MAYONNAISE
1tsp FRENCH MUSTARD
LEMON JUICE

For the garnish:
16 LETTUCE LEAVES
4 HARD-BOILED EGGS, thickly sliced
4tbls FINELY CHOPPED PARSLEY

1 Prepare the potatoes, carrots and swede or turnip and cut into 5mm/¼in dice. Cook them in lightly salted boiling water until just tender. Also cook the peas, separately. Drain, refresh in cold water and leave to cool.

2 Put the cooked root vegetables in a large mixing bowl with the peas. Add the celery and pickled cucumber. Cut the ham into 5mm/¼in dice and add to the bowl along with the spring onion tops. Using a large kitchen fork, mix the ingredients together thoroughly, but very gently to avoid breaking the softer vegetables.

3 Flavour the mayonnaise with the mustard and a few drops of lemon juice, then fold it into the ham and vegetable mixture. Put two lettuce leaves on each of eight individual plates and spoon the salad on top. Garnish with a slice of hard-boiled egg and finely chopped parsley.

Cook's tips

Vary the proportions of the different vegetables to taste, but take care to cook them only until just tender. Overcooked vegetables are bound to be crushed when the salad is mixed.

Use the centre slices of hard-boiled egg to garnish the salad; the remainder can be diced and added to the vegetables.

★ Beef in red wine

- *Preparation: 45 minutes, plus marinating*
- *Cooking: 3¼ hours*
- *Serves 8-10*

1.8kg/4lb BRISKET OF BEEF, boned and tied
75g/3oz PIECE OF PORK FAT
1 GARLIC CLOVE, crushed
25g/1oz BUTTER
3tbls OIL
1 LARGE ONION, chopped
1 CARROT, sliced
1 CELERY STALK, sliced
1tbls TOMATO PURÉE (optional)
SALT and PEPPER
1 BOUQUET GARNI (see Cook's tips, page 20)

For the marinade:
1 ONION, CARROT and CELERY STALK, chopped
4 PARSLEY STALKS
3 THYME SPRIGS
2 BAY LEAVES
600ml/1pt RED WINE, or half wine, half beef stock
50g/2oz RAISINS, tied up in muslin

1 Wipe the beef with absorbent paper. Cut the pork fat into small strips and rub them in the crushed garlic. Make small incisions in the joint with a sharp knife and push the pork lardons into them.

2 Put the meat in a shallow dish with all the marinade ingredients. Marinate in a cool place for 12-24 hours.

3 Heat the oven to 170C/325F/gas 3. Strain the marinade into a saucepan; discard the vegetables and herbs but reserve the raisins.

4 Heat the butter and oil in a flameproof casserole. Wipe the meat dry again to ensure that it seals and browns. When the butter stops foaming, add the meat and brown it quickly all over; take care not to pierce it when turning. Remove from the casserole with a slotted spoon.

5 Add the onion, carrot and celery to the fat remaining in the casserole and fry for about 5 minutes over medium heat until softened but not browned. Put the meat on top of the vegetables.

6 Heat the marinade, stir in the tomato purée, if using, and pour just enough over the vegetables in the casserole to cover them. Reserve the remaining marinade.

7 Season with salt and pepper to taste and add the bouquet garni. Cover tightly with a lid and braise for 2½ hours. Add the reserved raisins and cook for 30 minutes or until the meat is tender. Remove the raisins.

8 Remove the meat and keep it warm. Arrange the vegetables on a serving platter and keep warm. Skim the fat from the pan juices, add the reserved marinade and reheat. Taste and adjust the seasoning.

9 Slice the meat and arrange it on top of the vegetables. Pour a little of the gravy over the dish and serve the rest separately in a sauceboat. Garnish with freshly cooked vegetables.

Plaice with parsley butter

● *Preparation: 30 minutes, plus marinating*

● *Cooking: 15 minutes* ● *Serves 8*

8 x 225g/8oz PLAICE, cleaned with heads removed
8tbls OLIVE OIL, plus extra for greasing
4tbls FINELY CHOPPED ONION
4tbls FINELY CHOPPED PARSLEY
SALT and PEPPER
JUICE OF 1 LEMON
PARSLEY SPRIGS and LEMON SLICES, to garnish

For the parsley butter:
100g/4oz BUTTER, softened
2tbls FINELY CHOPPED PARSLEY
2tbls LEMON JUICE

1 Trim the plaice, cutting the fins away with scissors, and pat dry with absorbent paper. Using a sharp knife, score each fish diagonally through the skin. (Use the fish trimmings to make stock for future use; this can be frozen until required at a later date.)

2 Pour the oil into a large shallow dish and sprinkle in the onion and parsley. Season generously with salt and pepper; stir in the lemon juice. Lay the fish in the dish and turn once to coat. Marinate for 2 hours, turning occasionally.

3 Meanwhile prepare the parsley butter. Cream the softened butter with the parsley. Season with the lemon juice and salt and pepper to taste. Wrap the flavoured butter in greaseproof paper or foil and roll into a sausage shape. Chill for at least 1 hour or until needed.

4 Heat the grill to high and brush the grid with oil. Drain off excess marinade and lay four fish side by side on the grid. Grill, turning once with a fish slice and basting with the marinade for 2-2½ minutes on each side or until the fish flakes easily with a fork. Transfer to a heated serving dish and keep hot while cooking the remaining fish.

5 Cut the parsley butter into 1cm/½in slices. Transfer the plaice to heated serving dishes and put one or two pats of butter on each one. Garnish the dishes with parsley sprigs and lemon slices and serve at once.

★ *Potatoes parisienne*

● *Preparation: 45 minutes*

● *Cooking: 15 minutes* ● *Serves 8*

1.8kg/4lb WAXY POTATOES
SALT
50g/2oz BUTTER
2tbls FINELY CHOPPED PARSLEY
½tsp LEMON JUICE

1 Peel the potatoes. Using a parisienne cutter (melon baller) cut out as many perfect potato balls as you can. Cook the balls in boiling salted water until just tender, about 15 minutes. Drain them carefully.

2 Put the butter in a small pan and melt it over low heat. Remove from the heat and stir in the parsley and lemon juice.

3 Pour the hot butter sauce over the potatoes. Turn them gently into a heated serving dish and serve hot.

Cook's tips

It is essential to use a firm, waxy variety of potato, such as the pink Desirée, to make this dish. Floury types would break up and spoil the effect.

Use leftover bits of potato in soup or to make a purée. Keep them covered in water until ready to use or they will discolour.

Spinach with nutmeg

● ***Preparation:*** *10 minutes*

● ***Cooking:*** *15 minutes* ● *Serves 8*

1.8kg/4lb SPINACH
50/75g/2-3oz BUTTER
SALT and PEPPER
GRATED NUTMEG

1 Wash the spinach carefully in plenty of cold water to make sure every trace of grit has been removed. Discard any yellowing or damaged leaves and pull away the stems. If they are tender they will snap off at the base, but if they are tough the stem will rip along the whole length of the leaf.

2 Shake the leaves and stand in a colander to get rid of excess moisture. Pack them into a very large saucepan. You may need to use two saucepans for this amount of spinach. Put over a fairly high heat, cover tightly and cook in the water still clinging to the surface of the leaves. Do not add salt at this stage; shake the pan occasionally.

3 When you hear sizzling noises coming from the pan cook for 1-2 minutes longer, uncovering the pan to turn the leaves over with a fork so that the uncooked layer on top takes the place of the cooked layer below. Remove from the heat.

4 Drain the spinach in a colander, pressing it firmly to extract any remaining moisture. If desired chop the spinach using two round-bladed knives held one in each hand, with the blades cutting across each other scissor fashion.

5 Return the spinach to the dry pan, dress with the butter and season with salt and pepper to taste and a little grated nutmeg. Stir over low heat to melt the butter and heat the spinach through. Turn into a heated serving dish and serve hot.

Roquefort cheese and walnut savoury

● ***Preparation:*** *20 minutes* ● *Serves 8*

225g/8oz ROQUEFORT CHEESE, without rind
50g/2oz BUTTER, softened
100g/4oz SHELLED WALNUTS, coarsely chopped
8 SMALL CRISP LETTUCE LEAVES
8 LEAVES RADICCHIO
8 WATERCRESS SPRIGS, to garnish
TRIANGLES OF TOAST, to serve

1 Mash together the Roquefort cheese and the softened butter until well mixed, then pass the mixture through a vegetable mill into a bowl. Alternatively use a food processor. Add the walnuts and mix well.

2 Arrange the lettuce leaves on a large serving platter, hollow side up, and put a radicchio leaf inside each one. Divide the Roquefort mixture between the 'cups'. Garnish with watercress sprigs and serve as soon as possible, with triangles of toast. These can be placed in a fan in the centre of the serving platter and garnished with another sprig of watercress.

Variations

If Roquefort is too expensive, or simply unavailable, substitute another fine blue cheese such as Gorgonzola or Bleu d'Auvergne. Stilton is rather too hard but can be used if very ripe.

Orange-strawberry trifle

• *Preparation: making sponge, then 40 minutes plus soaking and chilling*
• *Serves 6-8*

2 LAYERS WHISKED SPONGE (see Cook's tips, below)
4tbls ORANGE MARMALADE
2tbls BRANDY
6tbls GRAND MARNIER
3 ORANGES
2 LEMONS
2tbls ICING SUGAR, sifted
450ml/¾pt DOUBLE CREAM

For the decoration:
150ml/¼pt DOUBLE CREAM, whipped
8 STRAWBERRIES

1 Make the whisked sponge and bake in two 18cm/7in sandwich tins. Turn onto a wire tray and allow to cool before using. Leave until cold.

2 Put the marmalade in a small bowl with the brandy and heat until well blended. Spread the mixture evenly over one layer of sponge. Sandwich the two layers together and put in a shallow 20cm/8in glass bowl. Sprinkle over 4tbls Grand Marnier, cover the bowl and leave to soak for 2 hours.

3 Grate the zest from two of the oranges and one of the lemons and put it in a small bowl. Squeeze the juice from the fruit and add it to the grated zest along with the icing sugar. Stir until the sugar dissolves.

4 Pour the cream into a large bowl and whip to soft peaks. Stir in the remaining 2tbls Grand Marnier and the fruit juice and sugar mixture. Pour the runny cream and juice mixture over the sponge layers. Cover and chill for at least 8 hours to allow the flavours to blend thoroughly.

5 About 30 minutes before serving remove the orange trifle from the refrigerator and bring to a cool room temperature. Using a piping bag fitted with a 1cm/½in star nozzle pipe eight rosettes of whipped cream between the edge of the glass bowl and the trifle. Arrange a strawberry on top of each rosette and serve the trifle straight away.

Cook's tips

To make a whisked sponge, put 4 egg yolks, 175g/6oz caster sugar, 1½tbls lemon juice and salt into a bowl. Whisk for 5 minutes until it leaves a trail when lifted. Sift 50g/2oz flour and 25g/1oz cornflour together a little at a time over the egg mixture, folding it in. Whisk the egg whites until soft peaks form, then fold into the sponge mixture gently with a large metal spoon. Divide into 2 prepared 20cm/8in tins and bake for 20-25 minutes in a pre-heated oven at 180C/350F/gas 4.

English fig tart

• *Preparation: making pastry case, then 20 minutes, plus chilling*
• *Cooking: 40 minutes*
• *Serves 8*

23cm/9in PASTRY CASE (see Fruity treacle tart, p.18)
1 EGG WHITE, beaten
800g/1¾ lb CANNED FIGS
2tbls KIRSCH
150ml/¼ pt DOUBLE CREAM

For the almond filling:
2 LARGE EGGS
5tbls CASTER SUGAR
100g/4oz GROUND ALMONDS
6tbls DOUBLE CREAM
JUICE AND FINELY GRATED ZEST OF 1 LARGE LEMON
1-2 drops ALMOND ESSENCE

1 Brush the half-baked pastry case with the beaten egg white. Leave the case in its tin on a baking tray. Heat the oven to 200C/400F/gas 6.

2 Prepare the almond filling: put the eggs in a bowl with the caster sugar and whisk until thick and creamy. Add the remaining filling ingredients and beat vigorously with a wooden spoon until smoothly blended.

3 Fill the pastry case with the almond mixture and bake for 30 minutes until it is puffed and firm to the touch. Cool on a wire rack.

4 Drain the figs and reserve the syrup. Cut the figs in half and drain on absorbent paper. Arrange the halves in concentric circles over the tart, leaving a narrow border around the outer edge.

5 Put 50ml/2fl oz of the reserved fig syrup in a small saucepan with the icing sugar and heat until the sugar has dissolved. Put the pan over medium heat and boil until the syrup has reduced by half. Add the kirsch and coat the figs with the syrup. Allow the tart to cool, then chill.

6 Just before serving whip the cream until thick. Fill a piping bag fitted with a star nozzle and pipe the cream round the outer edge of the tart.

EASTER DINNER FOR SIX

Poached eggs en brioche · Stuffed saddle of lamb · Buttered turnip and courgette strips · Mixed vegetable salad · Russian Easter pudding

TRADITIONAL DISHES FROM different countries make this an Easter dinner to remember.

Eggs are a must, so begin with a luxurious French starter, Poached eggs en brioche, served with Hollandaise sauce and a garnish of red caviar. Spring lamb has long formed the main course for Easter meals in many countries; Stuffed saddle of lamb, flavoured with watercress, orange and onion, comes from Britain. Serve this with roast potatoes and two other vegetable dishes, one hot, one cold: Buttered turnip and courgette strips, plus colourful Mixed vegetable salad.

Finish with spectacular Russian Easter pudding, or Pashka, similar to cheesecake but lighter.

Table Talk

If you feel that the Russian Easter pudding might not appeal to some of your guests, choose a suitable alternative dessert. In Spain, an ice cream cake is the traditional finish to an Easter feast - Pineapple ice cream cake, page 174, is a tangy variation. Or you could serve English Simnel cake, originally made by girls in service for Mothering Sunday, the day they were allowed to visit their families. Add an extra festive touch to your Easter table by decanting the wine into an elegant glass decanter.

Wine Ideas

Roast lamb is traditionally partnered by a red Bordeaux, or claret. If it's to be a no-expense-spared occasion, pick one of the famous Burgundy names like Nuits-St. Georges or Châteauneuf-du-Pape. Otherwise go for an equivalent wine of similar style – Château La Jaubertie 1986 Bergerac, a wine from the Bergerac region in France right next door to Bordeaux, would be ideal.

Countdown

Two days before
Drain the cheese for the Russian Easter pudding.

The day before
Make the Russian Easter pudding to the end of step 4 and chill until needed.

In the morning
Bake or buy the brioches for Poached eggs en brioche. Prepare the vegetables for Buttered turnip and courgette strips and store in plastic bags in the refrigerator.

Four hours before
Take the saddle of lamb out of the refrigerator to come to room temperature.

Two hours before
Prepare and cook the Stuffed saddle of lamb; keep hot. Prepare the Mixed vegetable salad.

1 hour before
Unmould and decorate the Russian Easter pudding; return to the refrigerator until ready to serve.

40 minutes before
Cook the Buttered turnip and courgette strips; keep hot.

20 minutes before
Make the Hollandaise sauce for the Poached eggs en brioche and keep over warm water until needed. Prepare and warm the brioches and cook the eggs for Poached eggs en brioche.

Before serving the main course
Make the gravy for the Roast saddle of lamb.

★ Poached eggs en brioche

● *Preparation: making brioche plus 20 minutes*

● *Cooking: making Hollandaise sauce, then 15 minutes*

● *Serves 6*

6 SMALL BRIOCHES
MELTED BUTTER
4tbls WHITE WINE VINEGAR
6 LARGE VERY FRESH EGGS
6tsp RED CAVIAR
300ml/½ pt HOLLANDAISE SAUCE (see Cook's tips, below)

1 Heat the oven to 170C/325F/gas 3. Make the Hollandaise sauce and keep over warm (not hot) water until ready to use.

2 Remove the top from each brioche and hollow out the centre with a teaspoon to make a cavity big enough to hold a poached egg. Brush inside the brioche cases with melted butter, arrange on a tray and heat for 6-8 minutes in the oven.

3 Meanwhile pour 7.5cm/3in water into a large frying pan. Add the vinegar and bring to the boil, then reduce to heat to a very gentle simmer. Break three of the eggs into separate cups. Slip them carefully into the water, then raise the heat until the water is just beginning to bubble. Reduce it to low and poach the eggs for 4 minutes.

4 Using a slotted spoon, transfer the eggs to a bowl of warm water to keep warm. Poach the remaining eggs in the same way.

5 Put the brioches on a heated serving dish. Drain the eggs thoroughly on absorbent paper and trim neatly with scissors. Put an egg in each brioche cavity. Spoon over a little Hollandaise sauce and top with 5ml/1tsp caviar. Serve as soon as possible with the remaining sauce.

Cook's tips

Brioches should be available in most French bakeries. If you cannot get them or make your own, use heated hollowed-out dinner rolls or small tart cases.

To make Hollandaise sauce, put a double boiler containing hot, not simmering, water over very gentle heat. Stir together 1-2tsp lemon juice, seasoning, 4 egg yolks, and a 1cm/½in cube cut from 100g/4oz of unsalted butter. Add a second cube of butter whilst whisking. The sauce will begin to thicken. Add the remaining butter, cube by cube as each one melts, stirring continually. Adjust the seasoning if necessary.

Scalloped crab

● *Preparation: 15 minutes*

● *Cooking: 15 minutes* ● *Serves 6*

350g/12oz CANNED CRABMEAT
4 SLICES WHITE BREAD, crusts removed
75g/3oz BUTTER
3-4tbls OLIVE OIL
1tbls FLOUR
2tbls MUSTARD POWDER
2tsp CURRY POWDER
150ml/¼pt MILK
2tbls DOUBLE CREAM
1tsp WORCESTERSHIRE SAUCE
BLACK PEPPER
6tbls TOASTED BREADCRUMBS (see Cook's tips, page 101)

1 Heat the oven to 180C/350F/gas 4. Drain the crabmeat and turn it into a mixing bowl. Dice the bread and fry in 40g/1½oz butter and the olive oil until golden brown on all sides. Drain on absorbent paper, then add to the bowl with the crabmeat.

2 Prepare the sauce: melt the remaining butter in a heavy saucepan. Add the flour, mustard and curry powder and stir over low heat for 1 minute to make a pale roux. Gradually add the milk, stirring constantly, bring to the boil, then simmer for about 5-6 minutes until the sauce is smooth and thick.

3 Add the cream and Worcestershire sauce and season with pepper to taste. Pour the sauce over the crabmeat and bread mixture and fold in gently.

4 Fill six individual 150ml/¼pt heatproof scallop shell dishes or ramekins with the mixture and sprinkle each serving with 1tbls toasted breadcrumbs. Bake in the oven for 10 minutes and serve piping hot.

★ Stuffed saddle of lamb

● *Preparation: coming to room temperature, then 20 minutes*

● *Cooking: 1½-2 hours* ● *Serves 6*

1.1kg/2½lb SMALL SADDLE OF LAMB, boned weight
50g/2oz BUTTER
3 LARGE ONIONS, very finely chopped
2 BUNCHES WATERCRESS, finely chopped
1 LARGE ORANGE, peeled and chopped
½tsp POWDERED BAY LEAVES
2 FRESH ROSEMARY SPRIGS
2 GARLIC CLOVES, peeled but left whole
2tbls REDCURRANT JELLY
1tbls DIJON MUSTARD
2tbls PORT
SALT and PEPPER
ROAST POTATOES, to serve

1 Ask the butcher to bone the saddle but not to roll and tie it. Melt the butter in a saucepan over medium heat, add the onions, cover with a lid or foil and cook very gently for 15 minutes until soft but not coloured.

2 Put the onions and their juices into a large bowl, add the watercress, orange and bay leaves and stir well.

3 Turn the lamb on its back, skin side down, and open out. Put one sprig of rosemary and one garlic clove on each side, then lay the onion and watercress stuffing down both sides. Carefully fold over the outer flaps, then tie with string in several places.

4 Turn the lamb skin side up and put it on a rack in a roasting tin. Heat the oven to 200C/400F/gas 6.

5 Put the redcurrant jelly into a small saucepan over low heat and stir with a wooden spoon until it begins to melt. Remove from the heat, stir in the mustard and port and mix well.

6 Season the lamb with salt and pepper and paint the skin with the redcurrant jelly mixture. Cook in the oven for 1 hour 5 minutes for pink lamb, 1½ hours for well-done, basting occasionally.

7 Transfer the lamb to a heated serving dish and put back in the turned-off oven. Pour excess fat from the tin, then put the roasting tin over medium heat and add 6tbls water and seasoning. Bring to the boil, stirring to scrape all the sediment off the tin. Strain the gravy into a heated sauceboat and serve with the lamb.

Roast fillet of beef

● ***Preparation:** coming to room temperature, then 15 minutes*

● ***Cooking:** 45 minutes, plus resting* ● *Serves 6*

1.1kg/2½lb FILLET OF BEEF, stripped of fat
40g/1½oz BUTTER, melted
SALT and PEPPER
24 FRESH ROSEMARY LEAVES
1 BAY LEAF, crumbled

For the garnish:
25g/1oz BUTTER
350g/12oz MUSHROOMS, thinly sliced
WATERCRESS SPRIGS

1 At least 2 hours before you intend roasting the beef, remove it from the refrigerator so that it comes to room temperature.

2 Heat the oven to 220C/425F/gas 7. Tuck the narrow end of the fillet under to make the joint an even thickness and tie it neatly with string. Brush generously with the melted butter and season with pepper to taste

3 Sear the meat on all sides in a shallow roasting tin set over high heat until well browned (3-4 minutes). Put it on a rack in the roasting tin and sprinkle with the rosemary leaves and crumbled bay leaf. Add 4tbls warm water to the tin and roast to taste. Allow 18-22 minutes per kg/8-10 minutes per lb for very rare to rare; 30-36 minutes per kg/14-16 minutes per lb for medium rare to medium. Remove from the oven and leave in a warm place to settle for 15 minutes.

4 Meanwhile prepare the garnish. Melt the butter in a frying pan and fry the mushrooms over medium heat until just tender – about 4-5 minutes. Add the lemon juice, stir and keep warm.

5 Before serving, remove the string and transfer the joint to a heated serving dish. Season with salt to taste and garnish with the mushrooms and watercress sprigs. Carve into thick slices.

Braised celery mornay

● ***Preparation:** making stock, then 20 minutes*

● ***Cooking:** 1¼ hours* ● *Serves 6*

3 HEADS CELERY
SALT and PEPPER
4tbls MELTED BUTTER
200ml/7fl oz CHICKEN STOCK
2tbls LEMON JUICE
SALT and PEPPER
FLAT-LEAVED PARSLEY, to garnish

For the cheese sauce:
40g/1½oz BUTTER
1tsp FRENCH MUSTARD
3tbls FLOUR
425ml/¾pt MILK
75g/3oz GRUYERE CHEESE, grated

1 Heat the oven to 190C/350F/gas 4. Remove the outer stalks from the celery and trim one-third from the tops. Cut each celery heart in half lengthways to make six portions.

2 Bring a large saucepan of salted water to the boil. Add the celery hearts, cook for 5 minutes only, then drain.

3 Brush a large shallow ovenproof dish with butter. Lay the celery hearts in side by side, cut side down. Pour in the remaining melted butter plus the stock and lemon juice. Season with salt and pepper to taste. Cover the dish with a double thickness of foil and cook in the oven for 1 hour or until the celery hearts are tender.

4 Meanwhile make the cheese sauce. Melt the butter in a saucepan, then stir in the mustard and flour. Cook for 2-3 minutes over low heat to make a pale roux, stirring frequently. Gradually add the milk, stirring constantly. Bring to the boil and season with salt and pepper to taste. Simmer for 1-2 minutes.

5 Heat the grill to high. Drain the liquid from the braised celery hearts into the sauce. Stir to blend thoroughly. Reserve 4tbls of the grated Gruyère cheese and stir the rest into the sauce until well mixed. Taste and adjust the seasoning and pour the sauce over the celery hearts.

6 Sprinkle with the reserved cheese and grill for about 10 minutes or until the top is browned. Garnish with parsley and serve at once.

★ Buttered turnip and courgette strips

● ***Preparation: 15 minutes***

● ***Cooking: 20 minutes*** ● ***Serves 6***

700g/1½lb TURNIPS
700g/1½lb COURGETTES
50g/2oz BUTTER
8tbls CHICKEN STOCK
SALT and PEPPER
2tbls FINELY CHOPPED PARSLEY

1 Peel and trim the turnips. Cut them lengthways into thin strips, then into strips 5cm x 5mm/2 x ¼in. Wipe the courgettes, top and tail them and cut in the same way as the turnips.

2 Melt the butter in a large saucepan, pour in the stock and mix together. Add the turnip strips and simmer gently for 5 minutes, tossing frequently with a large metal spoon. Season generously with salt and pepper.

3 Add the courgette strips and cook for a further 10 minutes or until both vegetables are tender when tested. Toss the vegetables together carefully from time to time to ensure even cooking.

4 Transfer the turnip and courgette strips to a heated serving platter. Pour over the cooking juices. Sprinkle with parsley and serve hot.

★ Mixed vegetable salad

● ***Preparation: 35 minutes, plus cooling***

● ***Cooking: 15 minutes*** ● ***Serves 6***

½ CAULIFLOWER, weighing about 225g/8oz
175g/6oz LARGE FRESH BROCCOLI SPEARS
100g/44oz FRENCH BEANS
225g/8oz TOMATOES
½ CUCUMBER
2 CELERY STALKS
SALT and PEPPER

For the dressing:

2tbls WINE VINEGAR
LEMON JUICE
1 GARLIC CLOVE, finely chopped
6-8tbls OLIVE OIL
2tbls FINELY CHOPPED PARSLEY
2tbls FINELY SNIPPED CHIVES

1 Put a large saucepan of salted water on to boil. Meanwhile, start preparing the vegetables. Break the cauliflower into florets and cut off the base of any hard stalks. Rinse in cold water. Cut away any stalks and large leaves from the broccoli and rinse. Top, tail and rinse the beans.

2 When the water is boiling gently add the cauliflower florets, broccoli and green beans and cook for 5 minutes.

3 Meanwhile make the dressing. Put the vinegar in a small bowl and season with salt, pepper and lemon juice to taste. Add the garlic and beat in the olive oil until the mixture emulsifies. Stir in the parsley and chives.

4 When the vegetables are cooked but still crisp, drain thoroughly and put in a bowl. Pour the dressing over while they are still warm. Toss carefully with your hands so as not to break the florets; leave to cool.

5 Blanch, skin and seed the tomatoes, then cut each one into eight wedges. Peel the cucumber and quarter it lengthways, then remove the seeds and cut the flesh into 2.5cm/1in lengths. Prepare the celery and cut into 2.5cm/1in slices.

6 Add the tomato wedges, cucumber and celery to the dressed vegetables and toss carefully. Transfer the salad to a glass serving dish.

Variations

Add sliced cooked carrots for extra colour; substitute finely chopped spring onion tops for the chives if these are not available.

★ Russian Easter pudding

• Preparation: 12 hours draining, then 30 minutes plus 12 hours chilling **• Serves 6-8**

700g/1½lb COTTAGE or CURD CHEESE
50g/2oz BLANCHED ALMONDS, chopped
50g/2oz MIXED CANDIED PEEL
50g/2oz SEEDLESS RAISINS, chopped
100g/4oz GLACE CHERRIES, chopped
125g/4½oz BUTTER, softened
2 EGGS
100g/4oz CASTER SUGAR
50ml/2fl oz CLOTTED, DOUBLE or SOURED CREAM
½tsp ROSE-WATER
BLANCHED ALMONDS, GLACE CHERRIES, CANDIED FRUIT AND ANGELICA, to decorate

1 Drain the cottage or curd cheese by hanging it in a large piece of muslin over the sink or a bowl for at least 12 hours.

2 Rub the drained cheese through a sieve into a large bowl. Mix the almonds, candied peel, raisins and glacé cherries with the butter, then stir the mixture into the cheese.

3 Whisk the eggs with the sugar until they are pale yellow and frothy, then add the mixture to the cheese and whisk thoroughly to eliminate lumps. Whisk in the cream and rose-water and continue mixing until the cheese and egg mixture is completely smooth.

4 Line a clean terracotta flower-pot large enough to hold the pudding with two layers of muslin. Turn in the pudding, fold the ends of the cloth over the top and cover the top with a small plate weighted down to press the contents. Stand the pot upright in a large saucer to catch the whey and put in the refrigerator for at least 12 hours

5 When ready to serve, unfold the muslin and carefully turn the pudding out onto a flat serving dish. Decorate with almonds, glacé cherries, candied fruit and angelica.

Cook's tips

In Russian this traditional pudding is known as Pashka. It forms the centrepiece of the Easter table and is decorated with the Cyrillic letters XB which stand for "Christ is Risen".

Pineapple ice cream cake

• Preparation: preparing sponge batter, freezing ice cream, then 30 minutes

• Cooking: 30 minutes **• Serves 6-8**

WHISKED SPONGE BATTER (see Cook's tips, page 168)
450g/1lb CANNED CRUSHED PINEAPPLE
BUTTER, for greasing
300ml/½pt DOUBLE CREAM
3tbls ICING SUGAR
GRATED CHOCOLATE or CHOCOLATE CURLS

1 Heat the oven to 180C/350F/gas 4. Take one-quarter of the pineapple and drain it well in a sieve, reserving the juice. Add the drained pineapple to the whisked sponge batter and fold in well.

2 Butter two 20cm/8in sandwich tins, then line the bases with two circles of greaseproof paper and butter these as well. Divide the sponge mixture between the tins and bake for 25-30 minutes until the cakes have shrunk away from the sides slightly and they are springy to the touch.

3 Allow the cakes to cool for a few minutes, then invert onto a clean cloth. Peel off the greaseproof paper, turn the cakes right way up onto a wire rack and leave until cold. Meanwhile purée the remaining pineapple and reserved juice in a blender or food processor.

4 Whip the cream in a large bowl until soft peaks form, then fold in the sugar. Combine the pineapple purée with just over half the whipped cream, folding lightly together until thoroughly mixed.

5 Divide the mixture between two 20cm/8in sandwich tins and freeze for 1-1½ hours. Stir the ice cream with a fork or a whisk, then return the mixture to the freezer for 2½-3 hours.

6 Just before serving, wipe the bottom of the sandwich tins with a cloth wrung out in hot water. Put one layer of sponge on a serving plate and turn one ice cream layer on top of it. Cover with a second sponge layer. Turn the second ice cream layer out onto a plate, then gently slide it into position on top of the other layers. Smooth the top if necessary.

7 Spread the remaining whipped cream around the sides of the cake, flicking it with a palette knife to form little peaks. Sprinkle the top with grated chocolate or chocolate curls and serve at once.

Index

Picture Credits

Bryce Attwell: pages 49, 50, 52 (right), 99 (right), 130 (right), 144 (right), 172 (left), 174 (left). Tom Belshaw: pages 51 (right), 117 (right), 147 (left). Paul Bussell: pages 31, 40, 48 (right), 58 (right), 60 (right), 69 (left), 108 (left), 123 (left), 125 (right), 141, 143 (right), 144 (left), 145, 146, 147 (right), 150 (right), 153 (left), 171 (left), 172 (right), 173 (left). Chris Crofton: pages 63 (left). Alan Duns: page 76 (left). Laurie Evans: pages 30 (left), 47 (left), 53 (left), 70 (right), 71 (left), 88 (right), 113 (right), 114 (left), 117 (left), 122, 123 (right), 126 (right), 129 (left), 133, 140, 155 (right), 157, 159 (left). Edmund Goldspink: pages 52 (left), 162 (left). Melvin Grey: pages 38 (left). John Hollingshead: pages 67, 73, 79, 115. James Jackson: pages 33 (right), 45, 65 (right), 77 (left), 86, 94 (right), 98, 101 (right), 119 (right), 121, 124, 126 (left), 138 (left), 162 (right), 169, 170, 171 (right). Chris Knaggs: pages 34 (right), 42, 57 (right), 58 (left), 62, 66 (left), 89, (left), 92, 100 (left), 102 (left), 106 (left), 118 (left), 136, 137 (right), 155 (left), 156 (left). Don Last: page 160. Michael Michaels: pages 97, 103 and 109. Peter Myers: pages 25, 27, 28 (left), 29 (left), 33 (left), 36 (right), 37, 51 (left), 54, 55, 56, 59 (right), 64 (right), 66 (right), 84 (right), 85, 90 (right), 95 (left), 99 (left), 102 (right), 116, 127, 129 (right), 131 (left), 132, 134, 135 (right), 137 (left), 139, 143 (left), 150 (left), 151, 153 (right), 154, 156 (right), 163, 174 (right). Roger Phillips: pages 26, 64 (left), 101 (left), 152. Ian Reid: page 104. Paul Webster: pages: 46 (right), 48 (left), 119 (left). Paul Williams: pages 29 (right), 43, 44, 45 (right), 46 (left), 47 (right), 57, 114 (right), (left), 63 (right), 65 (left), 87 (left), 111 (left), 112 (right), 128, 138 (right), 142 (left), 158, 159 (right), 173 (right).